American Boarding
School Fiction,
1928–1981

American Boarding School Fiction, 1928–1981

A Critical Study

ALEXANDER H. PITOFSKY

McFarland & Company, Inc., Publishers
Jefferson, North Carolina

LIBRARY OF CONGRESS CATALOGUING-IN-PUBLICATION DATA

Pitofsky, Alexander H.
    American boarding school fiction, 1928–1981 : a critical study / Alexander H. Pitofsky.
       p.   cm.
    Includes bibliographical references and index.

    ISBN 978-0-7864-7865-1 (softcover : acid free paper) ∞
    ISBN 978-1-4766-1662-9 (ebook)

    1. American fiction—20th century—History and criticism. 2. Boarding schools in literature. 3. Boarding schools—United States. 4. Students in literature. I. Title.
PS379.P56 2014
813'.509—dc23   2014024229

BRITISH LIBRARY CATALOGUING DATA ARE AVAILABLE

© 2014 Alexander H. Pitofsky. All rights reserved

No part of this book may be reproduced or transmitted in any form or by any means, electronic or mechanical, including photocopying or recording, or by any information storage and retrieval system, without permission in writing from the publisher.

Cover image © 2014 Jupiter Images/Thinkstock

Printed in the United States of America

McFarland & Company, Inc., Publishers
  Box 611, Jefferson, North Carolina 28640
    www.mcfarlandpub.com

Acknowledgments

I am grateful to my colleagues at Appalachian State University for the support they provided while I worked on this book. Special thanks to Tom McLaughlin, Dave Haney, Mark Vogel, and Craig Fischer for commenting on early drafts of the chapters and listening patiently while I thought out loud about boarding schools and school fiction.

Many thanks to the staffs of the libraries of Appalachian State University, Davidson College, North Carolina State University, the University of Georgia, the University of North Carolina at Chapel Hill, Wake Forest University, the Groton School, the Lawrenceville School, and Phillips Andover Academy.

I'm indebted to Christopher Buckley and the late Louis Auchincloss for responding so graciously to the questions I sent them about their novels and the years they spent in boarding school.

A version of Chapter 1 appeared in *Studies in American Culture* in 2010 and a version of Chapter 2 appeared in *Papers on Language and Literature* in 2013. I thank both journals for their permission to reprint those materials here.

Most of all, I'd like to thank my parents, Robert and Sally Pitofsky, my children, Jackson and Marina Pitofsky, and Leslie Lawley for all of their patience and encouragement.

Table of Contents

Acknowledgments   v
Introduction: "The Freshest Boy" and the Prep-School Myth   1

1. Masculine Competition and Boarding-School Culture in *The Catcher in the Rye*   11
2. Unseen Academy: John Knowles's *A Separate Peace*   33
3. Campus Politics and Endless Adolescence in *The Rector of Justin*   54
4. Sexuality, Gothic Melodrama, and Boarding-School Fiction: James Kirkwood's *Good Times/Bad Times*   77
5. "That was what made the school so useless": Anti-Prep Broadsides and *A Good School*   108
6. Isolation and Conflict in *Tea and Sympathy* and *Peace Breaks Out*   134

Conclusion: An Indestructible Myth   160
Chapter Notes   173
Works Cited   187
Index   195

The chief wonder of education is that it
does not ruin everybody concerned
in it, teachers and taught.
—Henry Adams

Almost any world seems preferable,
when you're an adolescent,
to the world you're in.
—John Updike

Introduction:
"The Freshest Boy" and the
Prep-School Myth

In F. Scott Fitzgerald's short story "The Freshest Boy" (1928), Basil Lee endures a miserable semester at a private academy called St. Regis.[1] When the headmaster, Doctor Bacon, hears about Basil's troubles, he wonders how one 15-year-old managed to alienate virtually everyone at the school:

> Beneath the cynical incrustations of many years an instinct stirred to look into the unusual case of this boy and find out what made him the most detested boy in school. Among boys and masters there seemed to exist an extraordinary hostility toward him, and though Doctor Bacon had dealt with many sorts of schoolboy crimes, he had neither by himself nor with the aid of trusted sixth-formers been able to lay his hands on its underlying cause. It was probably no single thing, but a combination of things; it was most probably one of those intangible questions of personality [60].

Sensing that Basil needs some time away from his schoolmates, Doctor Bacon arranges for him to go to a Broadway musical. Basil's luck improves as soon as he gets to Manhattan. His chaperone, a teacher named Mr. Rooney, goes on a drinking binge, allowing Basil to explore the theater district on his own. Basil opens a letter from home and learns that his mother wants him to transfer to a school in Europe. His joy and relief are overwhelming: "No more St. Regis! No more St. Regis! He was almost strangling with happiness.... No more Doctor Bacon and Mr. Rooney.... He need no longer hate them, for they were impotent shadows in the stationary world that he was sliding away from, sliding past, waving his hand" (69). In the theater's lobby,

Introduction

Basil spots Ted Fay, the captain of the football team at Yale. (Fay is modeled on one of Fitzgerald's childhood idols, an All-American fullback named Ted Coy.[2]) Basil watches Fay leave the theater with an actress after the show. Then he follows the couple to a hotel tearoom, where the actress tells Fay that she has decided to marry a theater impresario. After he witnesses Fay's disappointment, Basil changes his mind about his mother's proposition:

> He did not understand all he had heard, but from his clandestine glimpse into the privacy of these two, with all the world that his short experience could conceive of at their feet, he had gathered that life for everybody was a struggle, sometimes magnificent from a distance, but always difficult and surprisingly simple and a little sad.... Suddenly Basil realized that he wasn't going to Europe. He could not forego the molding of his own destiny just to alleviate a few months of pain. The conquest of the successive worlds of school, college and New York—why, that was his true dream that he had carried from boyhood into adolescence, and because of the jeers of a few boys he had been about to abandon it and run ignominiously up a back alley! [74, 75].

On the surface, this passage seems to focus on three enviable characters—a football hero, a star on Broadway, and a prep-school student soaking in his first visit to New York. But instead of highlighting the trio's youth and good fortune, Fitzgerald laces the passage with melancholy. These characters struggle like everybody else. Life is *always* difficult, Basil concludes, *always* a little sad, even when it seems "magnificent from a distance." Near the end of the story, Basil's reputation as "the most detested boy" at St. Regis begins to fade. He makes a friend or two after Christmas vacation and then, during a basketball scrimmage, one of the other boys calls him "Lee-y." The nickname was hard to pronounce, but it was an improvement on everything else his schoolmates had called him. "They would all forget eventually," Basil thinks, "maybe during the summer. There would be new fresh boys in September; he would have a clean start next year" (76).

Before Fitzgerald wrote "The Freshest Boy," the most popular narratives set at British and American boarding schools—Thomas Hughes's *Tom Brown's Schooldays* (1857), Talbot Baines Reed's *The Fifth Form at St. Dominic's* (1887), Ralph Henry Barbour's *The Half-Back* (1899) and *For the Honor of the School* (1904), P. G. Wodehouse's *The Pothunters* (1902), *Tales of St. Austin's* (1903), and *The Gold Bat* (1904),

Introduction

Owen Johnson's *The Lawrenceville Stories* (1908–11), Arnold Lunn's *The Harrovians* (1913), and many others—featured thrilling victories, lighthearted humor, or both.³ Tom Brown and his friends strike back at the notorious bully Flashman, for instance, and the cricket trophies and other prized objects lost and stolen in Wodehouse's tales of "eccentric masters and nefarious schoolboys" (Watson 162) are returned to their rightful owners. *The Lawrenceville Stories* introduced this kind of narrative to thousands of American readers. Owen Johnson's fictional version of the Lawrenceville School is a paradise for rowdy, underachieving students. In the classroom, they fire spitballs and resist the urge to doze off during lectures. They watch in astonishment while a "frail and undersized" (14) boy eats forty-nine pancakes in one sitting, breaking a local record. They give their peers nicknames like Fire Crackers, the Uncooked Beefsteak, and the Tennessee Shad. And to escape from the school's routines, they go to a soda fountain called The Jigger Shop and order as many drinks as they can on credit:

> Half drugstore, half confectioner's, the Jigger Shop was the property of Doctor Furnell, whose chief interest in life consisted in a devotion to the theory of the millennium, to the lengthy expounding of which an impoverished boy would sometimes listen in the vain hope of establishing a larger credit. On everyday occasions the shop was under the charge of "Al," a creature without heart or pity, who knew the exact financial status of each of the four hundred odd boys, even to the amount and date of his allowance. Al made no errors, his sympathies were deaf to the call, and he never (like the doctor) committed the mistake of returning too much change [7].

On the rare occasions when Johnson's schoolboys suffer, their problems are short-lived and described by the narrator in a mock-epic style. When a student known as The Prodigious Hickey is chastised by school officials twice in one day, for example, he seethes with resentment and dreams about "single-handedly defying the whole organized, hereditary and entrenched tyranny that sought to crush him ... [about] matching his wits against the hydra despotism, perhaps going down gloriously like Spartacus, for the cause, but leaving behind a name that should roll down the generations of future boys" (13).⁴

In "The Freshest Boy," by contrast, the students at St. Regis range from unfriendly to merciless, Mr. Rooney is mean-spirited, and Doctor

Bacon seems jaded, a middle-aged school official "whose original real interest in boys was now tempered by the flustered cynicism which is the fate of all headmasters..." (59). Unlike previous heroes of school fiction, Basil Lee has nothing—no close friend, no adult mentor, no athletic or academic distinction—to take his mind off of his loneliness and disappointment. In spite of Basil's troubles, however, Fitzgerald's rendering of boarding-school culture is not entirely bleak. The outcast eventually realizes that he has brought his unpopularity on himself. "He saw now," the narrator explains, "that in certain ways he had erred at the outset—he had boasted, he had been considered yellow at football, he had pointed out people's mistakes to them, he had shown off his rather extraordinary fund of general information in class. But he had tried to do better and couldn't understand his failure to atone. It must be too late" (61). Basil's first year at school is punishing, but by the end of the story he seems to benefit from it. As soon as he kicks the habit of showing off in front of his peers, his situation starts to improve.

Malcolm Cowley once described "The Freshest Boy" as "a minor classic of prep-school life" (308). In this book, I want to suggest that it is more than that. By infusing the story with unhappy memories of his own first year at boarding school,[5] Fitzgerald introduced a new kind of school narrative. The novels, short stories, and films discussed in the following chapters pay scant attention to sports, upper-class male bonding, religion, practical jokes, and other subjects emphasized in nineteenth- and early twentieth-century fiction set at boarding schools. Instead, most of them feature variations on Fitzgerald's approach in "The Freshest Boy": an emotionally volatile teenager; a series of painful incidents; an open-ended conclusion in which the student survives his campus ordeal, but can't seem to put his anguish behind him. (The American school literature of the period examined in this book focuses almost exclusively on boys' schools, but there are of course many private academies for girls and most of the well-known American prep schools that originally enrolled only boys became coeducational by the 1970s. Several novels published in the past ten years, including Curtis Sittenfeld's *Prep* [2005], Anna Shapiro's *Living on Air* [2006], Anita Shreve's *Testimony* [2008], and Pamela Erens's *The Virgins* [2013], pay close attention to the experiences of female characters at boarding schools.)

Introduction

The thought that he was reformulating school fiction may not have crossed Fitzgerald's mind. As several critics have noted, Fitzgerald wrote the "Basil stories" for the money. The market for his short fiction peaked in the late 1920s, and throughout his career he viewed most of the stories he published in *The Saturday Evening Post, Esquire,* and other popular magazines as throwaways that produced a regular stream of income while he worked on novels that would make his name as a "serious writer." In particular, Jackson Bryer and John Kuehl explain, Fitzgerald worried that if he republished the Basil stories—along with several stories featuring Josephine Perry, a supremely confident young socialite—as a book, readers would think of them as his latest novel:

> Fitzgerald's dread lest "Basil and Josephine" seem a novel is understandable. He had not produced a full-length piece of fiction since *The Great Gatsby* (1925) and he hoped *Tender Is the Night* (published on April 12, 1934) would revive his reputation for serious long fiction. By 1934, most readers knew of him only as a popular writer who contributed stories like the Basil and Josephine series to the *Post* and other mass circulation magazines. These readers might very well regard a book of Basil and Josephine as "watered goods." Fitzgerald, who regarded the story—with its hack-work connotations and its literal potboiling function in his life—as less "artistic" and "serious" than the novel, was thus understandably uneasy [x].

Similarly, Matthew J. Bruccoli observes that Fitzgerald was "a little embarrassed by the Basil series: not by the stories themselves, most of which were excellent, but by the circumstance that he was writing stories about adolescents for the *Post*" (*Some Sort of Epic Grandeur* 266).

Regardless of Fitzgerald's motives, "The Freshest Boy" marks a turning point. American writers of the post–World War II era stayed clear of the moral lessons and schoolboy antics in previous works about prep-school life and, like Fitzgerald, accentuated dark humor and teenage angst. J. D. Salinger's *The Catcher in the Rye* (1951) is narrated by a prep-school misfit even more restless and demoralized than Basil Lee. John Knowles's *A Separate Peace* (1959) and *Peace Breaks Out* (1981) echo Fitzgerald by examining the destructive impulses of students without casting blame on the school they attend. Louis Auchincloss's *The Rector of Justin* (1964) highlights several adult characters' juvenile attitudes concerning a prep school and its legendary founder.

Introduction

James Kirkwood's *Good Times/Bad Times* (1968) features a student who endures a string of harrowing experiences at a private academy. And Richard Yates's *A Good School* (1978) challenges the received opinion that Northeastern boarding schools are the *ne plus ultra* of American secondary education. British school fiction has also grown darker since the 1920s. Novels such as James Hilton's *Goodbye, Mr. Chips* (1934), R. F. Delderfield's *To Serve Them All My Days* (1972), J. K. Rowling's Harry Potter series (1997–2007), and Meg Rosoff's *What I Was* (2007) blend the comedy, nostalgia, and moral didacticism of traditional British school literature with plots centering on grief and violence. In his bibliography of English schoolboy stories, Benjamin Watson attributes this change to the repercussions of World War I. The genre, he explains, "originated in an atmosphere that was effectively destroyed by [the war]. A solid wall of differences divides pre-war from post-war stories. The former celebrate English public schools as noble institutions engaged in character building for the good of the nation. The latter deride the stuffiness of public school values and tend to show the schoolboy as the victim rather than the beneficiary of the system" (ix).

A Good School was not a commercial success, but *The Rector of Justin* and *Good Times/Bad Times* were national bestsellers and *The Catcher in the Rye* (more than sixty-five million copies sold) and *A Separate Peace* (more than nine million copies sold) are among the most popular American novels of the past fifty years.[6] What can account for the broad appeal of these mournful school narratives, most of which are set in and around the World War II era and focus on characters who are white, male, Protestant, and privileged? The percentage of Americans who have attended a preparatory school is minuscule. In *The Best of the Best: Becoming Elite at an American Boarding School* (2009), Rubén A. Gaztambide-Fernández estimates that only a tenth of one percent of the nation's sixteen million secondary-school students attend elite private academies. Political and social commentators, moreover, rarely express much sympathy for the preppie. Indeed, well-to-do WASPS may be the only demographic group in the United States that can be ridiculed without fear of backlash. Say whatever you like about George H. W. Bush's vacation compound in Maine and his penchant for golf, boating, and other country-club pastimes—nobody is likely to take offense. To the contrary, Governor Ann Richards provoked gales of laughter at the 1988 Democratic National Convention by mocking Bush's Yankee Brahmin background: "Poor George. He can't help it. He was born with a silver foot in his mouth." A year later, Jim Hightower, Commissioner of the Texas Department of Agriculture, famously said that Bush "was born on third and thinks he hit a triple." Similarly, Walt Harrington argues that patricians like Bush have no business commenting on the economic challenges faced by less privileged Americans: "He can preach a renewed American opportunity, equal opportunity, but his life is testament to what can happen when one boy is more equal than others.... Hearing Bush preach the American Gospel ... is still like listening to a very tall man praise the virtues of being very tall. I think: *Yeah, that's easy for you to say*" (161).

Suspicious attitudes about WASP elites have also been commonplace in *Dead Poets Society* (1989), *Scent of a Woman* (1992), and other recent films set at American prep schools. The picture-perfect campuses in these films conceal disturbing things: bigotry, snobbery, mental illness, conspiracy, cheating scandals, sadistic teachers, you name it. The representations of boarding-school culture in the movies have become so unflattering, and so predictable, that the time seems ripe for a different approach. The surest way for filmmakers to revitalize the genre would be to turn their attention to characters whose schooldays are troubled by problems that originate off-campus. (To their credit, the creators of *The Simpsons* avoid most of the clichés of prep-school cinema in "The Bart Wants What It Wants," an episode that begins at Springfield Preparatory School. When the studious, talented Lisa Simpson lays eyes on the school's "lush and verdant" campus and well-equipped classrooms, she cries "I belong here!" and refuses to leave.)

The popularity of American school fiction also seems curious because the nation's prep schools are less prestigious than they used to be. David V. Hicks, a former rector of St. Paul's School, reports that "the American boarding school—Andover, Choate, Groton, St. Paul's, and others—is in trouble, an endangered species of the independent school genus" (523). Since 1985, enrollments at private schools have increased by twenty percent, but enrollments at private boarding schools have decreased by almost ten percent, in part because of critiques such as Louis M. Crosier's *Casualties of Privilege* (1991), "which describe these schools as places where drug use, bullying, eating disorders, and sexual activity are 'the common currency of social acceptance and individual prowess.' In an era of increasing violence and disorder, teen pregnancy and sexually transmitted disease, addictive and destructive pressures and temptations, parents hesitate to entrust their children to schools that are either unwilling to acknowledge their destructive aspects or unable to assert control over them" (Hicks 524).

Nevertheless, most Americans seem familiar with what I have come to think of as the prep-school myth. More specifically, it is widely assumed that private academies are ideal places for young people to prepare themselves for exceedingly bright futures. These institutions are posh and exclusive, American counterparts of British public schools such as Eton, Rugby, Harrow, Charterhouse, and Westminster. They have long roots in the nation's history. Phillips Academy Andover, for example, can boast that "Paul Revere designed its school seal and John Hancock signed [its] Act of Incorporation" (Sargent 64). Their academic programs, the myth continues, are unmatched, and most of their graduates are destined for high-powered careers in finance, medicine, media, government, and the law. They are, as Gaztambide-Fernández argues, schools in which students "internalize elite status and convince themselves that they deserve what they get" (1).

In "The Freshest Boy," Fitzgerald stresses the distance between the prep-school myth and the reality Basil finds at St. Regis. While traveling to the school from his home in the Midwest, Basil, an avid reader of school fiction, can hardly wait to join a community steeped in prestige.[7] The problem, as he sees it, is that a schoolmate named Lewis Crum interrupts his daydreams by insisting that the campus environment at St. Regis is harsh and repressive. "You wait!" Crum tells the newcomer. "They'll take all that freshness out of you" (56). Like an adolescent Don Quixote, Basil refuses to give up the idealistic notions he has drawn from books without a fight, so he suffers one humiliation after another until he begins to see St. Regis in a clear-eyed way. To understand Fitzgerald's reformulation of prep-school fiction, it is important to notice what is *not* examined in "The Freshest Boy." Fitzgerald is reputedly one of America's leading observers of the moneyed elite, the writer who asserted that the rich are "different from you and me,"[8] but, with the exception of one passage in which Basil cringes at the thought that he is "one of the poorest boys at a rich boys' school" (59), the story has nothing to say about social class. Prep schools tend to be associated with right-wing politics, but the story does not contain a single reference to America's political landscape circa 1910. Unlike most authors of school literature, Fitzgerald does not locate his fictional academy in an attractive pastoral setting. Eastchester, New York, the narrator tells us, was a "suburban farming community, with a small shoe factory. The institutions which pandered to the factory workers were the ones patronized by the boys—a movie house, a quick-lunch wagon on wheels known as the Dog and the Bostonian Candy Kitchen" (62). "The Freshest Boy" does not even pose questions about education. The reader learns that Basil's grades were poor during his fall-semester ordeal, but apart from that the schoolwork assigned at St. Regis is not mentioned at all. (As Arthur Powell observes, when Americans discuss independent schools, they usually pay more attention to issues relating to class than to those relating to education: "[I]ssues of economic privilege have traditionally overshadowed issues of educational practice in public consciousness of independent schools. When success or scandal gets them in the papers, their names are usually preceded by 'exclusive' or 'elite.' Their existence symbolizes both the advantages conveyed by privilege and the insulation of privilege from the presumed melting pot of public education" [4].)

What Fitzgerald does examine is Basil's misery when his boarding-school dreams are displaced by a nightmare. In this passage, for instance, Fitzgerald turns the reader's attention away from everything but the schoolboy's "despair and self-pity":

> Had these slights, so much the bitterer for their lack of passion, been visited upon Basil in September, they would have been unbearable. But since then he had developed a shell of hardness which, while it did not add to his attractiveness, spared him certain delicacies of torture. In misery enough, and despair and self-pity, he went the other way along the street for a little distance until he could control the violent contortions of his face. Then, taking a roundabout route, he started back to school [65].

This emphasis on the ways in which prep-school life can give rise to anguish and disappointment is what Salinger, Knowles, Auchincloss,

Kirkwood, Yates, and other writers inherited from "The Freshest Boy." From the 1950s through the 1970s, American school narratives shared a certain somber mood and a certain revisionist agenda. They depicted the Northeastern prep school as a sphere in which there is much to endure and little to enjoy. They insisted that every boarding school is only a school, not an enchanted academy in which highly privileged young people are placed on the fast track to unlimited success. The authors of these works, in other words, try to complicate and, if possible, to dispel the prep-school myth. That has turned out to be a difficult task. The idea that a small number of students at exclusive private academies savor the best of everything while gaining enormous social and economic advantages seems as deeply ingrained in American culture as it is in the imagination of Fitzgerald's unhappy teenager in "The Freshest Boy."

* * *

A few words about terminology:

- Strictly speaking, the terms "boarding school" and "preparatory school" are not interchangeable. Private day schools, for instance, are preparatory schools, but not boarding schools. The terms are generally used as if they were synonymous in American historical, literary, and journalistic discourse, however, so I will use them that way here.
- The officials who run prep schools are usually called headmasters or headmistresses, but at some institutions the top administrators are known as principals, deans, or (at church schools) rectors.
- At some private schools, each year of study is known as a "form." First form corresponds with seventh grade at an American middle school. Sixth form corresponds with senior year at an American high school.

1

Masculine Competition and Boarding-School Culture in The Catcher in the Rye

> *If you get on the side where all the hot-shots are, then it's a game, all right—I'll admit that. But if you get on the other side, where there aren't any hot-shots, then what's a game about it?*—J. D. Salinger, *The Catcher in the Rye*

American audiences have a knack for misinterpreting cultural icons. As the biographer James Lincoln Collier points out, Louis Armstrong is frequently mistaken for a "cheerful, eager-to-please entertainer who mugged his way through his songs, talked a little comic jive talk, and occasionally played the trumpet" (3).[1] Gordon Gekko, the villain of Oliver Stone's *Wall Street* (1987) and *Wall Street: Money Never Sleeps* (2010), has become a role model for would-be financiers. Michael Douglas, who won an Academy Award for his first performance as Gekko, "often expresses his astonishment at the many Wall Street males who have sought him out in public places just to say, 'Man, I want to tell you, you are the biggest reason I got into the business. I watched *Wall Street*, and I wanted to be Gordon Gekko'" (Lewis 128). And somehow, through another process of mass-audience distortion, J. D. Salinger's *The Catcher in the Rye* (1951) has been tagged as the story of a teenager who despises "phonies." When Salinger died in 2010, references to Holden Caulfield's aversion to insincerity were everywhere. The London *Times* described *The Catcher in the Rye* as a "first-person account of a late adolescent for whom everything is in suspense; he seeks to make contact, but meets only 'phonies' (the book gave this word an added dimension which it has not lost)" (1). The satirical website *The Onion* also stressed Holden's contempt for "phonies," in an article that imitates the tone and rhythm of his voice:

> BUNCH OF PHONIES MOURN J. D. SALINGER
> CORNISH, NH—In this big dramatic production that didn't do anyone any good (and was pretty embarrassing, really, if you think about it), thousands upon thousands of phonies across the country mourned the death of author J. D. Salinger, who was 91 years old for crying out loud. "He had a real impact on the literary world and on millions of readers," said hot-shot English professor David Clarke, who is just like the rest of them, and even works at one of those crumby schools that rich people send their kids to so they don't have to look at them for four years [1].

More recently, the *New York Times* noted that Salinger's efforts to have his name removed from the J. D. Salinger Scholarship at Ursinus College were practically inevitable because for decades he had "done everything possible to protect his privacy from the same stinking phonies who'd so unnerved Holden Caulfield" (Kourkounis A1). (Salinger enrolled at Ursinus in 1938, but dropped out after spending only three months there.) Holden's "war against the phonies" (Pinsker 13) has also played a central role in critical discussions of *The Catcher in the Rye*. Arthur Heiserman and James E. Miller, Jr., were among the first to characterize the wanderings of Salinger's antihero as a "frenzied search for the genuine in a terrifyingly phony world" (223), and many have agreed, including David Castronovo, who recently labeled Holden as a character who believes "there is something ... dead and phony and disgusting about the arrangement of things" (57). Similarly, Dan Wakefield observes that "[t]he things that Holden finds so deeply repulsive are things he calls 'phony' and the 'phoniness' in every instance is the absence of love, and, often, the substitution of pretense for love" (197). Ihab Hassan concludes that "Holden is motivated by a compelling desire to commune and communicate, a desire constantly thwarted by the phoniness, indifference and vulgarity that surround him" (163). Charles McGrath, moreover, argues that Salinger's preoccupation with "phonies" has become passé: "In general what has dated most in Mr. Salinger's writing is not the prose ... but the ideas. Mr. Salinger's fixation on the difference between 'phoniness,' as Holden Caulfield would put it, and authenticity now has a twilight, '50s feeling about it. It's no longer news, and probably never was. This is the theme,

1. Masculine Competition and Boarding-School Culture

though, that comes increasingly to dominate [Salinger's work]: the unsolvable problem of ego and self-consciousness, of how to lead a spiritual life in a vulgar, material society" ("Still Paging Mr. Salinger" C1). These commentators have overstated the significance of Holden's "war." He complains about insincerity, to be sure, but the *bête noire* that irks him throughout the novel is masculine success. From a naval officer he meets in New York to his brother D.B. (a Hollywood screenwriter), male characters linked with prestige, authority, wealth, and fame drive Salinger's narrator into fits of resentment. Given Holden's jaundiced view of successful men, his misadventures at three Northeastern prep schools should not come as a surprise. He tries to distance himself from the greed and arrogance he associates with "hot-shots," but prep-school life circa 1950 offered no refuge from aggressive masculine competition. Accordingly, Holden's prospects at the end of the novel are dimmer than most critics have recognized. A young man of his generation could conceivably avoid contact with "phonies," but how could he disengage himself from America's pervasive culture of competition and success?

"Where there aren't any hot-shots"

Holden Caulfield begins his indictment of successful men by describing his brother's career in the movie industry as a form of prostitution: "He just got a Jaguar. One of those little English jobs that can do around two hundred miles an hour. It cost him damn near four thousand bucks. He's got a lot of dough, now. He didn't *use* to. He used to be just a regular writer, when he was home. He wrote this terrific book of short stories, *The Secret Goldfish*, in case you never heard of him.... Now he's out in Hollywood, D.B., being a prostitute" (4). This passage introduces a pattern that repeats over and over in *The Catcher in the Rye*—male characters connected with wealth and status are almost certain to elicit a hostile reaction from Salinger's antihero. Holden has nothing to say about his brother's occupation except that it pays well. In New York, D.B. was a "regular writer," a literary craftsman unconcerned about commercial success, but now Holden is convinced that his brother has become a Hollywood "hot-shot." As

Bernard Oldsey points out, "D.B. has been Holden's idol; but the idol is crumbling, may even have crumbled.... Holden has already lost one brother to death and is extremely reluctant to admit having lost the other to Hollywood" (210). What kind of work has D.B. done since he moved to Los Angeles and "prostituted himself" (124)? Has he written musicals? Westerns? Crime films? How did he make the transition from short stories to screenplays? Holden does not address these questions because his attention is riveted to the "dough" his brother has earned.² Similarly, Holden assumes that there must be something deplorable about Mr. Ossenburger, a funeral-services tycoon: "I lived in the Ossenburger Memorial Wing of the new dorms.... It was named after this guy Ossenburger that went to [Pencey Prep]. He made a pot of dough in the undertaking business after he got out of Pencey. What he did, he started these undertaking parlors all over the country that you could get members of your family buried for about five bucks apiece. You should see old Ossenburger. He probably just shoves them in a sack and dumps them in the river" (22). Holden's sardonic sense of humor is in top form here, but his remarks about Ossenburger's business practices are a smokescreen. Holden dislikes the tycoon because he came to Pencey in a "big goddam Cadillac" and gave a speech in which he "[told] us all about what a swell guy he was, what a hot-shot and all" (22, 23). Holden knows very well that few status symbols match the impact of an expensive new car. While other young men his age look forward to owning a sports car or a luxury sedan, Holden views the Jaguar and the Cadillac as unmistakable signs that his brother and Ossenburger have sold out.

Holden's descriptions of male celebrities are equally caustic. At a nightclub in New York City, he ridicules the showmanship of a popular musician:

> Ernie's a big fat colored guy that plays the piano. He's a terrific snob and he won't hardly even talk to you unless you're big shot or a celebrity.... I certainly like to hear him play, but sometimes you feel like turning his goddam piano over. I think it's because sometimes when he plays, he *sounds* like the kind of guy that won't talk to you unless you're a big shot.... He had a big damn mirror in front of the piano, with this big spotlight on him, so that everybody could watch his face while he played.... I'm not too sure what the name of song was that he was playing when I came in, but whatever it was, he was really stinking it up.... You

1. Masculine Competition and Boarding-School Culture

should've heard the crowd, though, when he was finished. You would've puked. They went mad [104–05, 109–10].

Holden pans Ernie's performance, but the real object of this rant is the musician's fame—the mirror, the spotlight, the applause. Holden considers himself something of a music aficionado, but he prefers entertainers who work in obscurity. (Later in the novel, he lavishes praise on the kettle drummer in the orchestra at Radio City Music Hall and a half-forgotten jazz singer named Estelle Fletcher.) During intermission at a Broadway show, Holden—reenacting an incident in F. Scott Fitzgerald's short story "The Freshest Boy"—catches a glimpse of a famous young man. When Basil Lee spots Ted Fay, the captain of Yale's football team, the very idea that he and the All-American are members of the same audience fills him with awe. This celebrity sighting, the reader suspects, is a moment that Basil will remember for the rest of his life:

> As [Basil] took out his ticket, his gaze was caught and held by a sculptured profile a few feet away. It was that of a well-built blond young man of about twenty with a strong chin and direct gray eyes. Basil's brain spun wildly for a moment and then came to rest upon a name—more than a name—upon a legend, a sign in the sky. What a day! He had never seen the young man before, but from a thousand pictures he knew beyond the possibility of a doubt that it was Ted Fay ... [70].

For Salinger's teenager, by contrast, the sight of a well-known young man is intensely annoying: "Some dopey movie actor was standing near us, having a cigarette. I don't know his name, but he always plays the part of a guy in a war movie that gets yellow before it's time to go over the top. He was with some gorgeous blonde, and the two of them were trying to be very blasé and all, like as if he didn't even know people were looking at him" (164–65). Even Sir Laurence Olivier's performance in his film adaptation of *Hamlet* leaves Holden unimpressed: "I just don't see what's so marvelous about ... Olivier, that's all. He has a terrific voice, and he's a helluva handsome guy ... but he wasn't at all the way D.B. said Hamlet was. He was too much like a goddam general, instead of a sad, screwed-up type guy" (152). *A terrific snob. Some dopey movie actor. I just don't see what's so marvelous.* Throughout his narrative, Holden suggests that male celebrities and other "hot-shots" do not deserve the acclaim and other rewards they receive. He repeatedly questions their abilities and reputations, suggesting that they are full of themselves and overrated.³

In the section of *The Catcher in the Rye* set at Pencey Prep, Holden looks askance at his roommate's reputation as a boarding-school ladies' man. Ward Stradlater brims with confidence because he is "madly in love with himself" (36). He seems dapper because he helps himself to the most stylish items in Holden's wardrobe. And in violation of Pencey's rules, Stradlater drives his dates around in a car he borrows from his basketball coach. "In every school I've gone to," Holden complains, "all the athletic bastards stick together" (56). In the nightclub episode, Holden skewers Ernie and then takes aim at the musician's audience. He rails against a young man whose clothes suggest that he may attend an Ivy League university: "On my right there was this very Joe Yale-looking guy, in a gray flannel suit and one of those flitty-looking Tattersall vests. All those Ivy League bastards look alike" (111–12). Then he ridicules the machismo of a naval officer: "He was one of those guys that think they're being a pansy if they don't break around forty of your fingers when they shake hands with you. God, I hate that stuff" (113).⁴ Taken together, these passages demonstrate that successful men exasperate Holden even more than the "phonies" who also grate on his nerves. Most of the characters Holden labels as "hot-shots" have done nothing in particular to set him off. D.B. shows sustained concern for his troubled younger brother. Instead of spending his weekends relaxing with his girlfriend, a British actress, he brings her to Holden's hospital room. (To give the brothers time to speak privately, or perhaps to avoid the sight of a 16-year-old in physical and emotional distress, the actress quickly excuses herself and walks to a ladies' room on the other side of the building.) Ernie's performance seems to dazzle everyone in the nightclub except for Holden. The movie actor tries to blend in with the crowd at the theater. And by overreacting to the sight of an "Ivy League bastard" in what he calls a "flitty-looking" vest, Holden inadvertently reveals his own belligerence and homophobia. (In a 1972 article that speculates about the course of Holden's life after the incidents recounted in *The Catcher in the Rye*, Stefan Kanfer suggests that the angst-ridden teenager eventually outgrew his reflexive contempt for Ivy Leaguers: "Maybe you were one of those who felt that … all along I was a conformist manqué. You were right. Boy, were you right!

1. Masculine Competition and Boarding-School Culture

For a while. A long while. At first I bought the whole shot. My head got straight; I went to Columbia—after I said I would never go to any of those phony Ivy schools—and even tried a year of law school. I wore a Tattersall vest. I even wore a hat, for God's sake. Not a red hunting cap, I mean a hat. A whaddyacallit. A fedora" [50].)

The most noteworthy "hot-shot" in *The Catcher in the Rye* may be Holden's father. Mr. Caulfield is not exactly a character (he never appears, not even in Holden's recollections of his childhood), yet he plays an important role in the novel. Salinger provides only a few basic facts about Mr. Caulfield. He is a partner in a corporate law firm. He owns an apartment on the Upper East Side and a vacation home near a lake in Maine. He has invested in a string of Broadway shows. He is a member of at least one country club. He sends Holden to boarding schools and expects him to earn strong grades and move on to an elite college. He has a hot temper—for instance, he becomes "quite touchy" (1) when people disclose private information about him. In short, Mr. Caulfield is a "hot-shot" *par excellence*. Holden does not seem to view his father with much affection, and the reader senses that the busy father and the bereft, erratic son do not spend much time together. Nevertheless, Mr. Caulfield differs from other "hot shots" mentioned in *The Catcher in the Rye* in that Holden does not seem to consider him dishonorable or ridiculous. Mr. Caulfield lost his son Allie to leukemia, but he has not allowed his grief to overwhelm him. Unlike Holden, Mr. Caulfield has mourned, recovered, and gotten on with his life. He is a "hot-shot" who has suffered, and that, in his son's mind, distinguishes him from other wealthy, prominent men. Holden recognizes that he lacks his father's capacity to suffer, survive, and keep moving forward. He notices that his mother lacks that capacity, too. Since Allie's death, she has endured bouts of anxiety and insomnia and generally "hasn't felt too healthy" (140). Does Holden admire his father's resilience? Does it bother him that his father is still prosperous, still in one piece? Salinger leaves these questions unanswered. All the reader knows for sure is that Holden seldom mentions Mr. Caulfield and does everything he can think of to postpone telling his father about his latest boarding-school fiasco.

Though Holden passes judgment on male characters throughout *The Catcher in the Rye*, he pays little attention to their interactions with women. For him, the term "hot-shot" signifies a man who thrives in competition with other men. Accordingly, Holden becomes suspicious and agitated whenever he encounters male characters who are rich or successful. As Michael Kimmel points out, this kind of preoccupation with masculine competition plays a central role in American gender politics:

> In large part, it's other men who are important to American men; American men define their masculinity, not as much in relation to women, but in relation to each other. Masculinity is largely a homosocial enactment.... From the early nineteenth century until the present day, much of men's relentless effort to prove their manhood contains this core element of homosociality. From fathers and boyhood friends to teachers, coworkers, and bosses, the evaluative eyes of other men are always upon us, watching, judging [7].

Similarly, David Leverenz writes that for many American males the most powerful fear is "not fear of women but of being ashamed or humiliated in front of other men or being dominated by stronger men" (451).[5] These observations help to explain why millions of young readers have felt an affinity with Holden, a character far too privileged to serve as a representative teenager of his (or any other) time. Salinger's antihero is unconventional in many ways, but when it comes to his resentment of successful men, and his tacit assumption that he will never join their ranks, Holden speaks for countless adolescents.

When Holden turns his attention to female characters, the tone of his narrative usually becomes less abrasive. He describes Selma Thurmer, the daughter of Pencey's headmaster, as "a pretty nice girl.... What I liked about her, she didn't give you a lot of horse manure about what a great guy her father was" (5, 6). He is charmed by Mrs. Morrow, the mother of a former schoolmate, even though he despises her son Ernest. He enjoys sharing a meal with two nuns and also praises his mother, his sister Phoebe, his friend Jane Gallagher, and the hat-check girl at the Wicker Bar in Manhattan. It seldom enters his mind that women or girls may turn out to be "hot-shots." He unwinds in their company, holding back the sarcasm he uses in most of his conversations with male characters. As Edwin T. Bowden argues, Holden feels more at ease with women because his relationships with them tend to be based on affection, not competition: "The one line of communica-

1. Masculine Competition and Boarding-School Culture

tion for Holden, the one way of establishing contact with others, is that of affection. And Holden is always quick to offer affection as well as to respond to it" (60). Granville Hicks notes that most of the objects of the young man's affection are female: "He is not only full of tenderness for his sister Phoebe and all children; he is touched by persons casually met on his pilgrimage—by the woman on the train, by the girls in the nightclub, by the nuns in the station—and wants to make them all happy. In the end he feels sorry even for those who have hurt him" (212). When Holden criticizes female characters, they are usually guilty of Caulfield's cardinal sin: they let it be known that they admire male "hot-shots." In the Edmont Hotel, he seethes after Bernice, a tourist from Seattle, crows about catching a glimpse of Peter Lorre:

"I and my girl friends saw Peter Lorre last night," she said. "The movie actor. In person. He was buyin' a newspaper. He's *cute*."
"You're lucky," I told her. "You're really lucky. You know that?" She was really a moron [93].

Similarly, Holden can hardly contain his irritation when Sally Hayes tells him that a student from Harvard and a cadet from West Point have been "[c]alling her up *night and day*" (138) and when she pauses to chat with an acquaintance from Andover. The compliments Holden pays to female characters, then, should not be interpreted as some sort of protest against the sexist attitudes of his era. He enjoys spending time with women and girls for a self-serving reason: it temporarily frees him from the company of "hot-shots."

Because Holden dislikes successful men, he habitually abstains from activities that involve masculine competition. He is not expelled from boarding schools because he lacks academic ability. Two of his former English teachers, Mr. Antolini and Mr. Hartzell, affirm that he is a talented writer and he reads novels by Thomas Hardy, Ring Lardner, Isak Dinesen, and W. Somerset Maugham in his spare time. As Antolini points out, Holden fails at school because he makes "absolutely no effort at all" (242).[6] In spite of his keen interest in athletics, Holden is disgusted by other characters' competitive impulses. He ridicules a young man who bores his date with a detailed description of a professional football game, but he also mentions that he attends the tennis championships at Forest Hills every summer. Apparently, he prefers the performances of amateur tennis stars—professionals were ineligible to compete at Forest Hills until 1968—to those of the "hot-shots" in the National Football League. At school, he pokes fun at the athletic rivalry between Pencey Prep and Saxon Hall. In New York, he pities a group of young women when he imagines that within a few years most of them will marry "dopey guys ... Guys that get sore and childish as hell if you beat them at golf, or even just some stupid game like ping-pong" (160). And to keep his distance from the sordid business of winning and losing, he serves as an equipment manager at school instead of trying out for a team.[7] By calling attention to Holden's reluctance to compete, Salinger suggests that his narrator's predicament as a boarding-school misfit was inevitable from the start. As David V. Hicks explains, athletic competition has always been a cornerstone of prep-school life: "[Athletics] toughened up the boys and girls, taught them perseverance and courage, and emphasized the need for teamwork and loyalty to others. Games—likely to be the most enduring legacy of these schools—stoked the furnace of ambition and fired the will to excel. All of this physical exertion not only heightened the drama of life, but tempered the character of the athlete, who was expected at all times to show grace in victory and equanimity in defeat" (529).[8] Thus, it is not hard to understand why Holden, a young man with no discernible "furnace of ambition," "will to excel," or desire to be "toughened up," has struggled to find a niche at the prep schools he has attended.

When Holden mentions recreational activities he has enjoyed (ballroom dancing, playing with his brother Allie's toy sailboat in a pond in Central Park, tossing a football with two of his classmates at Pencey) they have little to do with competition. And in conversations and reveries about the future, he rules out every potential occupation that would force him to engage in competition. The common denominators of the "careers" that do appeal to him—recluse in the New England woods, ranch hand in Colorado, deaf-mute auto mechanic, "catcher in the rye"—are silence, isolation, and the absence of any form of masculine competition. More conventional possibilities, such as a legal career like his father's, are out of the question because they would involve vying with "hot-shots" for money and status:

> Lawyers are all right, I guess—but it doesn't appeal to me ... I mean they're all right if they go around saving innocent guys' lives all the time,

1. Masculine Competition and Boarding-School Culture

and like that, but you don't *do* that kind of stuff if you're a lawyer. All you do is make a lot of dough and play golf and play bridge and buy cars and drink Martinis and look like a hot-shot. And besides. Even if you *did* go around saving guys' lives and all, how would you know if you did it because you really *wanted* to save guys' lives, or because you did it because what you *really* wanted to do was be a terrific lawyer, with everybody slapping you on the back and congratulating you in court when the goddam trial was over, the reporters and everybody ... [223–24].

The trouble with Holden's desire to shun competition is that he does not live in silence and isolation. Because he lives on the Upper East Side and on the campuses of Northeastern prep schools, he is constantly reminded that other characters do not view success the way he does. With the exception of Holden, the Caulfield family is crowded with high-achieving males. Mr. Caulfield's practice is so lucrative that he takes the family to Maine every summer, where they golf and attend dances at a country club. D.B. is an accomplished, versatile writer. Even Allie showed incipient signs of brilliance. "He was two years younger than I was," Holden recalls, "but he was about fifty times as intelligent. He was terrifically intelligent. His teachers were always writing letters to my mother, telling her what a pleasure it was having a boy like Allie in their class" (49–50). Holden's continual exposure to successful male characters bothers him because he is more competitive than he is willing to admit. He does not seem to mind being kicked out of Pencey Prep, but it's galling to hear about students who attend Andover, Choate, Princeton, Harvard, West Point, and other exclusive institutions. (Holden's contempt for elite schools seems to have sprung directly from Salinger, who told the journalist Lillian Ross that he hated "every school and college in the world, but the ones with the best reputation first" [22].) Holden does not seem to mind abstaining from sports, but it's galling to think that his roommate is one of the best athletes at Pencey. And although he does not seem to mind that he never went past holding hands with Jane Gallagher, it's galling to think that she is dating the self-assured, sexually experienced Stradlater.

One possible explanation for Holden's dim view of competition is that Salinger wanted *The Catcher in the Rye* to convey, among other things, a teenager's articulation of concerns like those highlighted in

David Reisman's *The Lonely Crowd* (1950), C. Wright Mills's *White Collar* (1951), and other studies of America's "social character" published in the early 1950s. Reisman, for example, posited that endless competition and status-seeking diminishes the individuality of white-collar workers.[9] Similarly, Mills warned that the nation's corporate culture had redefined the personal characteristics of employees as "commodities in the labor market":

> In a society of employees, dominated by the marketing mentality, it is inevitable that a personality market should arise. For in the great shift from manual skills to the art of handling, selling, and servicing people, personal or even intimate traits of employees are drawn into the sphere of exchange and become commodities in the labor market. Whenever there is a transfer of control over one individual's personal traits to another for a price, a sale of those traits which affect one's impressions upon others, a personality market arises.... In all work involving the personality market ... one's personality and personal traits become part of the means of production. In this sense a person instrumentalizes and externalizes intimate features of his person and disposition [182, 225].

Holden probably would not take issue with these findings. After all, he blasts several characters who seem to personify the conformity and mercenary impulses highlighted by these and other social commentators of the era. His disdain for his brother's screenwriting career, for example, seems in step with Mills's admonitions about "personality markets" which transfer "control over one individual's personal traits to another for a price." Early in his career, D.B. wrote poignant short stories based on childhood memories. Now he cranks out formulaic screenplays for his employers in Hollywood studios. Nonetheless, Salinger suggests that bereavement, not ominous trends in the nation's "social character," is the principal source of Holden's desire to go "where there aren't any hot-shots" (12). As Louis Menand points out, most of Holden's emotional distress seems to stem from memories of Allie's death: "[Salinger] wasn't trying to expose the spiritual poverty of a conformist culture; he was writing a story about a boy whose little brother has died. Holden, after all, isn't unhappy because he sees that people are phonies; he sees that people are phonies because he is unhappy. What makes his view of other people so cutting and his disappointment so unappeasable is the same thing that makes Hamlet's feelings so cutting and unappeasable: his grief" (84).[10] Gerald Rosen places this reading in a religious context, asserting that "beneath Holden's quarrel with his culture, there is always his quarrel with God, whom Holden can't forgive for killing his brother" (165). (Holden's grief, by the way, helps to explain his hostility toward Pencey's benefactor Mr. Ossenburger. Having mourned the loss of his younger brother, Holden finds the tycoon, who has gotten rich by peddling cut-rate funeral services, unspeakably crass.) Allie died as a promising child: he never had the opportunity to attend a prep school, join a varsity team, or launch a career. Hence, the thought of pursuing things denied to his brother fills Holden with guilt and he recoils when other characters do not share his misgivings about success.

The Pencey Chapters

In light of Holden's aversion to masculine competition, his erratic behavior at Pencey Prep is very much in character.[11] Salinger does not provide a full account of the time Holden spent at the school. The opening chapters of *The Catcher in the Rye* concentrate on several incidents which take place after the headmaster, Dr. Thurmer, notifies him that he has been expelled because of his fall-semester grades: four Fs and a C. The reader does not even receive a full account of Holden's experiences after the meeting with Thurmer. The Pencey chapters are limited to the hours leading up to Holden's decision to go home before the beginning of Christmas vacation:

> All of a sudden, I decided what I'd really do, I'd get the hell out of Pencey right that same night and all. I mean not wait till Wednesday or anything. I just didn't want to hang around any more. It made me too sad and lonesome. So what I decided to do, I decided I'd take a room in a hotel in New York—some very inexpensive hotel and all—and just take it easy till Wednesday. Then, on Wednesday, I'd go home all rested up and feeling swell [66–67].[12]

Holden's eagerness to leave Pencey is understandable. He is a dispirited figure early in the novel, a 16-year-old going through the motions of prep-school life even though he, his teachers, and his schoolmates know that he is not going to return after the holidays. Salinger stages a number of episodes in which Holden interacts with characters connected with the school, but at the same time he emphasizes his narrator's isolation. After Holden leaves Pencey's fencing equipment in a subway car, for example, he sits alone, "ostracized" by the students on the team: "We'd gone in to New York that morning for this fencing meet with McBurney School. Only, we didn't have the meet. I left all the foils and equipment and stuff on the goddam subway. It wasn't all my fault. I had to keep getting up to look at this map, so we'd know where to get off.... The whole team ostracized me the whole way back on the train" (6).[13] This blunder highlights Holden's sense of disengagement from Pencey: imagine how trivial a student's responsibilities as equipment manager of a school team must seem after he has been informed of his expulsion. As John Seelye points out, the timing of Holden's departure from the school is another telling sign of his disengagement: "Whether you style it a 'quest' or a 'flight,' Holden's trip has no final destination, being a passage without a rite. Notably, Holden's hegira takes place between the time he leaves Pencey and the official date the school will be let out, a time frame he invents for himself and, being disjoined from adult or social chronology, a period with no identifiable place in any conventional context" (27).

The annual football game against Saxon Hall unites the school community, but for Holden it serves as a stark reminder that he is an outsider:

> It was the last game of the year, and you were supposed to commit suicide or something if old Pencey didn't win. I remember around three o'clock that afternoon I was standing way the hell up on top of Thomsen Hill, right next to this crazy cannon that was in the Revolutionary War and all. You could see the whole field from there, and you could see the two teams bashing each other all over the place. You couldn't see the grandstand too hot, but you could hear them all yelling, deep and terrific on the Pencey side, because practically the whole school except me was there ... [5].

Holden has spent enough time at Pencey to have learned the name of the hill and the provenance of the cannon, yet he seems as detached from his schoolmates as a phantom watching the mortal world go on without him. He tries to seem nonchalant, but his narrative clearly indicates that he felt wounded and lonely the day he left Pencey. On

1. Masculine Competition and Boarding-School Culture

Thomsen Hill, he indulges in a few moments of sentiment, trying to say "good-by" to the school (7). On the way to the home of Mr. Spencer, his history teacher, he becomes so dejected that he feels as though he has become invisible.[14] Holden hopes the visit with Spencer will present another chance to "feel some kind of good-by," but the teacher disappoints him by holding forth on the subject of his failing grade. "I flunked you," Spencer says, "because you knew absolutely nothing.... But absolutely nothing. I doubt very much if you opened your textbook even once the whole term. Did you? Tell the truth, boy.... Do you blame me for flunking you, boy?" (15, 17). To prove that he bears no responsibility for Holden's F, Mr. Spencer reads aloud from the essay section of his final exam. Holden replies without protest to Spencer's self-exonerating questions, but this tactic hurts his feelings: "I don't think I'll ever forgive him for reading me that crap.... I wouldn't've read it out loud to *him* if *he*'d written it—I really wouldn't. In the first place, I'd only *written* that damn note so that he wouldn't feel too bad about flunking me" (17). As Jonathan Baumbach notes, Holden's behavior in this episode seems more thoughtful than that of his elderly teacher: "While Spencer, out of a childish need for personal justification, insensitively embarrasses Holden (already wounded by his expulsion from Pencey) the boy is mature enough to be kind to his conspicuously vulnerable antagonist. Holden accepts the full burden of responsibility for his scholastic failure so as to relieve Spencer of his sense of guilt" (58).

Holden's remaining hours at Pencey do nothing at all to cheer him up. He bickers with his suitemate Robert Ackley. He is overwhelmed by jealousy when he learns that his roommate has a date with Jane Gallagher. He agrees to write an English composition for Stradlater, but the paper, a description of Allie's baseball glove, stirs up some of his most unbearable memories:

> He got leukemia and died when we were up in Maine, on July 18, 1946.... I was only thirteen, and they were going to have me psychoanalyzed and all, because I broke all the windows in the garage. I don't blame them. I really don't. I slept in the garage the night he died, and I broke all the goddam windows with my fist, just for the hell of it. I even tried to break all the windows on the station wagon we had that summer, but my hand was already broken and everything by that time and I couldn't do it. It

was a very stupid thing to do, I'll admit, but I hardly didn't even know I was doing it, and you didn't know Allie [49, 50].

As if these tribulations weren't enough, Holden suffers a beating later in the evening after he provokes a fistfight with Stradlater.[15] Even during his last attempt to express his defiance before returning to New York, Holden cannot break away from the anguish and embarrassment which have shadowed him since he learned of his expulsion:

> When I was all set to go, when I had my bags and all, I stood for a while next to the stairs and took a last look down the goddam corridor. I was sort of crying, I don't know why. I put my red hunting hat on, and turned the peak around to the back, the way I liked it, and then I yelled at the top of my goddam voice, "*Sleep tight, ya morons!*" I'll bet I woke up every bastard on the whole floor. Then I got the hell out. Some stupid guy had thrown peanut shells all over the stairs, and I damn near broke my crazy neck [68].

Throughout the opening section of the novel, then, Salinger emphasizes that Holden is woefully out of place on the grounds of a private academy. His schoolmates are ambitious: they have come to Pencey to prepare for college, to make their marks as athletes, to compete and succeed. Holden, by contrast, wants to go home, to spend time with the only people who fully understand the grief he has suffered since Allie died. Holden's parents seem resolved to send him away, perhaps because they think a return to campus routines will ease his distress or perhaps because they can no longer stand the company of their traumatized son. (Salinger does not make the chronology of Holden's education entirely clear, but it appears that he started to attend boarding schools *after* his brother's death.) At any rate, they send Holden to California to recuperate instead of having him admitted to a hospital in New York and, despite his failure to make a go of it at three previous boarding schools, they arrange for him to attend yet another as soon as he regains his health.

One of the most puzzling features of the Pencey chapters is that Holden makes so few derogatory remarks about the school. Indeed, he suggests that he was treated reasonably well there. Pencey deserves some credit, after all, for taking a chance on a student with an abysmal academic record. After flunking out of Whooton School, Holden dropped out of a school called Elkton Hills, ostensibly because he dis-

1. Masculine Competition and Boarding-School Culture

liked his schoolmates and the headmaster: "One of the biggest reasons I left Elkton Hills was because I was surrounded by phonies. That's all. They were coming in the goddam window" (19). Holden argues that Pencey maintains its strong academic rating by expelling students at the bottom of every class, but Salinger undercuts that allegation. School officials warned Holden repeatedly that he was in danger of flunking out, but he concedes that he did nothing to avoid "the ax." And when the time came to notify Holden that he had been expelled, Dr. Thurmer sat down with him for an extended meeting. Holden considers the headmaster's advice worthless—life is "a game," Thurmer told him, and therefore it must be played by "the rules" (12)—but he also mentions that the conversation lasted for two hours and that Thurmer tried, in his way, to offer constructive advice. "He was pretty nice about it," Holden tells Mr. Spencer. "I mean he didn't hit the ceiling or anything. He just kept talking about Life being a game" (12). Thurmer could not have chosen an analogy less likely to make an impression on Holden, but then again he could not have known that the young man on the other side of his desk was determined to shun every form of competition. Joyce Rowe argues that Spencer pretends to express "fatherly interest" while upbraiding his former student (89), but Holden takes the teacher's claim that he is "trying to help" at face value: "'I'd like to put some sense in that head of yours, boy,' [Spencer said]. 'I'm trying to help you. I'm trying to *help* you if I can.' He really was, too. You could see that" (20).[16]

Holden has several opportunities to criticize Pencey, but he passes them up. On the train to New York, Mrs. Morrow asks what he thinks of the school. "Pencey?" he replies. "It's not too bad. It's not *paradise* or anything, but it's as good as most schools. Some of the faculty are pretty conscientious" (71). When one of the nuns praises Pencey, he decides not to contradict her: "'What school do you go to?' she asked me.... I told her Pencey, and she'd heard of it. She said it was a very good school. I let it pass, though" (145). Later, Holden has a similar exchange with a woman who works in the principal's office at his sister's elementary school: "She asked me where I went to school now, and I told her Pencey, and she said Pencey was a very good school. Even if I'd wanted to, I wouldn't have had the strength to straighten her out. Besides, if she thought Pencey was a very good school, let her think it" (261).[17] *It's not too bad. Let it pass. Let her think it.* These remarks are a far cry from Holden's normal conversational style. As we have seen, he seems incapable of "letting it pass" when other characters express their admiration of "hot-shots."

When it comes to Pencey, however, Holden keeps his disenchantment to himself.[18] Instead of calling attention to the school's faults, he implies that it was perfectly ordinary. Students gathered in the chapel for assemblies and in a dining hall for meals. His classes focused on standard subjects: poetry, history, and public speaking. And during his conversation with the nuns, he describes the English class he took there with something bordering on enthusiasm:

> "What have you read this year? I'd be very interested to know." She was really nice.
> "Well, most of the time we were on the Anglo-Saxons. Beowulf, and old Grendel, and Lord Randal My Son, and all those things. But we had to read outside books for extra credit once in a while. I read *The Return of the Native* by Thomas Hardy, and *Romeo and Juliet* and *Julius—*"
> "Oh, *Romeo and Juliet*! Lovely! Didn't you just love it?" She certainly didn't sound much like a nun.
> "Yes, I did. I liked it a lot" [144].

In spite of his troubles at Pencey, moreover, it seems that Holden did not find it hard to make friends there. He admired Ward Stradlater until he learned about the date with Jane Gallagher and he mentions that he got along well with several other schoolmates, including Mal Brossard, Robert Tichener, and Paul Campbell. Holden even implies that he initially felt at home at the school. He tells Phoebe that he joined a "secret fraternity" there (217), and if he had always been the embittered figure we see early in the novel, what can account for the Pencey Prep sticker Mrs. Morrow notices on one of his suitcases? This is not to say that Holden was fond of the school: he obviously considered it irritating and dull. The point I want to make is that Holden's resentment of "hot-shots" seldom informs his remarks about Pencey. Even when he criticizes the school, his complaints seem half-hearted. The students there pay too much attention to varsity football, divide into "dirty little goddam cliques," and chatter endlessly about "liquor and sex" (170)? The same could be said about students at thousands of other schools. Pencey's magazine advertisements ("Since 1888 we have been molding boys into splendid, clear-thinking young men" [4]) are pompous and misleading? Surely Holden understands that advertisers have been known to exaggerate the virtues of the commodities they are selling.

Holden rarely bothers to criticize Pencey, it seems, because the school is second-rate, not a training ground for "hot-shots." Throughout the novel, Salinger stresses Holden's grasp of the difference between the middling and the elite. He notices that the fathers of some of his schoolmates look gauche in their "suits with very big shoulders and corny black-and-white shoes" (19) because his parents take him shopping at Brooks Brothers. And after he arrives in New York, he is amused by three tourists who hope to meet celebrities in the Lavender Room at the Edmont Hotel: "[They] kept looking all around ... as if they expected a flock of goddam *movie stars* to come in any minute. They probably thought movie stars always hung out in the Lavender Room when they came to New York, instead of the Stork Club or El Morocco" (95–96). Holden does not explicitly identify Pencey as the "Lavender Room" of boarding schools, but he makes it clear that the school is mediocre at best. Agerstown, Pennsylvania does not carry the cachet of, say, Andover, Massachusetts or Lawrenceville, New Jersey. Thurmer's platitudes cause him to resemble a run-of-the-mill high school guidance counselor more than Endicott Peabody of Groton School, Lewis Perry of Phillips Exeter Academy, and other well-respected headmasters. Moreover, it is hard to imagine an elite school rolling out the red carpet for a graduate like Mr. Ossenburger:

> The first football game of the year, [Ossenburger] came up to school in this big goddam Cadillac, and we all had to stand up in the grandstand and give him a locomotive—that's a cheer. Then, the next morning, in chapel, he made a speech that lasted about ten hours. He started off with about fifty corny jokes, just to show us what a regular guy he was. Very big deal. Then he started telling us how he was never ashamed, when he was in some kind of trouble or something, to get right down on his knees and pray to God. He told us we should always pray to God—talk to him and all—wherever we were. He told us we should think of Jesus as our buddy and all. He said *he* talked to Jesus all the time. Even when he was driving in his car [22–23].

The setting of the film *Scent of a Woman* (1992) is a prep-school dystopia— a campus controlled by a conniving headmaster and arrogant rich boys who deliberately humiliate a working-class schoolmate. Salinger could have placed the opening chapters of *The Catcher in the Rye* in an equally repellent setting, but he imagined a different kind of prep school. When wealthy parents of the 1950s sent their children to private academies, teachers like Mr. Spencer and students like Robert Ackley were not what they had in mind. Holden seems indifferent to Pencey after his departure. In New York, he seldom mentions, or even thinks about, the school unless another character raises the subject. Something is tormenting Salinger's narrator, but Pencey seems too mundane to be the culprit.

Late in the novel, Holden reaches an impasse. He is ashamed to find that he is falling behind the "prep school jerks and college jerks" (109) who encircle him. To stop falling behind, he will have to compete at the next school he attends. Competition will force him to take on some of the traits he associates with "hot-shots." This, he fears, will make him feel ashamed. He believes, in other words, that the only alternative to disgraceful failure is disgraceful success. It is absurdly reductive to assume that one must choose between becoming a Trump or a "catcher in the rye." The vast majority of adults find some sort of middle ground between unbridled self-interest and the heroism of a dream figure whose only responsibility is to rescue endangered children.[19] Salinger stops short of indicating that his antihero has put away his childish attitudes about competition, but near the end of the novel it appears that Holden has begun to do so. In the episode that gives *The Catcher in the Rye* its title, Holden admits that his vision of the future is "crazy" as soon as he puts it into words:

> Anyway, I keep picturing all these little kids playing some game in this big field of rye and all. Thousands of little kids, and nobody's around—nobody big, I mean—except me. And I'm standing on the edge of some crazy cliff. What I have to do, I have to catch everybody if they start to go over the cliff—I mean if they're running and they don't look where they're going I have to come out from somewhere and *catch* them. That's all I'd do all day. I'd just be the catcher in the rye and all. I know it's crazy, but that's the only thing I'd really like to be. I know it's crazy [224–25].

Holden's reaction to his sister's ride on the carousel in Central Park also suggests that he has begun to reevaluate his social surroundings.

1. Masculine Competition and Boarding-School Culture

As Warren French points out, when Phoebe falls in line with the other children attempting to grab the gold ring, Holden watches the spectacle of competition in an uncharacteristically even-tempered way: "Holden is afraid that Phoebe may fall off the horse, as the kids he dreamed of protecting might fall off the cliff; but he has abandoned his vision of [the "catcher in the rye"] ... and he displays now an acceptance—if never approval—of things as they are on 'a sort of lousy day.'... He does not say anything to Phoebe, but he informs the reader that he cannot do anything to stop her, because 'the thing with kids is, if they want to grab for the gold ring, you have to let them do it and not say anything'" (44). James E. Miller, Jr., also suggests that the time Holden spends with Phoebe may be the source of his relatively hopeful outlook late in the novel: "Phoebe's spontaneous generosity expressed in her willingness to run away with him confirms his decision to stay, to become involved, and to rejoin the human race" (17). In Chapter 26, the novel's epilogue, Holden mentions that his parents have made arrangements for him to attend another prep school. He ridicules a psychiatrist who asks if he is going to "apply himself" there—"It's such a stupid question ... I mean, how do you know what you're going to do until you *do* it?"—but then he adds "I *think* I am" (276). From another character these words might seem inconsequential, but from Salinger's boarding-school misfit, a young man who has adamantly refused to compete, they indicate that he may have broken through the impasse. He realizes that he can compromise, a little, without becoming a "hot-shot."

Holden is, among other things, one of the most judgmental characters in American fiction, a narrator who describes dozens of characters and makes caustic remarks about nearly all of them.[20] As we have seen, the roster of male students, educators, business executives, and entertainers he denounces is particularly extensive. These characters are a diverse group in some ways, but they share one common characteristic: they are eager to "get ahead," to gain more money, prestige, or both. These ambitions seem commonplace in a novel set in America midway through the twentieth century, yet Holden finds them insufferable. Unlike most of his male contemporaries, he is determined *not* to get ahead, *not* to prepare himself for a prosperous future. His thoughts are anchored in his childhood, the days when Allie was delighting his teachers and scribbling poems in green ink on his baseball glove. Holden's assumptions about successful men suggest that his prospects at the conclusion of the novel are even dimmer than most critics have recognized. If his contempt for "phonies" were the main source of his anxieties, those anxieties could be allayed. A young man with his sharp eye for insincerity can readily avoid most of the "phonies" who cross his path, but how can an American male of his generation keep his distance from the nation's all-pervasive culture of competition? Unless Holden continues to compromise, making peace with the "hot-shots" who surround him, he faces two alternatives. He can continue to rail against masculine competition or he can take the path J. D. Salinger chose two years after he published *The Catcher in the Rye*: find a secluded hideaway and drop out of American society the way a traumatized adolescent drops out of school.

2

Unseen Academy: John Knowles's A Separate Peace

> *Someone made a long speech listing every infraction of the rules we were committing.... Someone else made a speech showing how by careful planning we could break all the others before dawn.* —John Knowles, *A Separate Peace*

American school literature tends to examine prep-school life in highly skeptical ways. One rare exception is John Knowles's novel *A Separate Peace* (1959).[1] Instead of raising doubts about exclusive independent schools, Knowles shields his fictional academy from criticism. First of all, he keeps the Devon School and its routines offstage throughout most of the novel. Second, when the student characters in *A Separate Peace* suffer physical and emotional trauma, Knowles makes it clear that their injuries are self-inflicted and therefore it would be unreasonable to hold Devon accountable. Knowles's efforts to turn the reader's attention away from the school have a paradoxical effect. On the one hand, they weaken *A Separate Peace* by making its main setting seem distant and elusive. On the other, they help to explain the novel's enormous popularity.[2] Because Devon never comes into focus, readers are free to fill the space Knowles leaves vacant with their most idealized notions about Northeastern prep schools.

Two Portraits of Prep-School Life

In John O'Hara's short story "Do You Like It Here?" (1939), a student named Humphrey Roberts is summoned to the housemaster's office and assumes that some sort of punishment is coming his way: "Roberts wondered what he had done. It got so after a while, after going to so many schools, that you recognized the difference between being 'wanted in Somebody's office' and 'Somebody wants to see you.' If a master wanted to see you on some minor matter, it didn't always mean that you had to go to his office, but if it was serious, they always said, 'You're wanted in Somebody's office'" (135). Roberts's suspicion proves correct. The moment he steps into Mr. Van Ness's office, the master swings his chair around, "putting himself behind the large desk, like a damn judge" (136). Van Ness asks Roberts to describe his family background, and then interrupts the boy's reply with a string of disdainful one-liners:

> "Well, I don't know. I was born at West Point, New York. My father was a first lieutenant then and he's a major now. My father and mother and I lived in a lot of places because he was in the Army and they transferred him. Is that the kind of stuff you want, Mister?"
>
> "Proceed, proceed. I'll tell you when I want you to—uh—halt." Van Ness seemed to think that was funny, that "halt."
>
> "Well, I didn't go to a regular school till I was ten. My mother got a divorce from my father and I went to school in San Francisco. I only stayed there a year because my mother married again and we moved to Chicago, Illinois."
>
> "Chicago, Illinois! Well, a little geography thrown in, eh, Roberts? Gratuitously" [137].

After these preliminaries, Van Ness gets to the point. He shows Roberts a wristwatch that was allegedly stolen from a room in the dormitory and placed in the master's office after he searched for it without success. Roberts insists (truthfully, the narrator tells us) that he has never seen the watch before, but Van Ness insinuates that he is lying: "Roberts, there is no room here for a thief! ... When I returned here after classes Monday afternoon, this watch was lying on my desk. Why? The contemptible rat who stole it knew that I had instituted the search, and like the rat he is, he turned yellow and returned the watch to me.... I do not know who stole this watch or who returned it to my rooms. But by God, Roberts, I'm going to find out" (139). Roberts repeats that he had nothing to do with the incident, but the master dismisses him coldly. Shaken by this confrontation, the accused student goes back to his room and curses Van Ness for treating him like a criminal: "Over and over, first violently, then weakly, he said it, 'The bastard, the dirty bastard'" (140).

By the end of the story, the reader knows a good deal about Roberts and his predicament. He has attended several boarding schools, largely because of his mother's troubled relationships with men. A few years earlier, he was sent away to school so he would not have to witness the end of his parents' marriage. Now, it seems, he has been sent away because his stepfather, an accountant, has had trouble finding steady employment. Van Ness's remarks are filled with a grating mixture of sentimentality, egotism, and self-pity. He makes a point of showing off his Phi Beta Kappa key, and then he holds forth, while abusing his authority over a 12-year-old, about the school and its "good name":

> I have a deep and abiding and lasting affection for this school. I have been a member of the faculty of this school for more than a decade. I like to think that I am part of this school, that in some small measure I have assisted in its progress.... I have not been without my opportunities to take a post at this and that college or university, but I choose to remain here. Why? Why? Because I love this place. I love this place, Roberts. I cherish its traditions. I cherish its good name [139].

While listening to Van Ness, Roberts realizes that there is something unconvincing about the master's account of the theft. Why would the culprit return the watch to Van Ness's office after the search failed? Why would the culprit take the unnecessary risk of sneaking in and out of the office? And why does the master imply, without a shred of evidence, that Roberts was the thief? He may be covering up for another student, or perhaps *he* stole the watch.[3] Steven Goldleaf argues that Van Ness's motives are beside the point: "[R]eaders differ over the events of the plot, namely, whether the watch was stolen and, if so, who stole it. But O'Hara has always held plot issues in low regard. The wonderfully controlled ambiguity stems from the Kafkaesque position [Roberts] is in, that of being forced to prove a negative proposition—that he did not steal the watch. Whether he stole the watch or not, his helplessness makes him cry out, 'violently, then weakly' at the end" (28–29). In any event, "Do You Like It Here?" is a *tour de force*: a five-page story that presents a vivid portrait of an American boarding school in the 1930s, from its dress code to the rules governing study halls.

In *A Separate Peace*, by contrast, John Knowles makes sure that the reader will not learn much about the Devon School. To begin with, the novel's early chapters take place during the first summer session in the school's 163-year history, a time in which "[t]he traditions had been broken, the standards let down, [and] all rules forgotten" (73). As Hallman Bell Bryant explains, Exeter's summer classes in the early 1940s were part of a special curriculum designed to help students graduate before serving in the armed forces: "Students had to work harder … because the academic program was accelerated through a plan called the Anticipatory Program, which graduated boys before they reached the draft age of eighteen" (3–4). In Chapter 1, Knowles's narrator Gene Forrester recalls that Devon's campus seemed almost deserted during the summer session of 1942:

> [We] passed the gym and came on toward the first group of dormitories, which were dark and silent. There were only two hundred of us at Devon in the summer, not enough to fill most of the school. We passed the sprawling Headmaster's house—empty, he was doing something for the government in Washington; past the chapel—empty again, used only for a short time in the mornings; past the First Academy Building, where there were some dim lights shining from a few of its many windows, Masters at work in their classrooms there; down a short slope into the broad and well clipped Common, on which light fell from the big surrounding Georgian buildings. A dozen boys were loafing there on the grass after dinner, and a kitchen rattle from the wing of one of the buildings accompanied their talk [19–20].[4]

These sentences epitomize the way Gene describes Devon throughout the novel. Instead of guiding the reader into campus buildings, he glances at their exteriors. Instead of recounting a meal served in the dining hall, he recalls a "kitchen rattle" heard from outdoors. Instead of presenting teachers at work, he offers glimpses of them through classroom windows. Gene and his schoolmates have presumably spent a great deal of time in the buildings mentioned in this passage, but in *A Separate Peace* there are two Devon Schools—the version familiar to insiders and the vague, remote version Gene presents to the reader.

The narrator of *Peace Breaks Out* (1981), Knowles's second school novel, shows no such reluctance to describe Devon. After Pete Hallam (Class of 1937) serves in the army in World War II, he returns to the school to teach history and physical education. The opening sentences of *Peace Breaks Out* reintroduce Devon in abstract phrases like those used in *A Separate Peace*. During the war, the narrator tells us, the school's "balanced eighteenth-century houses," "red-brick, no-nonsense nineteenth-century dormitories," "elaborate neo–Georgian twentieth-century class buildings," and "broad-sweeping Playing Fields," were among Hallam's most soothing memories of peacetime (1). After Hallam returns, however, the narrator speaks about Devon and its surroundings with great precision. Hallam's apartment, located on the ground floor of a dormitory, is described meticulously:

> The first thing he noticed, entering the apartment, was a fair-sized fireplace in the far wall, and he felt a small, atavistic ripple of pleasure at the sight of it, the hearth: barracks and bivouacs didn't have them. There were three scatter rugs on the floor, a rather battered desk and chair, a worn and comfortable looking easy chair by the fireplace, bookshelves, lamps, a couple of tables, two framed prints of Harvard scenes, narrow sash windows, a low ceiling, and a general sense of old-fashioned functionality [3].

This kind of detailed description of the interior of a campus building never appears in *A Separate Peace*. And when the fall semester begins, the reader is led into a classroom, where Hallam and a dozen students gather around a table to discuss common assumptions about American history. (Since the 1930s, Exeter has organized classes around the Harkness Plan, a pedagogical format that encourages teachers and students to "work together, exchanging ideas and information" ["History of Harkness Teaching" 1].[5] Arthur M. Schlesinger, Jr., was among the first students at Exeter to experience this approach. "I came to Exeter," he recalls, "at the beginning of the Harkness Plan.... We sat around tables and ... education became, not a performance, but a process" [106].) A "precociously jaded" student named Wexford muses that Hallam's course will probably fall short of "his intellectual standards" (14). Then one of his classmates, Eric Hochschwender, reveals with no apparent shame or hesitation that he is a bigot:

> Mix the decayed remnants of the aborigines with a lot of flotsam from England, religious fanatics here in New England, bankrupt aristocrats and indentured servants in the South, then add new floods of rejects from Europe, the dregs of inferior places like Ireland and Italy and the

Slav countries, pour on a few million savages from Africa, and what do you expect? A mongrel country getting bigger and bigger and winning wars because the land they've got is so rich in resources that they can defeat superior countries [17].

Wexford asks Hochschwender if he drew his opinions from *Mein Kampf*, Hochschwender takes offense, and the class begins a lively, wide-ranging discussion.

This passage has no counterpart in *A Separate Peace*. Like several other episodes in *Peace Breaks Out*, it suggests that Knowles could have described Devon in detail in *A Separate Peace* but chose not to do so. While some of the places and objects described in *Peace Breaks Out* could be found at any American secondary school, the narrator clearly indicates that Devon is posh and exclusive. The chapel is a miniature Gothic cathedral, with a bell tower on the roof and a baby grand piano in the basement. Visitors can watch the lacrosse team "hammering up and down the Playing Fields ... and crew shells skimming with their thin oars like huge delicate waterbugs across the shining water of [a nearby river]" (112). Unlike its precursor in *A Separate Peace*, this version of the Devon School is unmistakably elite, a school that educates the sons of financiers and political leaders. Knowles's first rendering of Devon is vague enough to seem familiar: a picturesque, but otherwise fairly ordinary American secondary school. The second rendering is specific enough to seem different from most of the nation's schools, public and private.

Mr. Prud'homme, the teacher in charge of Gene's dormitory, is a summer substitute, not a seasoned Devon master. When Gene and his roommate Finny realize that Prud'homme has not had time to learn most of Devon's rules, they commit one violation after another. Imitating upperclassmen who have started to train for military service, they climb a tree and jump from a high branch into the Devon River. They gamble, skip meals in the dining hall, and keep banned items, including an icebox and a radio, in their room.[6] Then they cut classes, leave the campus without permission, ride bicycles to the beach, and sleep there before hurrying back in time to attend morning classes. Prud'homme seems the antithesis of John O'Hara's hostile housemaster. He patiently reminds Gene and Finny that the school's normal policies are still in effect, but they ignore him, recognizing that the summer session has given them rare opportunities to make their own rules:

> This was the way the Masters tended to treat us that summer. They seemed to be modifying their usual attitude of floating, chronic disapproval. During the winter most of them regarded anything unexpected in a student with suspicion, seeming to feel that anything we said or did was potentially illegal. Now on these clear June days in New Hampshire they appeared to uncoil, they seemed to believe that we were with them about half the time, and only spent the other half trying to make fools of them. A streak of tolerance was detectable; Finny decided that they were beginning to show commendable signs of maturity [23].

Later on, Gene carelessly mentions the trip to the beach to Prud'homme, but the teacher is simply not interested in meting out punishments: "Summer lazed on. No one paid any attention to us. One day I found myself describing to Mr. Prud'homme how Phineas and I had slept on the beach, and he seemed to be quite interested in it, in all the details, so much so that he missed the point: that we had flatly broken a basic rule.... No one cared, no one exercised any real discipline over us; we were on our own" (55). Long after he published *A Separate Peace*, Knowles explained that Prud'homme's tolerant attitude is based on the author's memories of the faculty at Exeter in the early 1940s: "[C]ommenting on conditions at Phillips Exeter during the war in a 1972 interview ... [Knowles] remarked that ... nearly all of the school's younger faculty were away in service or doing war-related jobs. He added that, except for a few younger men who were 4-F, or unfit for military service, all of the teachers were between fifty and seventy years old.... The faculty, in addition to being older than usual, were in many cases not even regular Exeter staff but substitutes brought in from other schools or from retirement for the duration" (Bryant 3).

Finny seems particularly intrigued by the summer session's casual atmosphere. He wears a pink shirt to find out "what would happen if I looked like a fairy to everyone" (25).[7] He calls the group of students who go to the river every night The Super Suicide Society of the Summer Session, knowing that school officials would not approve of the name, much less the leaps from the tree, if they knew what he, Gene, and their classmates were up to. Dissatisfied with Devon's summer athletic program, Finny invents Blitzball, a contact sport played without helmets or pads. (Knowles's decision to focus attention on Blitzball instead of varsity sports also makes life at Devon seem ordinary and familiar. Countless readers can recall inventing games in their teens and teaching the rules to their friends. If Knowles had shown students competing as varsity athletes, Devon's top-notch playing fields and equipment would have signaled that it is a highly unusual institution, an academy that trains the elite.) And at a gathering hosted by Mr. Patch-Withers, a history teacher serving as substitute headmaster for the summer, Finny uses his school tie as a belt and explains that the gesture is meant to celebrate the Allies' first bombing raids in central Europe. Much to Gene's surprise, Patch-Withers, the "sternest of the Summer Sessions Masters," roars with laughter and Finny "[gets] away with everything" (25, 28).

A number of commentators have argued that *A Separate Peace* is an adolescent romance novel that has been mislabeled as a narrative about the impact of war on the psyches of young civilians. (See James Holt McGavran, "Fear's Echo and Unhinged Joy: Crossing Homosocial Boundaries in *A Separate Peace*" [2002]; Eric Tribunella, "Refusing the Queer Potential: John Knowles's *A Separate Peace*" [2009]; and Georges-Michel Sarotte, *Like a Brother, Like a Lover: Male Homosexuality in the American Novel and Theater from Herman Melville to James Baldwin* [1978].) Citing the night Gene and Finny spend together at the beach, the episode in which Gene tries on some of Finny's clothes (including the bright pink shirt the boys explicitly associate with "fairies"), and other passages, these critics suggest that most readers have, to paraphrase Tribunella's title, ignored the novel's "queer potential." That may be so, but the commentators who define the roommates' friendship as homoerotic beg the question. If Gene and Finny are attracted to each other, alone together in their dorm room every night, and largely unsupervised by faculty, why don't they "cross homosocial boundaries" in ways that go beyond roughhousing and jumping together from a tree? And if they are consciously involved in a same-sex flirtation, why would Gene find it astonishing that Finny gets away with trivial stunts such as using his school tie as a belt? It seems curious, moreover, that McGavran, Tribunella, et al. have labored to find hints of boarding-school homoeroticism in *A Separate Peace* when the subject has been examined closely and directly in other American novels, including James Kirkwood's *Good Times/Bad Times* (1968), Louis Auchincloss's *Honorable Men* (1986) and *The Education of Oscar Fairfax* (1995), and Norman Mailer's *Harlot's Ghost* (1991). (Chapter 4 discusses the depictions of homosexuality in these works.)

Knowles also turns the reader's attention away from Devon by staging a number of episodes in which Gene, Finny, and other students occupy deserted sites on campus or leave the school altogether. In the opening pages of the novel, Gene comes back to Devon fifteen years after graduation and spends his entire visit alone. As Bryant observes, "Gene's return ... is not that of the normal homecoming young graduate. He has not come back to the campus to be reunited with former classmates or to visit with old teachers. Although Gene is now a grown man, he still is haunted, as he tells us, by two fearful places that he wants to see now" (34). Gene eats his lunch alone at the Devon Inn. Then he walks down Gilman Street toward the school. The neighborhood is deserted—even the houses seem "more lifeless than ever" (11). Unlike many other American boarding schools, which are "self-isolated communities," Exeter is located *in* a town, not close to one: "[At Exeter,] the town merged almost imperceptibly into the Academy, and the Academy into the town: the students were not going merely to a boarding school but to the town of Exeter itself" (McLachlan 232).[8] While describing Devon's campus, Gene recalls that "[i]t was early afternoon and the grounds and buildings were deserted, since everyone was at sports" (11). He enters the First Academy Building, looks at the white marble stairs where Finny reinjured his broken leg, and then crosses a muddy field toward the Suicide Society's tree, marveling at the elegance of his old school: "Devon is sometimes considered the most beautiful school in New England, and even on this dismal afternoon its power was asserted. It is the beauty of small areas of order—a large yard, a group of trees, three similar dormitories, a circle of old houses—living together in contentious harmony.... Everything at Devon slowly changed and slowly harmonized with what had gone before" (12).

Several scholars have linked Gene's admiration of Devon's "contentious harmony" to his desire to stop blaming himself for Finny's death,[9] but they have paid little attention to the ways in which this episode highlights Gene's solitude. He crosses the campus of a large boarding school that is in session, yet he seems as isolated as a character in a Western passing through a ghost town. Then he approaches the river, gazes at the tree, and returns to the Center Common, alone. Part of Gene's solitude can be attributed to the weather (he mentions that he returned to Devon on a "wet, self-pitying November day" [10]), but even so this is the first of many episodes in which the reader is denied access to the school's everyday routines. The scenes by the river concentrate on a secluded site inside Devon's borders. In other passages, Knowles's characters wander off-campus. Before Finny suffers his first injury, he and Gene ride to the shore. While Finny recuperates, Gene visits him at his home near Boston after spending the month after the summer session "down South" (68) with his own family. During the fall semester, groups of Devon students leave the campus to harvest apples and to shovel snow that had "paralyzed the railroad yards of one of the large towns south of us on the Boston and Maine line" (93). Later on, Finny organizes a "winter carnival" in a nearby park and Gene travels to Elwin "Leper" Lepellier's home in a part of New England that seems far less inviting than the countryside near Devon:

> He lived far up in Vermont, where at this season of the year even the paved main highways are bumpy and buckling from the freezing weather, and each house executes a lonely holding action against the cold. The natural state of things is coldness, and houses are fragile havens, holdouts in a death landscape, unforgettably comfortable, simple though they are, just because of their warmth.... The Lepellier house was not far out of town, I was told. There was no taxi, I was also told, and there was no one, I did not need to be told, who would offer to drive me out there [139, 140].

Another device Knowles uses to keep Devon offstage is the emphasis he places on his characters' unofficial pastimes. Gene was a leading candidate for valedictorian, but he seldom mentions a class meeting, a lab report, or a reading assignment. This kind of indifference to schoolwork has long roots in boarding-school fiction. As P. W. Musgrave points out, Thomas Hughes's *Tom Brown's Schooldays* (1857) contains "few descriptions of work in school or of preparing for school lessons" (59); indeed, one early reviewer noted that "a boy might really infer from *Tom Brown* that he was sent to school to play at football, and that the lessons were quite a secondary consideration" (64). Similarly, although Finny is said to be "the best athlete in the school" (16), no one talks about his experiences as a member of Devon's football, hockey, baseball, and lacrosse teams. The reader learns that Finny has won the Galbraith Memorial Football Trophy, the Devon School Contact Sport Award, and the Bonaventura Ribbon (an award for outstanding hockey players), but these prizes create a mystique, not a direct representation of his athletic ability. Did he play in the infield or the outfield? Did he win championships, or was he a standout on unsuccessful teams? Instead of discussing Finny's performances as a varsity athlete, Gene recalls his friend's mastery of several quasi-athletic activities: Blitzball games, snowball fights, and leaps from the tree. And when Finny breaks a swimming record held by a Devon graduate named A. Hopkins Parker, he insists that he wants the feat to be unreported and unofficial:

> "My God! So I really did it. You know what? I thought I was going to do it. It felt as though I had that stop watch in my head and I could hear myself going just a little bit faster than A. Hopkins Parker."
> "The worst thing is there weren't any witnesses. And I'm no official timekeeper. I don't think it will count."
> "Well of course it won't *count.*"
> "You can try it again and break it again. Tomorrow. We'll get the coach in here, and all the official timekeepers and I'll call up *The Devonian* to send a reporter and a photographer—"
> He climbed out of the pool. "I'm not going to do it again," he said quietly.
> "Of course you are!"
> "No, I just wanted to see if I could do it. Now I know. But I don't want to do it in public" [43–44].

Gene recalls that he attended prayer services regularly, but he never describes the interior of Devon's chapel. He mentions that he and his classmates joined a number of school-sponsored organizations—Brinker Hadley, for instance, was a member of the Golden Fleece Debating Society, the Underprivileged Local Children subcommittee of the Good Samaritan Confraternity, the staff of the student newspaper, the choir, and a group called the Student Advisory Committee to the Headmaster's Discretionary Benevolent Fund—but in Gene's narrative these groups are nothing more than names. Devon's students and graduates are familiar with their contributions to campus life, Knowles suggests, but it is not necessary for the reader to know anything about them. Gene is certainly capable of presenting detailed narration (witness his descriptions of the sunrise at the beach, the winter landscape of Vermont, the rules of Blitzball, and the impact of World War II on the daily lives of American civilians), but when it comes to Devon he keeps the details to himself. For this reason, an early reviewer of *A Separate Peace* argued that the novel's setting is not "fully drawn": "Maurice Richardson ... applauded Knowles for his 'variations from conventional American attitudes' ... but concluded that the writing, though pleasing, did not quite convince because the school background was not as fully drawn as he felt 'institutional frameworks' should be" (qtd. in Bryant 13). When Knowles reflected on *A Separate Peace* in interviews and autobiographical writings, he described it as a kind of moral parable and insisted that its boarding-school setting was of little importance. In 1985, for instance, he wrote that "[the novel] is a story of growth through tragedy. Young people, on their deepest emotional level, respond to that. It makes not the slightest difference that the story's externals may be totally foreign to them. In the novel there is not a girl in sight; that means nothing—women of all ages and every background treat it as central to their view of life. It takes place among some privileged kids in a first-rate preparatory school; that doesn't mean anything either" ("My Separate Peace" 109). It seems incongruous, but there it is: the author of *A Separate Peace*, one of America's most famous boarding-school novels, was unwilling to acknowledge that it *was* a boarding-school novel. Instead of presenting his schoolboy characters as privileged young men in a rarified setting, Knowles presents them, to a large degree, as representative teenagers. They form friendships and rivalries. They cut classes and break rules. They do all sorts of reckless things when the adults on campus are not paying attention.

After Finny is hospitalized for the second time, Gene departs from his usual narrative approach by providing a detailed account of one day in his life at the school:

> I left the Infirmary and went to my 10:10 class, which was on American history. Mr. Patch-Withers gave us a five-minute written quiz on the "necessary and proper" clause of the Constitution. At 11 o'clock I left that building and crossed the Center Common where a few students

were already lounging although it was still a little early in the season for that. I went into the First Building, walked up the stairs where Finny had fallen, and joined my 11:10 class, which was in mathematics. We were given a ten-minute trigonometry problem which appeared to solve itself on my paper.

At 12 I left the First Building, recrossed the Common and went into the Jared Potter Building for lunch. It was a breaded veal cutlet, spinach, mashed potatoes, and prune whip. At the table we discussed whether there was any saltpeter in the mashed potatoes. I defended the negative.

After lunch I walked back to the dormitory with Brinker. He alluded to last night only by asking how Phineas was; I said he seemed to be in good spirits. I went on to my room and read the assigned pages of *Le bourgeois gentilhomme*. At 2:30 I left my room, and walking along one side of the oval Finny had used for my track workouts during the winter, I reached the Far Common and beyond it the gym. I went past the Trophy Room, downstairs into the pungent air of the locker room, changed into gym pants, and spent an hour wrestling. I pinned my opponent once and he pinned me once. Phil Latham showed me an involved method of escape in which you executed a modified somersault over your opponent's back [192].

I quote at length here because this passage has so little in common with every other description of prep-school life in *A Separate Peace*. As Kathy Piehl observes, "the one school day which Gene records in scrupulous detail is striking because of the rarity of such an occurrence in the rest of the book" (70). The topics covered in class discussions and homework assignments? The menu in the dining hall? Tactical advice given to a student by a wrestling coach? These are the kinds of details Knowles usually omits in *A Separate Peace*. Attentive readers will wonder why Gene's memories of the time he spent at Devon have suddenly become so specific. The answer comes into focus immediately after this passage. Gene is not particularly interested in the things he did that day; he lists them to show that he remembers everything about the day Finny died.

The Most Conservative Boarding-School Novel

In some ways, Knowles raises the suspicion that the authorities at Devon were negligent. Gene, Finny, and several other students went to the river over and over during the summer session, yet it never dawned on the faculty that the Suicide Society existed. All of Leper's peers knew that he was unprepared to serve in the military. He was one of the most childlike students at Devon, perpetually surrounded by "a protective cloud of vagueness" (204). (This is an interesting phrase—as I have been suggesting, Gene sees to it that "a protective cloud of vagueness" also surrounds the school.) Leper enlisted, moreover, for a breathtakingly naïve reason: he was captivated by "a recruiting film of ski troops, the 'white warriors of winter,' who glide silently as angels across pure fields of snow" (Bryant 86). A single conversation with a teacher or guidance counselor almost certainly would have led to a recommendation that he should wait until after graduation, but it seems that no such conversation took place. One could also argue that Devon's response to Finny's first injury was insufficient. Because school authorities concluded that no investigation was necessary, lingering rumors about the incident prompted Brinker Hadley to organize the mock trial that culminated in Finny's second injury and by extension his death. How could Devon justify this hands-off approach? As a character in Auchincloss's *The Rector of Justin* (1964) explains, boarding schools normally go out of their way to ensure that students will spend every hour of every day under faculty supervision: "'Fun' was defined in terms of group activity, such as football or singing ... the devil lay in wait for the boy alone, or worse, for two boys alone. The headmaster believed that adolescence should be passed in an organized crowd, that authority should never avert its eyes" (247). Why did authority avert its eyes at Devon? Wasn't the school's indifferent supervision largely to blame for the most destructive events in the novel?

Previous discussions of *A Separate Peace* have not addressed these questions. Devon has escaped criticism, it seems, because Knowles suggests that there is nothing to criticize. Teachers and other school officials are kept offstage throughout most of the novel, but when they do appear they are depicted in favorable ways.[10] Mr. Patch-Withers is elderly, yet he does not seem to have lost touch with his students. Prud'homme is one of the most underwritten characters in the novel, but his appearances leave the impression that he is broad-minded and unassuming. And Dr. Stanpole seems exceptionally thoughtful when he tells Gene the shocking news about Finny's first injury:

"I don't want any of these teachers flapping around him," [the doctor said]. "But a pal or two, it'll do him good."

"I suppose he's still pretty sick."

"It was a messy break ... but we'll have him out of it eventually. He'll be walking again."

"*Walking* again!"

"Yes." The doctor didn't look at me, and barely changed his tone of voice. "Sports are finished for him, after an accident like that. Of course.... As a friend you ought to help him face that and accept it. The sooner he does the better off he'll be. If I had the slightest hope that he could do more than walk I'd be all for trying for everything. There is no such hope. I'm sorry, as of course everyone is" [63].

Stanpole seems equally compassionate when he informs Gene that Finny has died: "'This is something I think boys of your generation are going to see a lot of,' he said quietly, 'and I will have to tell you about it now. Your friend is dead.... In the middle of [the operation] his heart simply stopped, without warning. I can't explain it. Yes, I can. There is only one explanation. As I was moving the bone some of the marrow must have escaped into his blood stream and gone directly to his heart and stopped it" (193). In spite of these two episodes, one commentator argues (not very persuasively, it seems to me) that Stanpole "is never able to communicate his compassion.... No adult in the book is a suitable model for a teen; there is no communication between boy and adult that seems natural or normal" (Ely 1129, 1130).

At times, Knowles seems to anticipate the charge that the Devon's faculty was negligent and counter it with mitigating evidence. All of the students in the Suicide Society, for example, knew that jumping from the tree was dangerous and strictly prohibited.[11] When Finny dares the others to follow after he and Gene make their first jumps, Leper appears to become "inanimate" and Bobby Zane and Chet Douglass refuse, "complaining shrilly about school regulations" (17). (Those regulations provided that only seniors were allowed to jump, under faculty supervision, as part of a military training program.) Knowles's implication is clear: reckless teenagers, not inattentive adults, were to blame for Finny's first injury. Similarly, Knowles suggests that the school should not be held responsible for Leper's nervous breakdown. At school, Leper seems eccentric but fundamentally healthy and content. Soon after he enlists, however, he becomes so unhinged that Gene cannot bear to hear about the circumstances that led to his desertion:

> "One day I couldn't make out what was happening to the corporal's face. It kept changing into faces I knew from somewhere else, and then I began to think he looked like me, and then he..." Leper's voice had thickened unrecognizably, "he changed into a woman, I was looking at him as close as I'm looking at you and his face turned into a woman's face and I started to yell for everybody, I began to yell so everybody would see it too, I didn't want to be the only one to see a thing like that" ...
>
> I said nothing, and Leper, having said so much, went on to say more ... as though his story would never be finished. "Then they grabbed me and there were arms and legs and heads everywhere and I couldn't tell when any minute—"
>
> "*Shut up!*"
>
> Softer, more timidly, "—when any minute—"
>
> "Do you think I want to hear every gory detail! Shut up! I don't care! I don't care what happened to you, Leper. I don't give a damn! Do you understand that? This has nothing to do with me!" [150–51].

Again, the implication is unmistakable—Leper's breakdown was self-inflicted. Devon did not promote early enlistment. Quite the opposite: the purpose of the summer sessions was to help students graduate *before* serving in the military. Leper deviated from the school's program, and the consequences of that decision speak for themselves. As Stephen E. Ambrose explains in *Citizen Soldiers* (1997), it was not uncommon for American troops in World War II to become deserters: "Desertion was a serious problem in the [European Theater of Operations], partly because it was relatively easy to do in Europe ... partly because of the never-ending nature of the combat, and partly because the Army tried to get deserters back to their outfits and give them a second chance, meaning deserters could figure there wouldn't be any punishment if they were caught" (343).[12] Leper's ordeal seems especially pitiable, however, because he never came close to a battlefield. He deserted and showed symptoms of what probably would be diagnosed today as post-traumatic stress disorder—emotional numbness, hallucinations, uncontrollable weeping—before he finished basic training.[13] Knowles also portrays the mock trial as a case of abysmal judgment on the part of students. Finny had not accused Gene of causing his injury; the two students remained close friends and roommates after the accident. School officials chose not to conduct an investigation, but Brinker Hadley refused to leave well enough alone and the other students at the trial followed his lead, even after he made the traumatized, psychologically unstable Leper his star witness. (As James Holt McGavran notes, it may be that what Brinker and the other students really want to investigate is Gene and Finny's unusually close friendship: "[The] unspoken motivation for that ultimately fatal event is not justice or truth—to find out who made Finny fall or to force him to accept his disability, as Brinker claims—but the other boys' combined homophobic fear and jealous curiosity at the closeness of his relationship with Gene and what the two of them might have been able to get away with" [80].)

Thus, *A Separate Peace* is, among other things, the most conservative American prep-school novel. Knowles's students suffer because they ignore Devon's traditions and authorities. Other American novelists of the 1950s and '60s encourage readers to view prep-school officials with suspicion. In J. D. Salinger's *The Catcher in the Rye* (1951), Dr. Thurmer, the headmaster of Pencey Prep, seems shallow and mediocre. He responds to Holden Caulfield's emotional and academic tailspin by expelling the lonely, haunted teenager and urging him to think of life as "a game" that must be played by "the rules" (12). Mr. Hoyt, the main authority figure in James Kirkwood's *Good Times/Bad Times* (1968), is a closeted gay man who becomes infatuated with Peter Kilburn, an 18-year-old student at his school. Hoyt seems harmless at first, but by the end of the novel his behavior turns compulsive and dangerous. And Mr. Knoedler, the headmaster in Richard Yates's *A Good School* (1978), is portrayed as a slick businessman intent on drumming up trade for his foundering school. These novelists raise doubts about prep-school traditions. They imply that the private academies of the Northeast are not all that they are cracked up to be and that the students, teachers, and administrators at those institutions are more troubled and confused than most Americans realize. Knowles, on the other hand, endorses the status quo at the Devon School. Things go wrong in *A Separate Peace* because teenagers substitute their own reckless impulses for the experience and judgment of their elders. If Gene, Finny, and their classmates had paid more attention to the instructions they received from Devon's faculty and administration, Finny would not have fallen from the tree, Leper would not have enlisted prematurely, Gene would not have been accused by his schoolmates, and Finny would not have lost his composure and fallen down the marble staircase in the Academy Building.

A Separate Peace *and Knowles's Alma Mater*

The reason Knowles does not raise doubts about his fictional academy in *A Separate Peace* is no mystery: he was a loyal graduate of Exeter and he modeled Devon on his old school. Salinger, Kirkwood, and other writers of American school literature lace their narratives with unhappy memories of boarding school, but Knowles uses his campus setting to celebrate Exeter, not to settle scores. Consequently, people associated with the school have generally taken pride in *A Separate Peace*. Exeter's Internet site, for example, features an elaborate tribute to the author and his book: a photo essay, a discussion of the 1972 movie adaptation directed by Larry Peerce, a page from the original manuscript of the novel, a selected bibliography, and an essay in which Knowles reflects on his education at Exeter. He begins the essay, titled "A Special Time, A Special School," by positing that few Exonians were more indebted to the school than he was: "Exeter was, I suspect, more crucial in my life than in the lives of most members of my class, and conceivably, than in the lives of almost anyone else who ever attended the school. It picked me up out of the hills of West Virginia, forced me to learn to study, tossed me into Yale (where I was virtually a sophomore by the time I entered), and a few years later inspired me to write a book, my novel *A Separate Peace*, which, eschewing false modesty, made me quite famous and financially secure" (1). Knowles struggled academically during his first year at Exeter and disliked most of his schoolmates, who seemed "too Eastern for me, too Yankee," but by the time he enrolled in the summer session of 1943[14] he had changed his mind about his new surroundings:

> The great trees, the thick clinging ivy, the expanses of playing fields, the winding black-water river, the pure air all began to sort of intoxicate me. Classroom windows were open; the aroma of flowers and shrubbery

floated in. We were in shirt-sleeves; the masters were relaxed. Studies now were easy for me. The summer of 1943 at Exeter was as happy a time as I ever had in my life.

Everything fit. There was a lively, congenial group of students in Peabody Hall that summer, many of them from other schools, accelerating like me. One was David Hackett from Milton Academy, on whom I later modeled Phineas in *A Separate Peace*. A great friend of Bobby Kennedy's, he later served under Bobby in the Justice Department. We really did have a club whose members jumped from the branch of a very high tree into the river as initiation. The only elements in *A Separate Peace* which were not in that summer were anger, envy, violence, and hatred. There was only friendship, athleticism, and loyalty [1–2].

Later in the essay, Knowles surveys his fondest memories of Exeter—movie nights in the gym, an outstanding Latin instructor, and the day he anchored a relay team that beat Andover in a swim meet. "You can see by now how I admire the school and love it," he concludes. "I found there a gorgeous world prepared to shape me up, and I tried to present and dramatize that [in *A Separate Peace*]" (2).

For those who have read *A Separate Peace*, the nostalgic tone of Knowles's essay will probably come as a surprise. If he associated Exeter with "friendship, athleticism, and loyalty," why is the novel based on his recollections of the school rife with "anger, envy, violence, and hatred?" If he regarded Exeter as a "gorgeous world" of memorable sporting events, superb teaching, and relaxed camaraderie, why does *A Separate Peace* pay so little attention to those features of life at Devon? And why have so many members of the Exeter community embraced a novel set in a facsimile of their school in which one student inflicts a crippling injury on his closest friend (perhaps accidentally, perhaps not), a second deserts his Army unit, and a third causes the death of a classmate by presiding over a mock trial in which another young man is accused of committing a vicious crime? The answer is that Knowles tries to have it both ways in *A Separate Peace*—he fashions an attractive portrait of his old school *and* saturates his plot with turmoil. Knowles wanted to write a novel that examines the destructive impulses of adolescent males. He decided that the main setting would be a private academy modeled on Exeter, but that decision posed the danger that readers would associate the school he "admired and loved" with anguish and death. The solution: *A Separate Peace* focuses almost exclusively on prep-school *students*. The school they attend is a lightly sketched backdrop.

For the most part, Knowles's efforts to turn readers' attention away from Devon have succeeded. Critics often describe the stories of Finny and Leper as anomalous, almost surreal. How could these things have happened at a school like Devon? In the early 1940s, everyone expected to hear about young men dying and becoming disabled overseas, but who could have foreseen casualties at an exclusive private academy? In "A Special Time, A Special School," Knowles writes that he was pleased to have written a prep-school novel that does not indulge in prep-school bashing: "The novel has one peculiarity for a school novel: it never attacks the place; it isn't an exposé; it doesn't show sadistic masters or depraved students, or use any of the other school-novel sensationalistic clichés" (2). What Knowles fails to mention is that he does not only avoid the "sensationalistic clichés" of boarding-school fiction in *A Separate Peace*: he avoids writing about boarding school. Even when Gene seems to be criticizing Devon, he is in fact commenting on his peers and himself. Early in the novel, he notes that "there were few relationships among us at Devon not based on rivalry" (45). And when Finny calls Gene "my best pal" at the beach, Gene's first thought is that "[i]t was a courageous thing to say. Exposing a sincere emotion nakedly like that at the Devon School was the next thing to suicide" (48).[15] In *The Catcher in the Rye*, Holden Caulfield praises his brother D.B.'s "The Secret Goldfish," a short story about a boy who "wouldn't let anybody look at his goldfish because he'd bought it with his own money" (2).[16] John Knowles's "secret goldfish," it seems, was Exeter. He prized his memories of the school so much that he refused to let readers see them in the turbulent first novel inspired by the years he spent there.

Knowles's depiction of Devon ultimately has a mixed effect on *A Separate Peace*. On the one hand, his reluctance to describe the school weakens the novel by making its main setting extremely (almost comically) vague. To write a school narrative that fails to show the audience a classroom, an assembly, the chapel, the football stadium, or the dining hall seems amateurish, even for a first-time novelist. Because the schoolboys in *A Separate Peace* move through an indistinct landscape, they seem more like archetypes than fully realized characters. Brinker, for example, functions as "the future politician," Leper as "the doomed naïf," and so forth. The students' actions, moreover, seem unreal at times because the novel's indefinite sense of place makes them hard to visualize. On the other hand, Knowles's unseen academy may help to explain the novel's extraordinary popularity. *The Catcher in the Rye, Good Times/Bad Times,* and other American school novels critique private academies so aggressively that they encourage readers to think twice about the lofty reputations of Northeastern prep schools. *A Separate Peace,* by contrast, raises questions about boarding-school students, not about boarding school. It suggests that the schoolboys at Devon were their own worst enemies and that school officials could not have prevented their mistakes. By providing a vague, incomplete portrait of Devon, Knowles allows readers to fill the empty space in the novel with their most idealized notions about prep-school life. *A Separate Peace* leaves open the possibility that picture-perfect secondary academies may actually exist. Maybe there are elite schools that offer the best of everything; maybe those schools can place young people on the fast track to unlimited success. Thus, in spite of Knowles's reluctance to describe everyday life at Devon, he produced his era's most attractive fictional portrait of an American boarding school.

3

Campus Politics and Endless Adolescence in The Rector of Justin

> *I clenched my fists and stared at the faded old Persian rug and prayed idiotically that it would sweep me up in the air and carry me far away from all the terrible things in Justin Martyr.*—Louis Auchincloss, *The Rector of Justin*

When Louis Auchincloss was a first-former at the Groton School, he confessed that he and two other boys had thrown rocks at a train. From that day forward, the future writer and Wall Street lawyer was "singled out for persecution.... So incessant was the daily hazing that [he] later likened getting around the Groton campus then to walking down a New York street at night now: 'You have to have one eye out for a mugger'" (Gelderman 37).[1] And that was only the beginning. Throughout the six years Auchincloss spent at Groton, schoolmates mocked his athletic incompetence and his "funny, almost English way of speaking" (50) so relentlessly that he often pretended to be sick and hid in the infirmary.[2]

Despite his unhappy memories, however, when Auchincloss made a prep school the main setting of his novel *The Rector of Justin* (1964), he did not follow F. Scott Fitzgerald, J. D. Salinger, and John Knowles by imagining a teenager in distress.[3] He focused on several adult characters associated with Justin Martyr, an Episcopal school thirty miles from Boston. This change in emphasis made it possible for Auchincloss to write the first American boarding-school novel that contains a comprehensive portrait of a school. By the end of *The Rector of Justin*, the reader learns a great deal about the history of Justin Martyr from the

1880s through the World War II era; its founding rector Francis Prescott and his family; David Griscam, the head of the board of trustees, and his family; and several teachers and graduates. Unlike previous authors of school fiction, Auchincloss surveys the elements that shaped an exclusive academy, including Prescott's towering reputation, Griscam's skills as a fundraiser, and the faculty's efforts to translate Prescott's ideals into academic and administrative routines. Whitney Balliett praises *The Rector of Justin* for dramatizing prep-school life without indulging in "brutal exorcising" or "genteel watercolors" (76). Similarly, David Parsell observes that "[f]or all its implicit tough-minded, clear-headed criticism of American private education, *The Rector of Justin* is in no sense an exposé, even less a denunciation; rather, it is the credible account of a durable American institution caught and portrayed in all its ambiguity" (52).

When *The Rector of Justin* was published in 1964, readers at Groton complained that Auchincloss had betrayed his alma mater. His portrayal of Frank Prescott, according to this interpretation, insults the memory of Dr. Endicott Peabody (Groton's founder and longtime rector) by suggesting that he was far more self-centered and ruthless than anyone connected with the school was willing to admit.[4] Auchincloss had not expected this reaction. As he explains in his memoir *A Writer's Capital* (1974), he thought of Peabody and Prescott as "near opposites":

> [W]hen I came to put my man together, I cast him in part in the mold of a non-teacher: Judge Learned Hand, the greatest human being that it has ever been my privilege to know. I tried to make my headmaster a man of giant intellect, of passionate idealism, of searing doubts, of mordant humor. All this, of course, availed me nothing with the Groton School alumni who took for granted, because certain facts and dates had been borrowed from the life of Endicott Peabody, that Peabody was the rector of Justin.... What particularly intrigued me about this willful identification of Peabody with my hero was that the two characters were near opposites. My Francis Prescott was complex, arrogant, witty, cynical, intellectual to his fingertips; Peabody was simple, straightforward, literal, and always sincere [35–36].

Similarly, in a speech titled "A Writer's Use of Fact in Fiction" (1984), Auchincloss explains that while preparing to write *The Rector of Justin* he "decided to take the dates and certain facts of the career of ...

Peabody, but I could not use his personality, which was too highly individual for my purpose. What I needed properly to dramatize the problems [a famous headmaster] ... would have faced was an almost morbid doubt and a mordant intellectualism. What I found I could use, at last, were some of the qualities of Judge Learned Hand. I even borrowed some of the stories that he had told me" (qtd. in Parsell 53).[5] In spite of the bruised feelings at Groton, *The Rector of Justin* climbed the bestseller lists, sold two million copies, and was nominated for the Pulitzer Prize and the National Book Award.

Auchincloss's detractors at Groton had good cause to be concerned about *The Rector of Justin*, but they were concerned for the wrong reason. If the novel were a *roman-à-clef* in which Prescott stands in for Peabody, it would be impossible to make sense of this entry in the journal of Brian Aspinwall, a teacher at Justin Martyr:

> I asked Dr. Prescott this afternoon his opinion of Peabody. He gave me one of his foxy, sidelong looks and snapped: "A man who considers that Theodore Roosevelt was America's greatest statesman and *In Memoriam* England's finest poem is well equipped to train young men for the steam room at the racquet club.... Cotty Peabody is a great man, in his way. What I really resent is that my graduates are not more different from his. For all my emphasis on the humanities and his on God, we both turn out stockbrokers!" [43–44].[6]

The speaker quoted in this passage is obviously not Endicott Peabody. He is one of Peabody's peers, a headmaster at another boarding school who knows Groton's founder well enough to call him "Cotty" and make fun of his opinions. *The Rector of Justin* is too complex to be labeled as a portrait of one legendary educator. Throughout the novel, Auchincloss exposes the juvenile attitudes of adult characters affiliated with his fictional academy. The six narrators who reflect on Frank Prescott's career often seem to forget that he is only a headmaster and Justin Martyr is only a school.[7] Some want to praise Prescott and others want to denounce him, but regardless of their motives they are united by their overreactions to Justin and its founder. By highlighting these characters' resentments and insecurities, Auchincloss raises questions previous school novelists had not considered. Do prep schools engender a kind of endless adolescence? Can an institution that has become as prestigious as Justin continue to guide students toward careers in

3. Campus Politics and Endless Adolescence

public service? Does a school that gains the world inevitably lose its soul? Accordingly, *The Rector of Justin* is, among other things, a cautionary tale. It warns that long-term exposure to an exclusive private academy may result in a severe case of arrested development.

The Aspinwall Papers

In the opening lines of his journal, Brian Aspinwall reports that he is about to join the faculty at Justin Martyr and worries that he is not up for the challenge. "I suppose all I have basically done since my seventeenth year," he writes, "has been to seek refuge in literature from the agony of deciding whether or not I am qualified to be a minister. Perhaps life in a church school will help me.... I am shy and lack force of personality, and my stature is small. I stammer when I am nervous, and my appearance is more boyish than manly. All this will be against me" (2). These flickers of self-doubt seem perfectly normal, but Aspinwall's first-year jitters soon give way to panic. One week into the fall semester, he complains that he is working under unbearable pressure: "I begin to wonder if I will ever be able to adjust my trudge to the noisy march of Justin. I had not imagined there could be so much noise. I have a constant sense of being about to be overwhelmed" (6). The words Auchincloss uses to convey the newcomer's fears—*trudge, march, noise, overwhelmed*—might have been drawn from the memoir of a combat veteran. This 27-year-old teacher reacts to his first days on a leafy campus in Massachusetts as if he has just parachuted behind enemy lines. When Aspinwall fails to take control of his dorm immediately, he thinks of the teenagers under his supervision as a pack of predators:

> My fourth form dormitory has been sizing me up, and now they have decided they can ride me. There were terrible squeals after lights tonight, and I was in a wretched quandary. How does one cope with forty fifteen-year-olds in the dark? Finally in a panic lest the sounds would come to the all-hearing ears of [the senior master], I strode to the door into the dormitory, turned on the overhead lights by the switch and called out in what I fear was a trembling falsetto: "Who is talking in this room?" Someone shouted back: "You are!" and the roar of laughter that followed must have been heard all over Lawrence House.... How can I afford to

admit that the boys were out of control? I can only pull out this journal and foolishly wish that I could climb inside of it and pull its covers close over my shamed and ridiculous head. Oh, Journal, if you could only hide me, if I could only turn myself into ink! Dear God, will I ever make a go at teaching? [7–8].[8]

Aspinwall may be the most hypersensitive character in any American novel of the past fifty years. He is such a fervent admirer of Samuel Richardson that he puts a portrait of the novelist on his mantel and uses *Clarissa* as a kind of literary sedative: "I shall now be able to read in peace another delightful chapter.... Escape? Who calls it escape? It's salvation!" (12). When Frank Prescott urges him to become a football coach, Aspinwall is embarrassed to admit that he knows nothing about the game. (The rector's passion for football, by the way, does seem to derive from memories of Endicott Peabody. As Geoffrey C. Ward points out, "[a]thletic distinction was central to real success at Groton, and football, wrote a school historian, 'was the Groton game *par excellence* ... [Peabody] trusted a football player more than a non-football player, just as the boys did'" [184].) When the rector's daughter Cordelia Prescott Turnbull slips on a negligée, mixes Martinis, and tries to seduce Aspinwall—"Are you a virgin, bunny? I'll bet you are" (216)—the teacher jumps to his feet and hurries out of her apartment. Aspinwall's journal is filled with this kind of inadvertent comedy, but it also introduces an idea that recurs over and over in *The Rector of Justin*: there is something about exclusive boarding schools that magnifies the most juvenile tendencies of adults. Within days after his arrival at Justin Martyr, Aspinwall starts to behave like a homesick schoolboy. There's a time to worry about hazing and unpopularity, Auchincloss suggests, but it ought to end before a man reaches his late twenties. Instead of seeing his entry-level teaching job for what it is, Aspinwall comes to Prescott's school in search of a new identity. He feels a "strong but still unmatured drive towards the ministry" (31), but can't tell if it amounts to a "calling." He has studied literature as an undergraduate at Columbia and as a graduate student at Oxford, yet he feels unqualified to teach at a secondary school. Instead of trying to chip away at what he calls "the timid and apprehensive side of my nature" (6), he hopes for a sudden transformation.

Aspinwall pulls himself together after his rocky debut and makes a surprisingly strong impression on the school's inner circle. By the end of the novel, he has become a confidant of Prescott, the rector's wife Harriet Winslow Prescott, the rector's old friend Horace Havistock, David Griscam, and several faculty members, but most of these characters seem to regard him as a promising young person. Prescott calls him "my boy" while teaching him how to deal with rowdy students, "dear boy" while mourning the death of Mrs. Prescott, and "young Brian" when Aspinwall witnesses a heated argument between the rector and Griscam (27, 36, 326). ("Young Brian" is 34 years old at the time of this incident.) Later, when Aspinwall suggests that some of Griscam's business tactics have shocked the rector, Griscam snaps, "Just remember, young man, that you can't make an omelet without breaking eggs" (329). Aspinwall also seems to find it hard to think of himself as an adult. When the rector thanks him for taking the time to read a Henry James novel to the ailing Mrs. Prescott, for example, his first impulse is to skip all the way back to his dormitory:

> "Aspinwall," he said, taking my elbow as he guided me to the front door, "you are very kind to devote so many afternoons to my wife."
> "Oh, it's my pleasure, sir. Truly I love it.... Mrs. Prescott is the most wonderful woman I've ever known!"
> The grip tightened on my elbow. "Bless you, my boy. Bless you for seeing that."
> Outside I almost ran back to the main door of Lawrence House, so full of emotion that it was all I could do to keep from skipping. What a man was this! A man who could read the later James and love his wife so tenderly, a man who could appreciate what a silly mite like myself, the reverse of all he expected in a master, could offer her and not hesitate to ask that mite to continue his offering. This was magnanimity on a scale for the gods. Looking up at the formidable dark tower of his chapel I laughed aloud in jubilation at the thought that there *might* at last be a place for me in Dr. Prescott's Justin [21].[9]

Aspinwall insists that he has benefited enormously from his experiences at Justin, but Auchincloss fills the teacher's journal with evidence to the contrary. Six years after his arrival, Aspinwall remains ineffectual as a teacher and as an authority figure: "I am again aware of whisperings and giggles in the back row of my classroom and odd noises in my dormitory after lights. The boys know that it is painful for me to give black marks and, all too naturally, they take advantage of this. Yet I have qualms about penalizing them for my own failure to be obeyed. If I were interesting, my classroom would be silent, and if I had a shadow of 'command presence' (instead of its opposite) there would be no moving between the cubicles at night" (284). (Groton's dormitories were so crowded and austere that the boys' living quarters were known as "cubicles," not rooms. See Jerome Karabel's *The Chosen: The Hidden History of Admission and Exclusion at Harvard, Yale, and Princeton* [2006] for a discussion of the "regime of Spartan deprivation" [28] at Groton and other Northeastern prep schools.)

By the end of *The Rector of Justin*, Aspinwall seems well-positioned to become Frank Prescott's Boswell. In addition to the notes about the rector he has collected in his journal, he is entrusted with unfinished manuscripts by Havistock, Griscam, and other would-be biographers, yet it seems unlikely that he will publish an account of his mentor's life. Sounding almost as frightened as he did in his first days at Justin, Aspinwall complains that he is in "a quandary." He would like to write about Prescott, but worries that he will fail to capture "the smallest hint of [the rector's] greatness." Then he asserts that he would prefer not to write a biography at all. Like Richardson (the creator of Clarissa Harlowe, Pamela Andrews, and Sir Charles Grandison), he wants to present a morally spotless protagonist:

> I am interested only in inspiring my reader, and I am very much at odds with my century in believing that to demonstrate the best by itself is more inspiring than the best with the worst. I want to reveal Dr. Prescott resplendent in the pulpit with his arms, so to speak, outstretched and his great eyebrows arched. I want the little figures like myself who might turn up on preliminary drafts washed out of the final picture. I know that we live in an age where the homely or psychological detail is considered all-important. We like heroes in shirt-sleeves, or, in other words, we don't like heroes. But things were not always that way.... I must stop rambling. I must cease my everlasting speculations. If I am ever to write anything, even if I give it my whole lifetime, I must still make a beginning. I must still make a mark on the acres of white paper that seem to unroll before me like arctic snows [339–40, 341].

Those acres of white paper, the reader suspects, are going to stay unmarked. Aspinwall's teaching job allows him to play a supporting role at a famous school, but it does not pull him out of his protracted

3. Campus Politics and Endless Adolescence

adolescence. In some ways, he seems even more naïve late in the novel than he did in the opening chapters. He concludes by daydreaming about writing a book that will leave out the faults that make Prescott interesting. He begins, on the other hand, by scheming to use his observations to "overtake" more forceful men:

> I have always wanted to keep a journal, but whenever I am about to start one, I am dissuaded by the idea that it is too late. I lose heart when I think of all the fascinating things I could have described had I only begun earlier. Not that my life has been an exciting one. On the contrary, it has been very dull. But a dull life in itself may be an argument for a journal. The best way for the passive man to overtake his more active brothers is to write them up. Isn't the Sun King himself just another character in Saint-Simon's chronicle? [1].

In the afterword to a recent edition of *The Rector of Justin*, Auchincloss suggests that Aspinwall is probably incapable of writing a book on any subject: "On the last page Brian has completed his researches and ... is picking up his pencil to start the biography. We never know, therefore, what he writes or even if he succeeds in writing it. Personally, I doubt if Brian would have been able to finish it. As I see him, he is the kind of perfectionist who would be constantly tearing up each page that he had written" (362).

"My share of his kingdom"

Cordelia Prescott Turnbull insists that she has always been her parents' worst disappointment. "I was born in 1895," she explains, "the baby of the family, the third of three girls, and because of complications attending my Caesarian birth it was decided that Mother should not be allowed to try again for the son whom she and Pa had so desperately wanted. Poor little fellow, I may have cost him his life, but when I think of the problems that any son of Pa would have had to face, it occurs to me that a wise providence may have known what it was about" (177). Her father, Turnbull adds, "took his revenge on me by a gleeful exercise of his sardonic sense of humor in the choice of my name. Imagine the lifetime of bad jokes that I have had to endure, as a third daughter with the name Cordelia" (177). As Turnbull's narrative progresses, it becomes increasingly clear that her cynicism, not her gender, has been the real source of her parents' disappointment. Her remark about her name, moreover, misses the point. Prescott's choice was hardly an act of vengeance; it aligns her with one of Shakespeare's greatest heroines and him with the capricious, destructive Lear.[10] (Turnbull repeatedly makes hyperbolic claims about characters who have offended her in one way or another. She describes her ex-husbands, for instance, in the most extreme language she can muster. Her first husband, she asserts, was "a monk"; the second was "carnal to a degree … I had not believed possible" [180, 209].)

The rector, Turnbull argues, was so preoccupied with his responsibilities at Justin Martyr that he neglected to raise his own daughters. They were placed in the hands of Mrs. Prescott, who "saw to it … that we received instruction even tougher than that meted out to the boys" (178). By Turnbull's lights, then, Harriet Prescott outperformed her husband as a parent and as an educator: "She was sometimes formidable and sometimes almost scaringly detached … but she always tried to make her girls feel that they were as important as Pa's sacred boys" (178). Turnbull could have cast her mother as a proto-feminist role model, but her point is not that Harriet Prescott was an extraordinary woman. Her point is that *she* was an extraordinary girl. Even though she had to cope with a career-obsessed father and an emotionally unreachable mother, Turnbull says, she was studying ancient literature and Darwin's theories early in her teens.

When Frank Prescott was not busy writing sermons and Sacred Studies lectures, Turnbull continues, he had a weakness for extramarital flirtations:

> I remember one summer at the Cape when Pa had been paying too much attention to a pretty neighbor (oh, yes, Mr. Aspinwall, that happened—you needn't look so shocked—maybe not actual infidelities, but cozy chats in windowseats and long, *long* walks on the beach) that Mother simply disappeared for three days. It turned out later that she had been in a hotel in Boston. When she came back, as seemingly cool and detached as ever, without offering the smallest excuse or explanation of where she had been, Pa, who had been frenzied by her absence, was a chastened man. He might have endured being left alone with his boys, but never with his girls [178–79].

3. Campus Politics and Endless Adolescence

Frank and Harriet Prescott found this incident so upsetting that they refused to discuss it for the rest of their lives. Nevertheless, Turnbull jumps at the chance to tell Brian Aspinwall, the man she thinks her father has chosen to write his biography, all about it. These passages, more than any other sections of Turnbull's narrative, reveal the depth of her hostility toward her parents. Like a desperate candidate trailing in the polls, she "leaks" every potentially destructive story she can remember, hoping that one will do the trick. He was preoccupied with "his sacred boys." She was "almost scaringly detached." He spent too much time alone with "pretty neighbors." She disappeared once, abandoning her family for three days, and then offered no "excuse or explanation." Turnbull suggests, in other words, that her parents' public image is largely an illusion. At Justin, they were entrusted with thousands of schoolboys, but at home they did a barely passable job of raising their own children. Turnbull seems especially eager to convince Aspinwall that Frank Prescott's failings as a parent stemmed from misogyny and repressed homosexuality:

> You're writing about a schoolmaster. Does he teach boys or girls? Boys. Very well, there's your first question. When did he begin to be attracted to his own sex? ... Everyone knows that Pa had a bee in his bonnet about perversion. And naturally, we all know that a completely normal man does not fear that sort of thing. We only fear what *threatens* ... He has always looked down on women. You have to have been his daughter to know how much. They don't really exist for him, except to satisfy a man's physical needs, bear his children and keep his house.... Only men are worthy of love, platonic love, and this love among men is stimulated by beauty of mind, beauty of soul, even beauty of body. Do you see? [174–76].

On several occasions, Turnbull boasts about using her relationships with men to strike back at her parents. She eloped at 17 because her first husband seemed the opposite of her father's conception of the ideal young man: "His name was Cabell Willets; he came of an old, devout Catholic family, and he had never in his life been away from his bigoted old mother, even to go to boarding school. He was mild and sweet and weak and ultimately stubborn. It's easy to see what he represented to me: he was the reverse in every respect of what Pa would have wanted a graduate of Justin to be" (179–80). Turnbull expected her father to be angry, but he did not play the role she envisioned:

"[We] were greeted back with smiles and open arms, and Pa told me, in a private conference, shaking his head in the gravest manner, that he, too, had had his doubts over the historic break with Rome.... Really! Anyone who hadn't known Pa would have thought he was making fun of me" (180). Several years later, Turnbull tried another tack, living in Paris with Charles Strong, a wounded World War I veteran and former standout at Justin Martyr:

> He was one of Pa's golden boys, Justin '11, senior prefect and football captain, a kind of American Rupert Brooke, at least in romantic appearance, blond, with sleepy grey eyes, a bit on the short side, but muscular and stocky, terribly serious and sincere, a savage tackle but gentle as a mother with children, honorable, naïve, charming, the kind of man who would protect his lady fair from a hundred wild Indians but whom *she* would have to protect from a swindling salesman—in short a magazine-cover hero, a Parsifal, Pa's ideal because the opposite of Pa [181].

Again, Turnbull hopes this relationship will infuriate her father, but the plan falls through when Prescott comes to Paris, inspires Strong to regain the faith he had lost during the war, and prays with him while Turnbull, annoyed by her father's influence on her lover, travels to Italy. While describing Strong's funeral, Turnbull rails against what she considers one of the rector's most unforgivable acts: "I shall never forget my last glimpse of [Strong's mother and sister] sitting primly on either side of Pa as their car drove away from the cathedral.... He had an air of having taken them ... under his big wings, of hugging to his benevolent chest all creatures but his own Cordelia. King Lear had not been content to deny me my share of his kingdom; he had seized the little principality that I had gained on my own. Obviously he felt that he had little to fear from filial ingratitude" (195). For Turnbull, then, virtually everything her father does, even his efforts to console mourners at a funeral, must be construed as part of an ongoing plot to control and belittle his youngest daughter.

As Turnbull discloses her own egotism and stormy marital history, Auchincloss raises the suspicion that she has been cataloguing her own problems and attempting to transfer them to her parents. Though she frequently refers to insights she has gained through psychoanalysis, she seems unaware that in her late forties she is still casting about for ways to flatter herself at her parents' expense:

3. Campus Politics and Endless Adolescence

> [Although the public] treated Pa and Mother with respect, it was the kind of respect that people might pay to the sovereigns of a small Pacific Island kingdom, more exotic than powerful, not quite to be taken seriously, perhaps even a bit ridiculous. I thought I could sense as a child among the graduates and the parents of the boys that curious half paternal, half protective, almost at times half contemptuous, attitude of men of affairs for academics, and I was determined that I should lead my own life in such a way as to be able ultimately to bid a plague on both kinds of houses. I would be neither sneered upon nor a sneerer. I would be an actress, a poet, a great artist and return to Justin only when Pa begged me, as a special treat, to come back and perform to the dazzled boys [179].

If there were any remaining doubts, Auchincloss eliminates them here—Turnbull's narrative is a paean to herself. She noticed the condescending attitudes of the graduates and their families, but her parents were oblivious. In the future, she predicts, the community at Justin will recognize that she is a "great artist" and the rector will ask her to come back and "perform to the dazzled boys." Her parents will continue to seem "a bit ridiculous," the alumni will continue to "sneer," and Cordelia will rise above them all. A number of commentators have argued that Turnbull's narrative sheds light on the rector's selfishness and hypocrisy. Parsell, for example, writes that "through Cordelia's testimony ... the reader clearly sees the dark side of Prescott's ostensibly inspirational behavior" (52). This interpretation gives Turnbull too much credit. She would like nothing more than to expose her father's failings, but her efforts backfire, focusing attention on her own bitterness. Among other things, her narrative demonstrates that a person does not have to be a student to be traumatized by boarding-school culture. Throughout her youth, Turnbull thought of Justin as a favored sibling, the Prescott "child" who received the largest share of her parents' attention. That conviction did not fade over time. Turnbull seems no less aggrieved in middle age than she was as a child. The immediacy of her resentment is the most striking feature of her narrative. Her mother has died, her father is over eighty years old, and in many cases she is recounting family quarrels that occurred decades earlier. Nonetheless, her emotional reactions seem as overwhelming as those of a teenager who has just been reprimanded by her parents and feels certain that they are in the wrong.

Palace of Lies

Cordelia Turnbull is the most vindictive character in *The Rector of Justin*, but Jules Griscam, the son of the chairman of Justin's board of trustees, runs a close second. First, like Turnbull, Jules insists that he is the most sophisticated member of his family. The device he uses to make this point is relentless cultural name-checking. David Griscam, Jules says, is so long-winded that he "would have talked the heart out of Keats and the sublime gaiety out of Mozart" (243). Frank Prescott might have become a talented performer, but "the perverted violence of his puritan conscience" caused him to dwindle into a schoolmaster. "As a young man ... he had strolled by the Thames reading Baudelaire and Rossetti," Jules explains. "He would have been a glorious repertory actor of the Henry Irving School, playing Iago one night and Tamburlaine the next" (247). During Jules's first year at Justin Martyr, his "Byronic pride" could not tolerate "the indignities of hazing" (246). When he was forced to endure "pumping," a hazing ritual that involved dunking the victim's head in a laundry sink, he was "borne up by the ecstasy of my passionate sense of wrong and the idea that, like the Count of Monte Cristo, I might have a lifetime for my revenge" (255). (Francis Biddle's description of "pumping" at Groton suggests that it resembled the "enhanced interrogation" technique known as waterboarding: "'[T]he fourth formers ... seized [the victim] and rushed him down the back stairs to the cellar, where he was turned upside down and held under the gush of a faucet ... until he had almost fainted.' Having suffered all the initial sensations of drowning, still retching and gasping, he was then asked if he fully understood the seriousness of his offense" [qtd. in Ward 183].[11]) Jules claims, moreover, that during his senior year, when he and several schoolmates built huts near the banks of a river, Prescott worried that the "independent Thoreaus camped on the very border of his village of robots" (249) were conspiring to undermine his authority.[12]

Secondly, Jules works tirelessly to annoy and embarrass his father. Again sounding very much like Cordelia Turnbull, Jules suggests that same-sex desire has been the main source of his father's loyalty to the rector: "The romance of his life—and this may explain some of Mother's domestic apathy—was Dr. Prescott. I am not well enough versed

3. Campus Politics and Endless Adolescence

in the new theories of Freud to be able to determine how much of this attraction was sexual; all I know is that his worship of the headmaster was of a jealous, proprietary kind and that it provided him with the only emotional excitement and quickening of the heart that I suspect his dry nature was ever to know" (245). The most curious feature of Jules's narrative is his conviction that Prescott thought of him as a nemesis, his opponent in a "long duel" (246). It would be more accurate to say that Jules's role in *The Rector of Justin* resembles that of Lucio in Shakespeare's *Measure for Measure*—he is a reckless, self-indulgent young man who puts himself in dangerous situations by repeatedly offending a more powerful character. If he had been imagined by a younger writer, Jules might have exuded something like the bravado of a 1960s student radical. In Auchincloss's hands, however, Jules is exasperating, a rich boy trying to convince the Brahmins at an exclusive prep school that he is a fearless dissident. When Prescott expels Jules and three of his classmates for committing an impulsive prank, Jules congratulates himself for getting in the "last word" against his enemy:

> "You've hated me from the beginning because you were shrewd enough to know that I saw through you. You had to get me before I got you!"
> "And when you saw through me, what did you see?"
> I was not taken in by his almost conversational tone of curiosity. I paused, but only to spit out the words more offensively. "I saw you weren't God. I saw that you don't even believe in God. Even in yourself as God. I saw you were only a cardboard dragon."
> "I will pray for you, Jules," he said in a very soft tone, almost a whisper. "And for your father."
> "And I, dear Doctor Prescott, will pray for you. Till we meet in hell!"
> This time his eyes really sparkled, and I knew it was my moment to turn about and march from the room. If he had won, I had had the last word. And a pretty magnificent last word, at that" [264-65].

Jules leaves the rector's office convinced that he has shaken Justin to its core, but in fact he has suffered a disastrous defeat. The prank—he locked Prescott in his study and hid the key, forcing the rector to climb through a window and down a ladder like "a great beetle" (259)—provokes the rector to expel him a few weeks before he would have graduated. The most harmful effect of this incident is that it seems to remove the possibility that Jules can outgrow his hatred of the rector, which, as Vincent Piket observes, has become "the rationale of his life" (155). David Griscam arranges for his son and the other expelled students to move on to Harvard, but Jules refuses to let go of his grudge. "I did not really believe in Harvard or in Father or in his dreary theories," he recalls. "Reality was gin and whiskey and poetry and fast driving and the evil memory of Justin Martyr" (270).

Jules's attempt to get even confirms that he has become virtually obsessed with his old headmaster. "To strike Dr. Prescott where he can be hurt," he tells the Harvard classmate who agrees to help him carry out the scheme, "one must commit an act of desecration on the school grounds.... After much thought, I have decided on three things. The face must be cut out of the portrait of Phillips Brooks [Prescott's mentor early in his career] in the school dining room.... The manuscript of the school hymn by Richard Watson Gilder in the library must be torn to shreds. And a hole must be poked through the figure of Justin Martyr in the altar window in chapel" (274–75). When these "acts of desecration" go awry, Prescott declines to press charges and visits Jules in jail, but his forgiveness is answered by another blast of contempt:

> "You built the school as your amphitheatre where through the decades generations of wondering boys could watch your Lacoon act. Oh, it was something! Until the devil peered out and saw his supposed victim strutting about on the rostrum, praying and preaching and exhorting, and realized that a new Barnum had put him on the boards and was making a fortune as a snake charmer."
>
> "And then what did he do?" Prescott's question came almost in a whisper.
>
> "Well, devils have a way of having the last word, you know," I said, looking at him hard, "particularly with those who are making a peepshow of God's mercy. Who are using God's things as props in vaudeville. And so it was that your beautiful academy, your palace of lies, should have at last a graduate ... who carries out your act to its ultimate degree and shatters for a gaping multitude the great glass window of your idolatry" [281].

Several critics have argued that the conflicts between Prescott and Jules wounded the rector and made him feel culpable when Jules died several years later in a one-car accident in the South of France.[13] Piket, for example, writes that "[Jules's] only satisfaction lies in having hurt

Prescott: the latter's will power and self-confidence are temporarily broken, as he acknowledges his failure in Griscam's case.... With the Rector's destruction, then, Griscam has also destroyed himself" (155–56). Similarly, Jonathan Yardley contends that Prescott "never quite recovers" (3) from his falling out with Jules. This reading is certainly plausible: after all, Prescott calls Jules's memoir "the record of my greatest failure" and tells Brian Aspinwall "I killed Jules. Or, not to be melodramatic, I sent him down the path that ended in his death" (240). Another possible interpretation is that these remarks illustrate the rector's mastery of campus politics. If Prescott thought of Jules's memoir as an account of the "failure" that "destroyed" him, what could he gain by giving it to Aspinwall and urging him to discuss its contents in his book? Perhaps he is using it to dispel lingering rumors about Jules's expulsion. Prescott asks Aspinwall not to quote directly from the memoir, but by presenting it to a would-be biographer who reveres him, he creates the possibility that he can exonerate himself without showing a trace of defensiveness. Jules's defiance was so blatant that readers at Justin would surely guess the identity of Prescott's antagonist and take offense when he calls the school a "disciplinary factory" (246) and its founder an atheist. And whether Aspinwall stresses Jules's tantrums or Prescott's patience, the rector can only benefit from further discussion of Jules's efforts to find a "chink in [Prescott's] armor" through which he could "jab the burning needle" (274).

Elsewhere in *The Rector of Justin*, Auchincloss presents accomplished adult characters who falter occasionally, revealing attitudes no less juvenile than those of Aspinwall, Turnbull, and Jules Griscam. Mr. Ives, Justin's senior master, takes Aspinwall aside and complains that he, like Mrs. Prescott, has suffered emotionally because of the rector's preoccupation with his school: "[S]he must have always known, as *I* have always known, that for every gram of love that comes back from Frank Prescott, a pound goes to the school.... That's the way things always are with great men. But sometimes, for aging wives and senior masters, it's a bit hard" (32). While helping Prescott with his mail, Aspinwall is astonished by the mean-spirited, self-inflating remarks of Justin's graduates:

> Some of the letters were childishly boasting. "You will observe from the letterhead that I am now a partner in..." or "Did you ever, Dr. P, expect

to address me as a fellow doctor?" In others the writers criticized Dr. Prescott bitterly, holding him responsible for unfortunate developments on the national or international scene, even the war itself. There was a shrill note to these, a "Now it can be told," an ultimate twisting, at a safe postal distance, of the old lion's tail. *See* what has come of your emphasis on football, Latin, cold showers, compulsory chapel, grace before meals or stiff collars on Sunday. "Would it interest you to know, Dr. P, how many of my formmates have been swindlers, dope addicts, alcoholics, lechers, pederasts? And whose fault was it, Dr. P?" ... I concluded that the common denominator of bad and good, favorable and unfavorable, was that in respect to Dr. Prescott most of his graduates had never grown up [40].

David Griscam claims that he worships Prescott, yet he never misses an opportunity to describe the rector's missteps or take partial credit for his success. In his notes toward a biography of Prescott, Griscam recalls that he convinced the rector to double Justin Martyr's enrollment and obtained funding for what he calls "my great project" (142) by covering up a cheating scandal involving the son of one of the school's richest benefactors: "[The] pledge came in the following month for exactly double the amount I had requested, and the great job of fund raising was at last completed. In the next two years the new dormitories, the chapel, the gymnasium, the handball courts, the wings to the Schoolhouse, the infirmary and six new masters' houses were erected, and by 1910 Justin Martyr had assumed very much the external appearance that it wears today ... and Francis Prescott took a long stride towards the deanship of New England headmasters" (162-63). These lines epitomize Griscam's mixed feelings about the rector. On the one hand, he celebrates Prescott's lofty reputation. On the other, he raises an implicit question: would that reputation exist if not for David Griscam and his "great project?" (Griscam's possessive attitude toward Justin Martyr seems to stem from his long association with the school. In addition to his years of service on the board of trustees, he was one of Prescott's earliest students. As Griscam explains in his notes toward a biography of Prescott, he enrolled at Justin only a few years after it was founded: "Justin Martyr in 1891 was only five years old, with forty boys, six masters and one big yellow barn of a building that stood up barely in the midst of a large field near the village of New Paisley, thirty miles west of Boston" [131]. Groton grew from equally humble origins, but by the turn of the twentieth century the school was so highly regarded that wealthy parents enrolled their sons there the day after the sons were born.) In some ways, Griscam suggests that Prescott was a liability during the process of expansion. He pretended to be cooperative in public settings, but "behind the scenes no Italian tenor of the Metropolitan could have behaved more outrageously.... He would describe himself pathetically to friends as David Griscam's dancing bear, led by a ring through its nose from laughing village to smirking town" (148). Griscam's message about Prescott, then, is perfectly clear: the rector has received no end of acclaim for the rise of his school, but he would not have accomplished nearly as much without the help of his brilliant, underappreciated junior partner.

Convictions of Failure

When Frank Prescott was five years old, his father, an officer in the Union army, was killed in the Battle of Chancellorsville and his "beautiful, grief-stricken mother ... quickly followed him to the grave" (64). Prescott had few friends at school. As Horace Havistock explains, he "cared too little for the opinions of others, and he could be brutally outspoken.... He was a silent, moody boy, and there was an air of truculent, rather unlovable superiority in his pale square handsome face..." (63). Prescott considered St. Andrew's, the private academy he attended, a perfect example of everything a boys' school should not be, and dreamed of presiding over a far more impressive institution.[14] He moved on to Oxford, attended divinity school at Harvard, took orders as an Episcopal priest, and founded a small church school. Over the next fifty years, Justin Martyr became an elite institution and Prescott became "probably the greatest name in New England secondary education" (2).

By any practical standard, this is a narrative about spectacular success: the story of an educator who set ambitious goals early in his career and reached them. Nonetheless, the elderly Prescott often seems morose. Like a tycoon haunted by the deals he failed to make, Prescott agonizes over the ways in which Justin has fallen short of his original aspirations. The rector's disillusionment is also reminiscent of the author's insistence in *The Education of Henry Adams* (1918) that his efforts to become well-educated have failed: "In age, looking back through the lens of his youthful expectations he had reason to consider that he had failed, regardless of what less idealistic observers might make of his remarkable literary career. Whether one finds his ambition inordinate or not may well depend on the daring of one's own aspirations" (Samuels viii). Parsell notes that the rector's regrets are particularly distressing to Aspinwall: "Brian at first sees in Prescott an exemplar of the strength and conviction ... [he] lacks. Delving deeper, however, Brian uneasily discovers the old man's gathering convictions of personal failure, convictions supported by mounting evidence that Prescott's lifelong dream of the perfect, 'unique' boys' preparatory school, a dream sustained at a tremendous cost in interpersonal relationships, has after fifty years resulted in an institution little different from others of the same type" (49). As Piket explains, the rector's dream was nothing less than to reinvent secondary education:

> [Prescott tried] to build a school in which boys might develop a degree of moral strength and integrity before being exposed to the large, practical and mercantilist world. Prescott's vision of life is profoundly holistic. In his educational plan, sacred studies, languages, mathematics and the sciences form integral parts of the development of a pupil's soul and character. As Justin is a church school, its education also includes religious service. Prescott tells Aspinwall that "There is no real distinction between the pulpit and the classroom. I tried to put God into every book and sport in Justin." ... The great impetus behind [the rector's] foundation of the school had been his perception of the mercantilism and political degeneration of America following the Civil War. By giving his pupils a broad, moralistic education, he hoped to broaden the moral basis of society [146, 148].[15]

After he retires, Prescott seems convinced that he has failed. He had hoped to train clergymen and elected officials, but most of Justin's graduates, like the graduates of other New England boarding schools, ended up "in the same business world ... he had meant to transform" (Piket 148).[16] Prescott becomes especially discouraged after David Griscam arranges for him to meet with the newest members of the school's board of trustees. One trustee, a bank president, complains that the school has drifted too far from its "traditions of honor and respectability." "Next year's first form," he says, "might have been garnered at Ellis

3. Campus Politics and Endless Adolescence

Island. Now I like to think I'm as democratic as the next guy, but where do we stop? Do we want to jettison altogether the principle of a Protestant school for boys of Anglo-Saxon descent?" (318). Then a second trustee, a former scholarship boy who earned an enormous fortune as a war profiteer, suggests that enrolling a few token black students might be a shrewd financial maneuver:

> "In these days a school must keep its eye on its tax exemption. The time may be coming when it will be politic to have a couple of coons to show the Revenue boys. Just to keep the record straight."
> Dr. Prescott's face was drawn to an expression of the tightest fascination.
> "Coons?" he said softly.
> "Negroes. We may come to that. Oh, a couple would do the trick. And some of them, you know, could pass for whites [321].

More than any other incident in the novel, this meeting convinces Prescott that he is a charlatan and that his school has always been a failed experiment:

> We sat for a few minutes more until suddenly Dr. Prescott started talking, in a low, somber tone, gazing into the fire. "I took my daughter Evelyn's youngest child to the circus in Boston last week. There was a clown in it who kept trying to escape from a round bright spotlight trained on him from the top of the house. Everywhere the bright circle remorselessly pursued him. Now I see that *I* was that clown. And the spotlight was the effort of all the rest of you to keep the truth from me."
> "The truth?" I burst out in dismay. "What truth?"
> Dr. Prescott looked at me as if he had forgotten my presence. But his tone was perfectly kind. "The truth about Justin Martyr, Brian.... I see that Justin Martyr is like the other schools. Only *I*, of course, ever thought it was different. Only I failed to see that snobbishness and materialism were intrinsic in its make-up. Only I was naïve enough to think I could play with that kind of fire and not get my hands burnt. But you, David, of course, understood all that. You even saw how to make a selling point out of my naïveté. You persuaded the world that the gospel of Prescott of Justin was the passport to good society. And the world believed it! When I urged the boys to go into politics or the ministry, they accepted it as Prescottism, so many lines of a lesson to be learned that had no relation to the real world at home. They learned their lines, yes. Some of them even enjoyed learning them. They had been told by their parents that to be a graduate of Justin would be a material aid in that real world. Ah, yes, reality.... Reality was the brokerage house, the

corporation law firm, the place on Long Island, the yacht, the right people" [323–25].

When readers at Groton objected to *The Rector of Justin* in 1964, this passage should have been their main concern. It's one thing if an angry, deluded character like Jules Griscam calls Justin a "palace of lies" and compares Prescott to a circus performer. It's another if the rector draws the same conclusions. (Prescott's dark mood in this section of the novel calls to mind Oliver Wendell Holmes's portrait of a headmaster in "The School-Boy" [1878], a poem written to commemorate the centennial of Phillips Academy Andover: "Grave is the Master's look; his forehead wears / Thick rows of wrinkles, prints of worrying cares; / Uneasy lie the heads of all that rule, / His most of all whose kingdom is a school" [259].) Schools like Justin Martyr, the rector maintains, have always been replete with "snobbishness and materialism." The "great headmasters" of his generation were little more than pitchmen who sold their academies to the wealthiest families in the Northeast. Prescott's efforts to turn privileged young men toward careers in public service have come to nothing. Students arrived at Justin Martyr expecting to use it as a stepping stone to Ivy League universities, high-paying careers, and exclusive country clubs, and that is exactly what they have done.[17] As Leigh Bienen writes, "The school succeeds and leaves its mark upon the pupils, who remember both the institution and its keeper; but at the end of his life [Prescott] must watch its founding ideals crumble in the face of a society which seems no longer able or willing to support institutionalized morality and ambition" (48). David Griscam was the school official at Justin who understood why parents send their children to exclusive private academies. By introducing him to the new trustees, Prescott concludes, Griscam "tore the scales off my eyes ... and made me see my lifework for the poor thing it was" (336). In *The Best and the Brightest* (1973), David Halberstam points out that Griscam's assumptions about boarding schools have always been more realistic than the rector's: "The overt teaching [at schools like Groton] was that the finest life is service to God, your family, and your state, but the covert teaching, far more subtle and insidious, was somewhat different: ultimately, strength is more important; there is a ruling clique; there is a thing called privilege and you might as well use it. That is the real world and it is going to remain that way, so you might as well get used to it" (51). Similarly, Carol Gelderman writes that "[p]arents sent their sons to [New England prep schools] to make friends with the right people, for these connections served well later on Wall Street and in Washington. No one sent a boy to Groton to become a priest" (36).

Throughout most of *The Rector of Justin*, Frank Prescott appears to stand above the juvenile attitudes of the characters who surround him. In the novel's closing section, however, Auchincloss stresses that the rector has some juvenile attitudes of his own. Not long after his retirement, Prescott lends his support to an uprising led by faculty members who disapprove of his successor: The Rev. Duncan Moore, the former rector of St. Jude's Church in Manhattan. Aspinwall recognizes that the insurgents are "carping critics" (295), but Prescott angrily defends his right to second-guess his successor: "'I tell you, Brian, you're a fusspot!' he exclaimed. 'We're only trying to devise a way to save what is best in Justin. This is not disloyalty.... What you must learn, Brian, if you are to be an effective priest, is that you belong to the church militant and that means you have to fight!'" (296). Prescott changes his mind after he discovers that the potential rectors on the board of trustees would be far more objectionable than Duncan Moore, but by then the damage is done. After five decades of running the school as he saw fit, Prescott fails to recognize that his participation in the plot against his successor is a breathtaking display of egotism.

By charting the life and times of Frank Prescott, Auchincloss raises questions previous authors of American school literature had not considered. Fitzgerald, Salinger, et al. created vivid portraits of individual boarding-school students, but *The Rector of Justin* examines boarding-school culture at large. On the one hand, in spite of his own unhappy experiences at Groton, Auchincloss suggests that there is much to admire in the leading Northeastern boys' schools, from their striking architecture to their efforts to weave academics, religion, athletics, and a commitment to public service into a worldview that can guide students and graduates throughout their lives. At the same time, Auchincloss emphasizes that the virtues of exclusive private academies are often accompanied by dangers. As the experiences of Brian Aspinwall, Cordelia Turnbull, Jules Griscam, and Frank Prescott illustrate, some adults associated with boarding schools lose sight of reality, expect too much of these institutions, and become no less aggrieved and demoralized than the adolescent protagonists of previous school narratives. In other words, *The Rector of Justin* raises serious doubts about the prep-school myth. The story of Frank Prescott's career at Justin Martyr suggests that there is no such thing as an ideal setting to prepare for a rewarding future. The rector worked for decades to create such a place, but all he managed to produce was one of the best schools in the country.

4

Sexuality, Gothic Melodrama, and Boarding-School Fiction: James Kirkwood's Good Times/Bad Times

> *I felt his hands on my back again. Only now, there was a difference; it was like they didn't know what they were doing there.... I felt his fists clench up and rest on my spine, and for a second I thought he was going to smash them down on me.—*
> James Kirkwood, Good Times/Bad Times

Few boarding-school novels are as innovative as James Kirkwood's *Good Times/Bad Times* (1968). First of all, Kirkwood examines homosexuality more candidly than any American school novelist had done previously, and after his breakthrough other authors of school literature stopped treating it as a taboo subject. Second, Kirkwood sets his novel apart by experimenting with the figure of the boarding-school headmaster. In the first half of the twentieth century, the Groton School's Endicott Peabody, Deerfield Academy's Frank Boyden, and other prominent headmasters were viewed with enormous respect. Accordingly, most American school narratives written before *Good Times/Bad Times* had stressed the dignity and competence of officials in charge of private boys' schools. Kirkwood diverges sharply from that approach, portraying Franklyn Hoyt, the headmaster of Gilford Academy, as a closeted, deeply neurotic gay man infatuated with Peter Kilburn, an 18-year-old who has recently enrolled at his school. By doing so, Kirkwood mixes school fiction and Gothic melodrama, a combination that earlier novelists had not attempted.

An Open Secret

Before James Kirkwood published *Good Times/Bad Times*, American authors of boarding-school fiction seemed to regard occasional references to homosexuality as an unpleasant but unavoidable feature of the genre. J. D. Salinger, John Knowles, and Louis Auchincloss acknowledge that homosexuality existed on prep-school campuses in and around the World War II era, but their references to the subject are fleeting and rare. Holden Caulfield's remarks about gay men are filled with the ignorance and hostility that pervaded mainstream American discourse about homosexuality circa 1950. While Holden waits for a former schoolmate to meet him at a hotel lounge in Manhattan, he notices a group of men seated at the bar and assumes that they are gay. "They weren't too flitty-looking," he recalls. "I mean they didn't have their hair too long or anything—but you could tell they were flits anyway" (142). Critical discussions of *The Catcher in the Rye* seldom mention this passage, but it is highly revealing. Many commentators have identified Holden as a rebel and an outsider, but some of his attitudes, including those relating to homosexuality, are in step with conventional opinion. He suggests that there is something suspicious, in one way or another, about gay men. Some grow their hair "too long." Others look so "normal" that they can readily pass for straight. Later on, Holden claims that adult homosexuals have tried to molest him "about twenty times since I was a kid" (193). Even if we attribute this high number of alleged incidents to Holden's tendency to exaggerate (e.g., his remark that his parents would have "two hemorrhages apiece" [1] if he disclosed any private information about them), this assertion makes it clear that he views gay men as predators, a threat he has experienced many times.

If not for Gene Forrester's prediction that his peers at the Devon School will suspect that his roommate Finny is a "fairy" if he is seen on campus wearing a pink shirt, *A Separate Peace* would contain hints of same-sex desire, but no direct references to the subject. Similarly, Louis Auchincloss refers to homosexuality from time to time in *The Rector of Justin*, but then he turns the reader's attention, very quickly, to less controversial subjects. As we have seen in Chapter 3, Cordelia Turnbull and Jules Griscam insinuate that their fathers may be closeted

4. Sexuality, Gothic Melodrama, and Boarding-School Fiction

gay men. And Frank Prescott tells Brian Aspinwall that throughout his career at Justin Martyr he worried about unusually close friendships between students:

> "[Y]ou never discouraged close friendships between boys, did you, sir?"
> "Did I not?" He grunted loudly. "I was one of the worst!"
> "Why, sir?"
> "Because, sir," he exclaimed loudly, driving his stick into the snow, "I did not think a hundred examples of David and Jonathan were worth one of sodomy!" [43].

Later in *The Rector of Justin*, Horace Havistock compares his lifelong friendship with Prescott to a certain type of marriage, but insists that there is nothing sexual about it: "The element of the female in my nature matched well with the masculine in his; in many ways our relationship was like that of a strong, single-minded husband and a clever, realistic wife. I quite realize that in the days in which I am writing, it will be impossible for a reader of the last sentence not to jump over a Freudian moon, but I belong to a simpler and less polluted generation. I have always gloried in my conception of friendship, and I will insist to my dying day that it has nothing of sex in it" (75).

In a sense, *The Catcher in the Rye*, *A Separate Peace*, and *The Rector of Justin* do not comment on homosexuality at all. They focus on straight characters' misconceptions about same-sex desire. Holden Caulfield believes that the men he sees at the bar are gay, but he is clearly speculating about their sexual orientation. He claims that gay men have tried to force themselves on him many times, but it seems that every one of these alleged attempts failed: he tells the reader that he was *threatened* repeatedly, not that he was molested. No one calls Finny a "fairy," but Gene Forrester worries that such a thing might happen if his schoolmates see Finny in his pink shirt. Moreover, Cordelia Turnbull and Jules Griscam imply that their fathers may have been attracted to each other for years, but as far as the audience can tell, the fathers' same-sex desires exist only in the imaginations of their children.

Given the obvious inclination of Salinger, Knowles, and Auchincloss to say as little as possible about homosexuality, Gore Vidal's story "The Zenner Trophy" (1950) seems almost prophetic. The plot is driven by the discovery of a sexual relationship between two students at a private academy for boys, but Vidal's characters refuse to name the transgression the young men have supposedly committed. If the word "homosexual" is prohibited on campus, how can school officials punish the offenders and cover up their alleged wrongdoing? Vidal suggests that the officials will need an assortment of vague, evasive phrases. Don't say that the students were caught in bed together: refer to their relationship as a "trying situation," "the revelation," "this distasteful business," a "vexing problem," "a disaster as vast as this one," or "the specter of all schools and the ruin of some." By using these and other circumlocutions, Vidal's educators get through an extended discussion of the students' affair without mentioning it in a straightforward way.

At the beginning of the story, the Principal of a school modeled on Phillips Exeter Academy explains that a crisis has arisen.[1] It has come to light that two students in the senior class are lovers. The main problem, as the Principal sees it, is that one of the young men is Flynn, who has just been given the school's most prestigious award for athletics. Kicking Flynn out of the school will be simple enough, but what, he asks, is to be done about the Zenner Trophy? During a conversation with Mr. Beckman, Flynn's faculty advisor, the Principal decides to take back the award and refuse to speak publicly about the expulsion:

> "Flynn of course can't have it now. I must say that I wish we hadn't made the announcement so far in advance ... but it's done and that's that and we'll have to make the best of it. I favor rewarding it but the Athletics Director tells me Flynn was the only possible choice ... our finest athlete." He paused. "Do you remember the day he pitched against Exeter? Marvelous!" [58].

Then the Principal sends Beckman to Flynn's dorm room to deliver the bad news. Beckman begins his meeting with Flynn with a sensation of "panic insecurely leashed" (64), but much to his surprise the student reacts to his punishment calmly. While packing his suitcases, Flynn explains that he knew he would be sent away and that he has earned enough credits to enroll at a university that has offered him a full athletic scholarship. Flynn's only objection to the way the "crisis" has been handled is that the Principal has explained the reason for his expulsion to his parents:

4. Sexuality, Gothic Melodrama, and Boarding-School Fiction

"[He has] written your parents."

"Written my parents *what*?"

"The ... the whole business. It's customary, you understand. The Principal wrote the letter himself, today, this morning as a matter of fact.... You must remember ... that the Principal was only doing his duty. You *were* caught, you know, and you *were* expelled. Don't you feel your parents deserve some sort of explanation?"

"No, I don't. Not like that, anyway. It's bad enough being kicked out without having that dumb bastard go and upset them. It's no way of getting back at me: I earn my own way. I can go to any school I want on a scholarship. Or I can turn pro tomorrow and make ten times the money that fool Principal makes. But why, I want to know, does somebody who doesn't even know me go out of his way to make such a mess for my family?" [66–67].

Thus, by presenting only three characters and two conversations, Vidal captures the prevailing homophobic attitudes at American boarding schools in the 1950s. It was an open secret that some students at private academies were gay or bisexual, but school officials chose to pretend that same-sex attraction did not exist at their institutions. If evidence of homosexuality became impossible to ignore or deny, the offenders were expelled to ensure that their "misconduct" would not hurt the school's reputation. The students are set to graduate in a week? There can be no exceptions. One of them is extremely popular and "the best athlete the school [has] produced in over a decade" (59)? There can be no exceptions. Compromise is not an option, the Principal assumes, when you are dealing with "the specter of all schools and the ruin of some." (Sawyer, Flynn's boyfriend, was so intimidated by the school community's hostility toward gay men that he went home "before anyone had a chance to talk with him" [53], leaving most of his belongings in his dorm room. The Principal initially describes Sawyer's departure as "cowardly," but then he concedes that it was "on the whole sensible for there could have been no doubt in his mind as to what our decision would be: by leaving he has saved us a certain embarrassment" [56–57].) Near the end of the story, Flynn tells Mr. Beckman that he cannot understand why his expulsion is necessary: "I still don't see why what I want to do should ever be anybody's business except my own.... [A]fter all, it doesn't affect anybody else, does it?" (70). Beckman tries to defend the Principal's actions, but his heart is not in it. "Not only was he sympathetic," the narrator tells us, "he was partisan, hopelessly identified with the other. He shuddered at the thought of the meeting between son and parents and he tried to think of what would happen" (68). Moments later, Flynn realizes why his advisor's remarks have been so mild and guarded. He, too, is gay, but no one else at the school knows about his sexual orientation. When Beckman offers to return the books Flynn has checked out from the school's library, Flynn suggests that the two of them might "get together some weekend" in Boston. "I should like that," Beckman replies (74).

Good Times/Bad Times *and "the specter of all schools"*

At the beginning of James Kirkwood's *Good Times/Bad Times*, Peter Kilburn is charged with killing Franklyn Hoyt, the headmaster of Gilford Academy. (Gilford is modeled on Brewster Academy, a prep school in Wolfeboro, New Hampshire, that Kirkwood attended for two years in the early 1940s.) After Peter is arrested, a criminal defense lawyer offers to represent him pro bono and asks him to write a complete account of the events leading up to Hoyt's death. Peter works around the clock on the document, partly to show his gratitude and partly to take his mind off of the media frenzy surrounding his arrest.[2] Early in his narrative, Peter recalls that he was sexually harassed just after he arrived at the local jail. An inmate known as "El Greco" began by singing a love song in the shower room and watching Peter's reaction. Then he went further, "soaping himself up and leering at me, singing *to* me, making sly little gestures, and getting a big kick out of it" (27). Peter looked away in confusion and embarrassment, but that only provoked El Greco:

> When I did this, he got an even larger jolt out of it and stopped singing and spoke to me in Greek. His tone was very insinuating. I turned my back to him and he gave a loud wolf whistle and slapped me on the ass. The two guards, who were standing in the doorway to the long, tiled shower room, laughed at this. The other prisoners, too. I told myself to keep cool. But then he started singing "I've Got a Crush on You" to me, in broken English, but he knew all the lyrics.
>
> Well, I've got a sense of humor and because of the implications in the newspapers and me being eighteen I can go along with a joke. But when

4. Sexuality, Gothic Melodrama, and Boarding-School Fiction

the other six prisoners joined in and one of the guards as well—the other one was too busy laughing to sing—then it got a little heavy-handed [27].

In some ways this passage, like the passages in *The Catcher in the Rye*, *A Separate Peace*, and *The Rector of Justin* mentioned earlier, has little to do with homosexuality. As the guards and the other adult prisoners recognize immediately, El Greco's antics are not a genuine attempt to flirt with Peter. They are a comic performance, a send-up of first-time prisoners' fears of sexual assault. Nonetheless, this passage is the first indication that same-sex desire will not be treated as an unmentionable subject in *Good Times/Bad Times*. It will be treated as a fact of life, a subject Kirkwood's characters often think about and discuss.

When Peter arrived at Gilford Academy, the first schoolmate who greeted him was Dennis Vacarro, a gay student who combines anxiety and shame with an unconcealed desire to find a boyfriend at the school. "I introduced myself," Peter writes, "and walked over and shook his hand, which was extremely damp; his face was sweaty, too. I said to come in but he looked back down the hall and said, 'No, better not, it's pretty late.' He glanced down at the floor, then up at me, and added, 'I could sneak up later, though, and we could talk.... Only talk, I don't mean anything else but just talk,' he said, making it a dead giveaway" (38–39). Most of the other students persecute Vacarro, but Peter's friend Jordan Legier spends some time getting to know the outcast and learns that he was a victim of childhood sexual abuse:

> Dennis and [Jordan] had many conversations and Jordan finally got him to tell how he started out. Of all people, Dennis' father had initiated him into sex, had made him perform certain acts when he was very young, like six or seven; Dennis had grown to like it and, at first, he even believed that's the way it was, that all good little boys obliged their fathers.... When Dennis was fifteen, his father up and walked out on his mother and him and settled down to live with a painter (male) in Key West, Florida. Jordan said Dennis was still looking for a father, still trying to please every male he could [148–49].

As James Levin observes in *The Gay Novel in America* (1991), this kind of facile explanation of how homosexual characters "got that way" was commonplace in American fiction before the 1970s: "[In] the last years of [that decade], there was not a single work speculating on the cause of homosexual behavior, a major question for earlier writers.... A greater sense of security among homosexually oriented men clearly led to less need for justification in fiction" (311). David Bergman notes that although many gay men have come to understand their sexuality in part through reading fiction about same-sex relationships, this "reliance on literature has not ... always been helpful. Even literature written by homosexuals has often presented gay life as a depressing, marginal, and unfulfilling experience dominated by violence, drugs, alcoholism, poverty, and prostitution. As Samuel R. Delany, the black science fiction writer, points out in an interview, gay men learned to speak about their sexuality in 'a rhetoric of despair and degradation'" (7).

Not long after Peter arrived at Gilford, he learned that a tragic incident had cast a pall over the campus. A few years earlier, Gilford had been regarded as a first-rate institution. "I don't mean like Exeter or Andover," Peter writes, "it was never a large school, or say in the top five, but it was a sound, well-thought-of prep school with a good standing. They still took day students, but they were in the minority. The boarding quota was full, with a waiting list" (70). The school's "good standing" vanished, however, after a senior at Gilford, the son of a United States Senator, committed suicide:

> The day before the Senator and his wife were due to arrive at the school—he was giving the graduation speech—a janitor found the boy's body in a corner of the boiler room at Logan Hall.
>
> He'd hanged himself with a belt. No note was left, but his mother found a diary among his things. He'd been having a relationship with his roommate (also captain of the football and ski teams) all year. His roommate had recently told him he was getting engaged that summer and planned to be married and they'd better not see one another after the end of school.
>
> The Senator started out from Washington to attend graduation and ended up at his son's funeral. Although the suicide itself couldn't be hushed up, they tried to hide the specific reason for it. As far as the newspapers were concerned, they were successful, but a local scandal around the school and village was impossible to suppress. The fact that nobody ever suspected what was going on made it a great item for gossip [71].

Gilford's board of trustees fired the headmaster and replaced him with Mr. Hoyt, but their damage-control strategy failed. The school "went into a decline," lost half of its enrollment, and "limp[ed] along" for

4. Sexuality, Gothic Melodrama, and Boarding-School Fiction

several years, unable to recover from the publicity surrounding the young man's death (71). In fact, Peter senses that Gilford is a troubled institution the day he arrives. He notices that the campus is "pretty … [and] almost graceful-looking," yet it seems that "some of its insides were missing. I sensed, from little things I heard, there was the ghost of a much better, healthier school hanging over Gilford" (70). Similarly, Jordan senses that all is not well at Gilford the first time he strolls around the campus:

> We walked on toward the edge of the lake. When we got to the water, Jordan turned around and stared up at the school. "Tell me, is this place…?" He broke off and didn't continue.
> "Is it what?"
> "As—sad as it seems?" …
> How's that for perception! He'd only arrived at two o'clock that afternoon. "Yes, I think it is," I told him. "Sad," I added, "that's a good word for it" [125].

At several points in his narrative, Peter mentions that he has some personal experience with same-sex desire. He identifies himself as heterosexual, but explains that before he left Los Angeles he and another boy were seduced by a male television actor. The actor invited them to his house in Laurel Canyon, served them drinks spiked with rum, "hauled out three albums of dirty pictures," and showed them an X-rated movie: "This actor was a master operator. One thing led to another and he finally had his oral way with first Boots and then me. Not only that, but he gave Boots a .22 rifle and me a suede jacket. Boots wanted to contact him again but he moved away soon after and we never did" (181, 182). (Kirkwood was a resident of Key West, like Dennis Vacarro's father, and a former television actor, like the man in this episode. Thus, though Kirkwood does not try to excuse or defend these characters, he accentuates things he has in common with them in addition to their misconduct.) After he describes the incident in Laurel Canyon, Peter observes that the line between friendship and homoeroticism can be difficult to draw. He explains, for instance, that he and Jordan often got into bed together at night, but only because "it would get chilly sitting around":

> Jordan would hardly ever touch me, not even with his leg or arm, when I'd be in his bed. We'd just be there talking, having, as we used to call it,

"News of the Week in Review," which was a post-mortem on the events of the day. Now that I look back on it, we liked each other so much I believe that's why we didn't play around, nobody wanted to chance spoiling the great relationship we had. I know that's part of it, aside from also knowing Jordan's tastes were much stronger for the opposite sex than for men. Me, too [182].

In earlier boarding-school novels, this kind of evening ritual would have seemed unusual, to say the least, but Kirkwood's depictions of homoeroticism are fundamentally different from those of his forerunners. As we have seen, American boarding-school narratives of the fifties and early sixties occasionally *refer* to homosexuality. Kirkwood, by contrast, presents a string of episodes in which male characters experience same-sex desire and talk about the subject in matter-of-fact ways.

Peter realizes that his narrative may create the impression that he is bisexual, but he never seems defensive about his sexual orientation. Yes, he writes, he and Jordan were tempted to "play around," but they abstained to avoid risking their friendship. They kissed at midnight on New Year's Eve, but that, he says, was simply the momentary impulse of two close friends at a raucous party: "It was a real kiss, and no matter what anybody might think, a perfectly right and fitting expression of our friendship for that time and place and for us. That's the only time there was any physical intimacy between us. Enough said" (259). They attended a performance of Puccini's *Turandot*, holding hands with tears in their eyes, but that speaks to the intensity of the opera, not to their sexual orientation. Jordan calls Peter "baby" and Peter defines his feelings for Jordan as "love," but Peter argues that he and his friend are not to blame if some readers do not understand that male heterosexuals can love each other. Unlike Holden Caulfield, Gene Forrester, and Frank Prescott, Peter and Jordan are not shocked or repulsed by homoeroticism. They have experienced that kind of attraction, but insist that they find it less powerful than their attraction to women. Moreover, both characters regard gay men with an empathetic, live-and-let-live attitude. As Levin points out, Peter and Jordan are the only students at Gilford who do not taunt and ridicule Dennis Vacarro, and their compassion is reaffirmed by their reactions to campus gossip about the nature of their friendship. Most of their school-

4. Sexuality, Gothic Melodrama, and Boarding-School Fiction

mates would have been incensed by rumors about their sexuality, but Peter and Jordan show an unusual willingness "to be labeled as homosexual when they are not" (Levin 234). This mislabeling may be an homage to Robert Anderson's play *Tea and Sympathy* (1953), in which a student at a New England preparatory school secretly pines for his housemaster's wife and is, at the same time, thought to be gay by his father, his schoolmates, and the housemaster.[3] Early in *Good Times/Bad Times*, Kirkwood drops in an allusion to Anderson's play. While Mr. Hoyt chastises Peter for a minor rule violation, the headmaster's wife brings in refreshments, but Hoyt orders her to take them away:

> I heard footsteps and some rattling sounds and the door opened. Mrs. Hoyt stood there carrying a large silver tray with cups and silver tea things and a plate stacked high with cookies. "Franklyn, I brought—"
>
> He waved her away with a hand. "No, Miriam," he said.
>
> She winced and ducked back a step, looking at me and then at him and said, "But I thought—"
>
> "Not now," he said, turning away from her and waiting for her to leave.
>
> "Yes, Franklyn," she said and backed out of the room.
>
> He turned around and looked at me closely. I remember thinking: No tea, and God only knows—no sympathy" [61].

When Jordan learns about Hoyt's infatuation with Peter, he asserts that most men are bisexual to one degree or another, and that those who recoil from their same-sex desires risk becoming psychologically unstable and possibly dangerous:

> Again I told Jordan how [Mr. Hoyt's actions] just didn't figure, with him being so uptight about things like that. "Exactly why it does figure," Jordan said. "Like guys who don't have a problem, if they come into contact with anything homosexual, they can just shrug it off. They can even have friends who swing that way and it doesn't drive them up the wall. But someone with a little iggie about it, who's fighting it off, they're the ones always screaming about the 'goddam faggots' and beating them up."
>
> "But what about the guy who killed himself here? [Mr. Hoyt's] never gotten over that little episode, so how could he ever—"
>
> "Sure he's never gotten over that. *Especially* that. What about those two guys? Nobody would have ever called them 'fruits'—they were attractive, popular, masculine. All his years at prep schools, [Mr. Hoyt] must have seen a lot of nonfruity guys he thought were fooling around.

I'll bet way deep down a little voice keeps nattering away at him: 'Hmn, it might not be all *that* bad'" [235].

Greg Varner argues that although the depictions of gay men in *Good Times/Bad Times* were "daring" in 1968, they seem retrograde today: "The novel is suffused with homoeroticism, but homosexuality is nervously (and unconvincingly) disavowed by [Peter] ... (It was not until the late 1970s, when openly gay writers such as Edmund White, Andrew Holleran and Larry Kramer all published novels with explicitly gay themes, that a daring novel such as *Good Times/Bad Times* would seem disingenuous and quaint because of its evasions)" (2–3). A 1975 magazine article about Kirkwood presents a similar conclusion. As Kirkwood's biographer Sean Egan explains, "[t]he gay magazine *Mandate* said ... [that the novel] does seem to beg the reader's credulity in those episodes dealing with the question of whether or not there was any actual sexual relationship between Peter and Jordan. The affection between them was so overwhelming that it's somewhat difficult to believe that nothing other than snoring went on beneath the bedcovers" (56). William Madison, moreover, contends that the most notable aspect of *Good Times/Bad Times* is "[the] energy Kirkwood's narrator expends in denying homosexuality. Despite whatever you may think, he says again and again, there was nothing sexual in his relationship with his best friend ... *Whatever you may have heard*, there was nothing 'funny' going on" (1).

Varner is correct to point out that Kirkwood's approach was bold for its time, but it is also true that the gay characters in *Good Times/Bad Times* are consistently associated with self-hatred, self-destruction, and criminality. Dennis Vacarro is openly gay, but ashamed of his sexuality. The Senator's son commits suicide after he is jilted by his boyfriend. Vacarro's father could have been prosecuted for molestation. The same could be said of the actor who seduced Peter and his friend, and of Mr. Hoyt, whose pursuit of Peter is discussed later in this chapter. As Levin points out, Kirkwood's rendering of Hoyt is so negative that it makes the novel as a whole seem "extremely critical of homosexual behavior" (234). Egan agrees, noting that "there is little denying that an unfortunate aspect to this book is the fact that there creeps into it a suggestion that homosexuality is 'wrong'" (228). Madison goes further, arguing that throughout *Good Times/Bad Times* "[homosexual] desire is treated as shameful ... the headmaster's recompense is death at the hands of the boy he craves" (1). Thus, although Kirkwood's treatment of same-sex attraction marks a turning point in American school literature, it marks a complex, and at times disturbing, sort of turning point. On the one hand, he raises the subject of homoeroticism candidly and often. On the other, the gay characters he imagines seem profoundly troubled, predatory, or both.

If readers want to argue that *Good Times/Bad Times* is the work of a self-hating gay man, the portraits of Franklin Hoyt, Dennis Vacarro, et al. present convincing evidence in support of that thesis. Another possible interpretation is that the novel is akin to the "Blaxploitation" films of the 1970s. Do movies like *Shaft* (1971), *Super Fly* (1972), and *Coffy* (1973) depict African Americans in flattering ways? Of course not: they are rife with toxic stereotypes about sex, drugs, and violence in predominantly black inner-city neighborhoods. In fact, these films reinforce so many racist assumptions that the NAACP and other civil rights organizations formed an ad hoc committee to express their concerns about them. Nevertheless, Blaxploitation movies were popular with black audiences because, unlike innumerable earlier Hollywood films, they do not marginalize black characters. As David Walker observes, "[in] the 1970s, black America was in need of an escape from the brutal reality of the past decade. The films that came along during the early part of the 1970s provided just such an escape, creating a fantasy world on the big screen where black men and women were the heroes" (viii–ix). Similarly, Yvonne Sims notes that the performances of Pam Grier and other African-American actresses in Blaxploitation films marked "a significant departure from the historical representations of black actresses and, through the writers, producers, and directors of the films [of the era], brought to the screen a new image of African-American femininity. It was goodbye to the headscarves worn by Mammy and the wavy hair of the Exotic Other, and a refreshing and political greeting to the woman with a natural hairstyle, modeled [on] civil rights heroines such as Angela Davis" (8–9). Kirkwood, it seems to me, uses a comparable approach in *Good Times/ Bad Times*. He reinforces negative stereotypes about gay men, but at the same time he presents a narrative in which gay characters are, by the standards of popular fiction in the 1960s, unusually visible and consequential.

After *Good Times/Bad Times* became a bestseller, American authors of school fiction let go of their previous reluctance to write about homosexuality. Louis Auchincloss, in particular, seems to have welcomed the chance to examine his characters' sex lives in ways that probably would have seemed out of the question earlier in his career. In *Honorable Men* (1986), Charles "Chip" Benedict enrolls at St. Luke's, an exclusive prep school in northern Massachusetts. During his first months there, Chip stays to himself because he wants to conceal what he thinks of as "the pollution ... of [his] mind" (52). The guilt generated by his homoerotic fantasies is especially powerful because his grandfather the Reverend Berwind, known at the school as "Mr. B," has just been promoted to headmaster after serving for many years as chaplain: "[A]t school, in chapel, in the pulpit, swaying to and fro to emphasize his moral points, the rich, melodious voice pouring forth his silver sentences, those gray eyes flashing in awful sternness, he was a saint, an angel, God even. But why did Chip have to be the only boy with God for a grandfather?" (48).

Chip keeps his fascination with "dirty things" in check until a student named Chessy Bogart suggests that they should ease the frustration of boarding-school celibacy by experimenting with gay sex. Chip refuses at first, but then he lets Bogart "slip into his bed" (60), immediately regrets that decision, and tries to convince himself that the encounter "never happened":

> Chessy was astonished at the violence of his friend's reaction. When Chip told him, the morning after the episode ... that they must no longer be friends, he protested vigorously, running after Chip's retreating figure and grabbing him by the arm.
> "Look, don't be an ass. It didn't mean anything. It's just till we get home and can see girls" ...
> Chip looked at him in horror. "I don't want to talk about it. I'm going to treat it as if it never happened. Maybe it didn't. Maybe it really didn't!"
> "You mean we just dreamed it?"
> "Yes!"
> "You must be crazy!"
> "It would kill my parents. If you ever breathe a word of it, I'll swear you're a liar!" [61].

4. Sexuality, Gothic Melodrama, and Boarding-School Fiction

Later, after Bogart is caught in bed with another schoolmate, he tells Mr. B that if homosexual experimentation is an expulsion offense it will be necessary to expel half of the students at St. Luke's, including his grandson. When Chip follows through on his threat to call Bogart a liar, he feels as if his one-night stand has been "cleared by the very gods" and that he has, for the first time, secured his grandfather's respect: "There was a distinct change thereafter in the way Mr. B treated him. He never called him 'Benedict' now, even in class, but always 'Charles.' It was as if Chip had passed through his period of probation, triumphantly, and could be recognized before the world as the staff on which the aging headmaster would confidently lean. Teachers and boys seemed to sense this, and as Chip, gaining confidence, and even a kind of happiness, took in the new friendliness of the campus, he became popular" (65). In several ways, the story of Chip Benedict's first year at St. Luke's echoes "The Zenner Trophy." Like Vidal's Principal, Mr. B has convinced himself that the young men at his school would never indulge in things he believes "no decent boy would do" (64). When that assumption turns out to be incorrect, he immediately banishes the offenders. Bogart is expelled for telling the truth, and Chip is rewarded for lying.

The story's conclusion poses a tacit question: was Mr. B shaken by the scandal because the students he expelled had sinned, or was he primarily concerned about the scandal's potential impact on his own reputation? After all, if he conceded that Bogart's claims were true, he would also have to concede that many of the students at St. Luke's have ignored the moral precepts in his lectures and sermons. Chip eases that concern by telling Mr. B what he wants to hear, and his lies transform him from a confused, guilt-ridden schoolboy to the young hero who had "saved the peace of mind of his parents" (65). A year later, on the day that Mr. B dies of a stroke, Chip almost discloses his role in the scandal at St. Luke's, but once again he is praised for concealing the truth:

> Afterwards, Chip's mother followed him into the next room, where she found him sobbing brokenly.
> "But, my darling boy, you must try to remember that you made him happy!" she cried, almost in surprise at such violent emotion. "Happy as nobody else ever made him. Even my own mother!"

"And yet I did something for which he would have expelled me, had he known."

Neither Matilda nor her husband was ever able to extract from their son another syllable as to what this act had been. They concluded that it must have been a prank that his natural grief for the old man had blown out of all proportion [67].

Auchincloss returned to the subject of boarding-school homo-eroticism in *The Education of Oscar Fairfax* (1995). Unlike Frank Prescott, Alcott Ames—the rector of St. Augustine's School—closely resembles Dr. Endicott Peabody. Consider these two descriptions of the real-life headmaster and his fictional counterpart. They contain so many overlapping words and images that Auchincloss seems to have used the first passage as a model for the second:

> Endicott Peabody had (he was then in his seventies) "command presence" as I have never seen it since, not even in four years of overseas duty in World War II. He was a very large man, with big hands and muscles, a square countenance, a mostly bald head, and a Roman nose dominated by gray eyes which were capable of the sternest, glassiest stare I have ever beheld.... When he laughed, his eyes became almost tender, and one could feel a great pull of affection toward him, but when he reprimanded, he was simply terrifying, like God in a Blake watercolor [*A Writer's Capital* 37].

> Doctor Alcott Ames ... was a large, strong man, with big arms and shoulders, a heavy, square balding head, glassy eyes and a prominent nose and chin. But his formidability was greatly lessened by the warmth of his tone and the cheer of his manner. He could be an impressive disciplinarian, and the whole school jumped at his command, but not even the smallest, timidest boy could quite escape the conviction—or at the very least the uneasy suspicion—that Alcott Ames was going to save his soul if Alcott Ames should expire in the process. In his booming sermons, when he spread out his arms and cried: "Christ is calling to you, boys! Christ is calling to you, if you'll only listen!" he gave evidence of a faith so invincible that it seemed almost to create for the unbeliever the very deity it invoked [*The Education of Oscar Fairfax* 25].

Philemon Sayre, Dr. Ames's oldest friend and the senior master at St. Augustine's, donated the money required to open the school and has "ever since been a cornucopia of beneficences, supplementing the slender salaries of the masters and the scholarships of the poorer boys" (26). (Sayre is modeled on William Amory Gardner, one of the richest

4. Sexuality, Gothic Melodrama, and Boarding-School Fiction

and most talented masters ever to teach at Groton. As Geoffrey Ward explains, "[Gardner's] fortune built both the small Tudor-style chapel in which [Franklin D. Roosevelt] first worshipped [at the school] and the majestic Gothic edifice that replaced it and was dedicated during his last year. But the rector's fondness for him went far deeper than that. Gardner was in fact a superb teacher, able to convey a richer sense of the world outside the school than any of the other masters" [188].) Sayre's wealth and Ames's "command presence" produced an outstanding school, but their friendship is tested when Sayre writes a book about what he calls "the pastoral years," the decade before St. Augustine's expanded from a school "designed for only two dozen masters and boys" to a "colony of four hundred young males subject to assemblies and roll calls and marches and highly competitive sports" (23). Auchincloss based the "pastoral" version of the school on the leading American preparatory schools of the early to mid-nineteenth century. As David V. Hicks explains, "[t]he time was ripe for a new model of education, and such men as Joseph Green Cogswell with his experiment at the Round Hill School had already begun to reinvent the American school in the image of the family living in a state of nature— or more precisely in a prepared environment, like the garden where nature is carefully arranged and tended. The European educational theory and practice of Johann Heinrich Pestalozzi ... influenced Cogswell, but his romantic theory of education came straight from Rousseau..." (525).[4]

The trouble at St. Augustine's begins when Sayre, a closeted gay man, asks two students, Oscar Fairfax and Grafton Pope, to help him get his manuscript ready to be published. The first time the students arrive at Sayre's house, they find him relaxing in the nude: "It was a day of freezing cold, and in his study we came upon the venerable scholar warming his backside before a bright fire in the grate. It was very literally what he was doing. His round pink body was exposed to us in its entirety, for he was wearing nothing but a Tyrolean cap with a scarlet feather and ankle-high black polished boots. One hand held a cigarette, the other the volume that he was intently perusing" (34). Fairfax apologizes for the intrusion and turns to leave, but Sayre calmly puts on a robe and invites the students into his study. Pope "passed the episode off as easily as if our host had been guilty of an unstraightened collar" (35), but it makes Fairfax uncomfortable, especially when the senior master rhapsodizes that Alcott Ames once had the body of "a god" and when he shows the young men a photograph, taken during "the pastoral years," of students and instructors from St. Augustine's skinny-dipping in a nearby lake:

> He turned the page and then turned it suddenly back with a rather foxy smile. "Ah, ah, this is not one to show the ladies." And having established our privilege, he turned the page a second time. "It's the way you caught me when you came in. A shot of our old swimming hole. The masters and the boys used to bathe together *in pueris naturalibus.*"
> Grafton and I examined the page with a quicker interest. The white figures of the bathers in and out of the creek were very white against the dark background, but few physical details could be made out. It was evident that no bathing suits were worn.
> "It's like that famous painting by Thomas Eakins; do you know it?" Mr. Sayre asked. "No false modesty. The innocence and beauty of an Eden, free of Eves and apodal tempters. Man in his youth and strength and fullness of purpose. So Greek. So light and sky clear [36].

While walking back to the school, Pope says that Sayre is "an old queen" and warns Fairfax that the master may have designs on him: "Do you suppose the old boy really believes the saggy protruding tummy and bony shanks he exposed to us were embodiments of the Hellenic spirit? Holy cow. I couldn't cover them up fast enough! But seriously, Oscar, I wouldn't go there alone again if I were you. You might find yourself caught in an embarrassing little game of snatch-and-catch" (37). Worried about the "jeers to which poor, innocent Mr. Sayre would be exposed" (38), Fairfax shows part of the manuscript to Mr. Carnes, an English teacher. Carnes agrees that the excerpt contains "a bit too much about masculine beauty" (39) and offers to pass it along to Dr. Ames. "Don't worry," he tells Fairfax. "Your name will not be mentioned. The headmaster, who, for all his deep faith, is highly conscious of the world, will know just what to do" (40).

Ames reads the excerpt, asks to see the rest of Sayre's manuscript, and then censors it ruthlessly. The confrontation between the old friends takes place offstage, but Auchincloss makes it clear that Ames gave Sayre a reprimand he will never forget. The next time Fairfax goes to Sayre's house, the senior master seems stunned and despondent:

4. Sexuality, Gothic Melodrama, and Boarding-School Fiction

He mumbled about things in a way I could not quite understand. He fidgeted with gadgets on his desk and kept looking away from me. I was, it gradually emerged, being dismissed as his assistant.... I shall never know whether he suspected me of having tipped off the headmaster or whether he simply associated me with what may have been the most painful incident in his life and wanted to see me no more. The headmaster ... must have been sufficiently blunt, for the printed version of "Saint Augustine's—The Pastoral Years" contained no descriptions of handsome young masters or lovely youths in communal swimming holes. Or anywhere else [41].

Moments later, when Sayre bursts into tears, there is no doubt that he has lost more than a few pages of his manuscript. This "painful incident" has destroyed Sayre's illusion that he and Dr. Ames are equals. Sayre was a powerful figure at the school when he kept his sexual orientation to himself, but that changed the moment he took a step out of the closet. Ames made him aware of something he should have already known: his friend has become his supervisor. Even though Sayre's financial contributions launched the school and even though he is an outstanding teacher and scholar, he stands well below Ames in the school's hierarchy. In the 1930s, headmasters at prep schools were straight. Gay instructors were tolerated, on the condition that they concealed their sexual orientation.

In Norman Mailer's *Harlot's Ghost* (1991), a CIA agent named Harry Hubbard (a.k.a. Harlot) describes St. Matthew's, the boarding school he attended, as a site dominated by same-sex desire. Hubbard stayed clear of the "goings-on all up and down the dorm," but then, during a school trip, he was molested by an assistant chaplain:

> When it was over, and I had been given an adolescent's peek into the firmament, he swallowed all the nourishment offered the parching of his mouth and began to sob in shame. Deep sobs. He was not a weak man physically ... [so] his sobs were strong.... I knew he was worried about his wife and children. "Don't worry," I said. "I'll never tell." He hugged me. Gently, I disengaged myself. I did it gently out of no noble funds of generosity, rather in the fear he would turn angry and grow rough [139].

Before Hubbard moves on to Yale, he is introduced to Hugh Montague, a former teacher at St. Matthew's who has become a senior official at the CIA. Montague had been attracted to boys as a young man, Hubbard explains, but he remained celibate, even though his lust was "the ongoing daily torment of his years at Harvard, then later [when he taught at] St. Matthew's.... Indeed, he had not entered the ministry for fear that he would ... dive deep into his impulses and betray his church" (144). The St. Matthew's section of the novel, then, concentrates almost exclusively on homosexuality. Mailer ignores virtually every other aspect of prep-school life. Indeed, he loads most of Hubbard's memories of St. Matthew's that do not pertain to same-sex desire into one long sentence: "Our soccer teams (it was the first prep school I knew to take soccer seriously), our football scrimmages at every class level, our Greek, Latin, daily chapel, and prayers before meals, our ice-cold showers from October to May (lukewarm in June and September), our button-down shirts and school ties for all occasions but sports (starched, white collar and shirt on Sundays) had now become an agreeable order of the day" (140). Thus, when it comes to depictions of same-sex desire, American boarding-school literature traveled a long distance between the 1950s and the 1990s. Salinger includes a few brief references to homosexuality; Mailer gives the reader little information about the school his narrator attended that is *not* related to the subject. This difference is mainly attributable to the rise of the gay rights movement and other social transformations of the sixties and seventies, but within the genre of school fiction, it started with James Kirkwood and *Good Times/Bad Times*.

Great Headmasters and Gothic Nightmares

In the first half of the twentieth century, the headmasters of a dozen Northeastern preparatory schools were among the most famous educators in the United States. Some might say that the reputations of Lawrenceville School's Mather Abbot, Deerfield Academy's Frank Boyden, St. Paul's School's Samuel Drury, Groton School's Endicott Peabody, Phillips Exeter Academy's Lewis Perry, Kent School's Frederick Sill, Phillips Academy Andover's Alfred Stearns, Choate School's George St. John, and the other "great headmasters" were overinflated. After all, their success derived largely from the financial contributions of some of the nation's richest families and from the prestige conferred

4. Sexuality, Gothic Melodrama, and Boarding-School Fiction

on their schools by exclusive universities, which admitted nearly all of their graduates.[5] Moreover, the prominence of the "great headmasters" allowed them to take disproportionate credit for the excellence of their schools. Today, it goes without saying that the management of a private academy requires a team of trustees, administrators, faculty, coaches, and staff. But that fact, as Louis Auchincloss illustrates in *The Rector of Justin*, has not always seemed so obvious. Over five decades, Frank Prescott, a composite portrait of the "great headmasters,"[6] came to be seen as more than a school administrator. He presided over Justin Martyr so long and so well that it was known as *his* school.

How did this apotheosis of a small group of educators take hold? It's hard to generalize about the "great headmasters," but most of them appear to have had two key traits in common. First, they operated in such a hands-on way that they ingrained their own values and personalities on their schools. Take, for example, this passage from *The Headmaster* (1966), John McPhee's chronicle of Frank Boyden's career at Deerfield Academy:

> [I]n his valley in western Massachusetts, Frank Boyden, who is eighty-six, continues his work with no apparent letup, sharing his authority by the thimbleful with his faculty, travelling with his athletic teams, interviewing boys and parents who are interested in the school, conducting Sunday-night vesper services, writing as many as seventy letters a day, planning the details of new buildings, meeting with boys who are going home for the weekend and reminding them of their responsibilities to "the older travelling public," careering around his campus in an electric golf cart, and working from 7 A.M. to midnight every day. If he sees a bit of paper on the ground, he jumps out of his cart and picks it up [8].

Given this sort of micromanagement, practiced over a 66-year career, it should not come as a surprise that many observers found it hard to distinguish between Boyden and his school. In *A Writer's Capital* (1974), Auchincloss recalls that Endicott Peabody's managerial style was equally painstaking:

> Groton School was everything to him. He had founded it, built it, nurtured it. He was present in every brick, in the soapstone basins of the lavatories, in the gleaming white columns of the porches, in the square, stout, uncompromising tower of the chapel.... Nothing that went on on the campus—in the kitchens, in the cellars, in the infirmary, as well as in the classrooms and on the playing fields—was beneath the rector's

notice.... He did everything himself, and his staff, from the senior master to the humblest kitchen maid, merely helped him in his great task [38].

Peabody seems to have had an especially powerful and lasting influence on his school's alumni. Auchincloss remained fascinated by him long after the author left Groton,[7] and as Ward observes, there was nobody Franklin D. Roosevelt respected more than the rector: "[I]t was Endicott Peabody himself whom Franklin professed to revere. 'As long as I live,' he wrote from the White House in 1934, 'the influence of Dr. and Mrs. Peabody means and will mean more to me than that of any other people next to my father and mother.' In paying such public obeisance to the rector, he was in part simply being a true son of Groton; he felt about Endicott Peabody pretty much the way most of the rector's boys had come to feel by the time they left his care" (189). Similarly, Carol Gelderman describes Peabody as the most dominant figure in Groton's history, a natural leader whose judgment and authority were hardly ever questioned:

> Groton and Endicott Peabody seemed synonymous to most people; he made the school in his image by virtue of his dominant nature and purposefulness. Even Theodore Roosevelt called him the most powerful personality he had ever encountered.... None of the other headmasters, and this was the era of great headmasters ... ever attained the fame of Endicott Peabody of Groton. He utterly dominated the school, the many strong men who served on his faculty, his board of trustees, and, of course, the students.... Like a benevolent dictator, the rector managed every detail of his school his way for more than half a century, even to decreeing its colors—red, black, and white—the same that had flown from his ancestors' ships in Salem harbor [34].

In *A World of Our Own: Notes on Life and Learning in a Boys' Preparatory School* (1970), Peter Prescott draws similar conclusions about George St. John, the headmaster of Choate School from 1908 to 1947:

> Part of [St. John's] genius lay in the building of buildings and the buying of land; more of it lay in the way he immersed himself in the life of the school, down to the most trivial detail. "I do not want to ask you for any rent," he wrote to one of his teachers, "but in a way you will be paying rent by keeping large areas clean and dusted" ... "The safety match," he advised the school's housekeeper, "which I recommend as infinitely better than the Vulcan Safety Match which we have been using, is called the Gold-Medal Safety Match" [53–54].

4. Sexuality, Gothic Melodrama, and Boarding-School Fiction

Lewis Perry, the Principal of Phillips Exeter Academy from 1914 to 1946, also made certain that he was directly involved in every aspect of campus life. As William G. Saltonstall explains, Perry worked closely with Exeter's faculty and trustees, but he also comforted homesick students, took part in the school's admissions process, and smoothed over seemingly trivial disagreements between students and teachers. When a Latin master told a student named James F. Oates, Jr., that he could not perform in a school play because his grades were too low, for instance, the Principal intervened, urged Oates to excel in his classes and onstage, and overruled the master's decision:

> "I made an engagement to see Dr. Perry at his home in the later afternoon," [Oates recalled]. Dr. Perry sat down in front of the fire and said, "What can I do for you, Jim?" I told him that Dr. Clark said I couldn't be in the play. After a little talk Dr. Perry said that when he went to college, whenever there was a play, he was in it, and he always did his best work in the month the play was produced. "And since I think that you are just like me, you can be in the play." ... This was a turning point in my life. I was given a chance, and I made good use of it. Pop Clark played his part and gave me the highest mark that I had had in the entire year in the month the play was produced [42].

The second trait shared by the "great headmasters" is that they encouraged some of the most privileged young men in the country to dedicate themselves to public service and, for the most part, they practiced what they preached. Peabody, Boyden, et al. had many opportunities to cash in on their ties to Wall Street and Washington, but most of them continued to serve as headmasters for decades, educating the sons and grandsons of their earliest students. Boarding schools are often associated with patrician self-importance but, as James McLachlan points out, most of the "great headmasters" came from middle-class homes and spent their careers teaching values prized by the middle class—diligence, polished manners, sportsmanship—to the sons of plutocrats: "[M]ost boarding-school headmasters were not rich Americans, but middle-income intellectuals, moralists, or clergymen, who would have blanched at the sight of an 'upper-class value,' and who were the heirs of educational traditions that transcended particular social classes. For most of their history, [Northeastern prep schools] have consciously educated their students to avoid, abjure, and despise most of what are traditionally thought to be aristocratic or upper-class values and styles of life" (13). Although these headmasters' attempts to snuff out the values of the very rich often failed, their determination to turn young Brahmins away from elitism and self-indulgence has played a crucial role in shaping their reputations.[8]

In *Good Times/Bad Times*, Kirkwood imagines a boarding-school administrator who has virtually nothing in common with the "great headmasters." In fact, it seems to me that the crux of the novel is a hypothetical question: how will school literature change if it concentrates on a headmaster who is deeply neurotic? During the first assembly Peter Kilburn attends at Gilford Academy, he notices that Mr. Hoyt has a number of curious physical characteristics:

> Just then Franklyn Hoyt strode out onto the stage from the wings and I had my first look at the headmaster. A tall, lean man, he had a walk that struck me right off as being unique. He tilted forward, springing ahead with each step off the balls of his feet. Although I later learned he was fifty-one, the walk was extremely youthful, belonging more to a lanky adolescent, except for the urgency in it. He radiated energy, hardly ever walking as if he were just walking, always as if he were going from one specific spot to another and without a lot of time to waste.... That morning, as he was walking, I also particularly noticed his hands. They were huge and seemed to swing independently of his body, even of his arms, like they'd been sewed on at the wrists [43].

Peter also recalls that there was something unsettling about the headmaster's smile. "It came too quickly," he writes, "seemed to strain his entire face, and left just as quickly. Oddly enough, when he smiled at me that first time, I felt more uncomfortable than at any other moment during our interview" (50). Stranger still, Hoyt has "a raised portion, like a carbuncle, about the size of a quarter, up over to the side of his forehead, close to the hairline. It had a slightly heightened reddish color, more than the rest of his face" (44). The more time Peter spends at Gilford, the more he learns to keep an eye on that "raised portion." Its color drains away, leaving a pale spot, every time the headmaster loses his temper.

Early in his narrative, Peter explains that Hoyt's first priority is to remove the stigma created by the death of the senator's son. To persuade "good solid New England families" (62) to reconsider Gilford,

4. Sexuality, Gothic Melodrama, and Boarding-School Fiction

Hoyt decides that the school must improve its standing in a competition known as the Point System:

> This was the second year of a seven-school league in the area for sports and other activities, such as debating and Glee Club. Each time two schools played a match, the winner scored ten points.... At the end of the year all the points were toted up and the number of points each school had determined its standing in the league. In the first year Gilford had not done too well; it came in sixth place—in other words, next to last.
>
> Mr. Hoyt was determined that the school would better its position this year. If he could work Gilford up to fifth or fourth or especially third place, the Board of Trustees would be impressed. This would be a sign that the school was gaining ground, not sinking farther into oblivion. To this end, Mr. Hoyt was a master organizer, verging on the fanatic. Hardly a morning assembly went by that he didn't speak of the competition, didn't urge every student to go out for any sport or activity in which he could help the school better its record [73].

As Peter's narrative continues, it becomes increasingly obvious that Hoyt's appearance and his eagerness to repair Gilford's image are relatively insignificant. The real trouble is the headmaster's infatuation with Peter. Kirkwood begins the story of Hoyt's destructive passion with a few understated clues. During the school assembly at which Peter sees Hoyt for the first time, the headmaster reciprocates by gazing at him: "When his eyes came to me, they stopped.... I felt that Mr. Hoyt was staring at me. I glanced over and he was, but looked away, diverting his attention to [a teacher] when our eyes met. I didn't look at him again during the assembly, because I could feel that he was, from time to time, looking at me" (43, 44). A few days later, Hoyt catches Peter imitating his ungainly way of walking and, instead of giving him the mild reprimand the situation calls for, he becomes unglued, snarling that Peter is "trash" and "a little Hollywood snip" (60). Then he warns that Peter will not be permitted to "contaminate" the "clean, decent boys" at the school:

> "Now," he said, going on in a perfectly matter-of-fact tone, as if he were going over my curriculum, "I suggest, if you have a dirty little bag of tricks up your sleeve, you just forget about them. The boys here may not be sons of great men, they may not come from the wealthiest families, but they're clean, decent boys. Most of them come from good solid

New England families and I don't want them contaminated." He looked at me. "You understand what I'm talking about?" I shook my head to the negative. "Oh," he said, picking up a pencil and fingering it, "I imagine you do. Any nasty little adolescent practices you might have picked up along the way in Hollywood."

I was so dumbfounded by this last statement that I stopped listening to him. He wasn't ranting any more, just talking on in a perfectly normal voice about the school and standards and studies (I believe) while I was wondering how anybody could condemn a person's entire character without knowing them [61–62].

Dirty bag of tricks? Nasty adolescent practices? The only offense Peter has committed is an attempt to mimic the headmaster's curious, forward-tilting stride. Hoyt clearly has more than campus discipline on his mind. The object of his desire has hurt his feelings, so he lashes out, trying to inflict a commensurate injury. Hoyt's anger recedes quickly, however. Soon after the episode in the headmaster's office, Peter notices that Hoyt has begun to stare at him again, in chapel and while Peter practices with the tennis team: "When I threw the ball up for my service ... I noticed a form standing behind the slightly opened Venetian blinds in a schoolroom on the third floor.... He remained there all during that game and one more, until we traded sides" (68). (Kirkwood's decision to make Peter a tennis player is more significant than it may appear. In the mid-twentieth century, tennis was widely regarded as the least "manly" varsity sport at American boys' schools. Tom Lee, the main character in *Tea and Sympathy*, is suspected of being gay in part because he plays tennis instead of a rugged team sport like football or crew. And in *A World of Our Own* [1970], Peter Prescott recalls that the Choate School's athletic director "[shook] his head, much as his predecessor ... used to shake his, when he heard that a boy wanted to go out for fall *tennis*. 'Only fairies go out for fall tennis,' he would tell the new boys, most of whom thought fairies lived in the kind of books they hadn't read for years. 'Are *you* a fairy?'" [41].[9])

When Peter emerges as the top-ranked player on Gilford's tennis team, helping the school move higher in the Point System standings, Hoyt's infatuation becomes practically unconcealed. He coaxes Peter to join Gilford's glee club and perform one of Hamlet's soliloquies, offers to meet with him for daily rehearsals, orders a costume (black

4. Sexuality, Gothic Melodrama, and Boarding-School Fiction

tights, a dance belt, ballet slippers, and a jumper with puffy sleeves), and asks Peter to model it for him:

> "Try on the tights now and we'll see if they're a good fit." Unfortunately, after a bit of tugging and straightening around which I knew he would do if I didn't, they seemed to fit.... "Mmn, mmn," he muttered, "they look fine. Turn around and hold your shirt up.... Are those jockey shorts you're wearing?"
> "Yes."
> "Yes, they show through your tights. We'll have to—perhaps Mrs. Hoyt can dye a pair of your shorts black." He kept staring at me. "Step over closer here." He motioned to me and I stepped up nearer to him until he was looking right up at me. "Or perhaps you should wear an athletic—"
> "Mr. Hoyt, do I have to wear black tights?"
> "Why?"
> "Well, I don't know..."
> "Why Peter," he said, almost amused. "You're not embarrassed? You have good legs, nothing to be embarrassed about" [111–12].

Jordan Legier warns that the headmaster's infatuation may be dangerous long before Hoyt comments on Peter's underwear and the shape of his legs. Peter, on the other hand, clings to the notion that Hoyt is probably just a harmless eccentric. Kirkwood does not make the reasons for Peter's lack of concern entirely clear, but he suggests that his otherwise perceptive narrator misjudges Hoyt for two reasons. First, unlike Jordan, the scion of a wealthy Southern family, Peter is a scholarship boy. One of his father's friends arranged for him to spend his senior year at Gilford and paid for his tuition, room, and board. Hence, although Peter knows that the school does not measure up to the exclusive academies he has read about in prep-school literature, he finds it hard to criticize Gilford and Hoyt. Second, Peter underestimates Hoyt's volatility because he is the son of an alcoholic. For several years, Peter has pitied his father, an actor whose drinking problem derailed a successful career, so it may be that Peter takes Hoyt's actions in stride because that has become his standard response to adult misbehavior. As the addiction specialist Janet G. Woititz explains, children of alcoholics are often "manipulated into making excuses for and covering up for [their parents] ... and, as a result, they unknowingly become part of the disease pattern" (1).

At any rate, Hoyt's violent mood swings cause a series of alarming incidents. Sensing that something is terribly wrong with her husband, Miriam Hoyt suffers a nervous breakdown. After one of Peter's performances as Hamlet, the headmaster is unable to keep his hands off of his protégé: "He took another step to me and put the palm of his hand on my cheek and jaw, almost cupped my face in his one hand it was so large. He looked at me for a long time. Then he said, 'Jesus, you're some boy. Some boy!'" (196). Hoyt is overwhelmed by jealousy when he sees Peter and Jordan dining together at a local restaurant. After Peter sprains his back while skiing, Hoyt stops by his room at night to check on him and then, when a doctor mentions that Peter might heal more quickly if he is given alcohol rubdowns, insists on serving as the young man's masseur. "I don't have any kind of a complex about people touching me," Peter explains, "but the idea that he, Franklyn Hoyt, was going to be applying his hands to my back was something I never would have thought of in my wildest imagination. As I got into position and heard him drag over the desk chair and settle himself in it, I realized I was tensing up as much as if I were expecting a snake to be dropped on me" (219). Once again, Peter tries to convince himself that Hoyt is basically harmless, but the headmaster's second nocturnal visit cannot be explained away. Hoyt returns to Peter's room, warns him that Jordan is a "decadent weakling ... without regard for any of the moral principles that govern decent conduct" (225), and then gives Peter a massage that stops just short of a sexual assault:

> About that time I heard him moving on the chair and then another cold splash of alcohol hit the small of my back. It got the top part of my pajama bottoms wet and I felt his hands touch them, then tug them loose and peel them down a ways from my waist. I started to get panicky as he spread the alcohol around the top part of my backside.... He stopped, picked up the bottle and dumped about a full pint in the small of my back so that it splashed right over my behind and trickled down in the crack, running down between my legs and wetting more of my pajama bottoms. He felt around with his hand, sort of grunted, as if to say, Um-hmn, they're wet all right, and then started tugging them down further.... He curled those huge fingers down under the waistband of my pajamas and, in spite of my efforts, managed to tug them all the way down off my backside, so they were finally resting halfway along my legs down by my knees [228].

4. Sexuality, Gothic Melodrama, and Boarding-School Fiction

Even after this incident, Peter does not report Hoyt to the police. He and Jordan agree that "the probability of another incident was slim, that what had happened was a freakish slip" (236). This miscalculation soon results in the deaths of Jordan and Hoyt. When the headmaster barges into Jordan's room the next day and finds Jordan and Peter lying in bed together (in a non-sexual way), he accuses them of "degeneracy" and suddenly shifts from unrequited lover to demonic avenger: "The look on his face will always be with me. First surprise, turning quickly to shock, then the coldest, most angry, knowing look I've ever seen. He just stood there staring at us, aiming a laser beam that could have sliced steel. After a while he began nodding his head up and down like a judge who'd just decided on the verdict—guilty—and also the penalty—death" (239). Jordan tells Hoyt that the "dirty little games" he has been envisioning are "all in [his] mind," and the headmaster becomes so enraged that Peter imagines he is about to "explode right there and splatter all over the walls" (240). A few days later, Hoyt finds Peter and Jordan in bed together again, strikes Peter in the face, yanks Jordan (whose chronic heart disease has been flaring up) out of his room, and hauls the ailing student across the campus to his residence:

> I heard the front door slam and was able to see them after they'd gotten off the porch and away from the building. Mr. Hoyt had a hand under Jordan's armpit. He was holding him up high on that side so that Jordan was walking all lopsided. He was also so much shorter than Mr. Hoyt he was dangling as if Mr. Hoyt had hold of a puppet. At one point, Jordan stumbled and his knees buckled and I let out a little sound. But Mr. Hoyt had a firm grasp and jerked him upright, still sort of dragging him along without even stopping to see how he was [274].

In chapel the next morning, Hoyt announces that two students were caught in bed together and says that an angry God has "struck [one of them] down by inflicting him with chronic ill-health" (279).

In the closing chapters of *Good Times/Bad Times*, the floodgates open and Hoyt commits one deranged act after another. As soon as Jordan's heart trouble seems to have stabilized, Hoyt punches him in the face. The next day, hours after Jordan's fatal heart attack, the headmaster tells Peter that his friend was lucky to have died young because otherwise he would have been "doomed to a misspent life" (310). Hoyt pressures Peter, at the height of his grief, to confess that he and Jordan had been lovers. He slaps Peter so hard that he knocks him to the floor. Peter flees to a bus station, but Hoyt tracks him down and forces him to return to Gilford. When Peter tries to escape again during a late-night snowstorm, the headmaster chases him across the campus, knocks him to the ground, and, once again, threatens him with sexual assault: "'Is this—this—what he did—hmn?—like this?' I screamed no, meaning no and for him not to do it, and kept fighting to move my head. 'No? No? ... What was it like? ... Wasn't it like this—hmn, hmn?' And for a brief second I felt his thin lips, cold and rubbery and tough, press down on my mouth. An awful moment—shuddering—like lizards and snakes crawling all over me" (329). Peter breaks free and hides in a boathouse, but Hoyt finds him, shouts obscenities about Jordan, and assaults him again. Wild with terror and grief, Peter kills the headmaster in self-defense, striking him on the head with an iron boathook.

For many readers, the first reaction to these incidents is likely to be a grim kind of amusement. This is melodrama: the showdown between predator and victim is over the top, devoid of the subtlety and playful humor that inform the first nine tenths of *Good Times/Bad Times*. On second thought, however, it is difficult not to marvel at Kirkwood's boldness and creativity. By staging Hoyt's emotional and psychological collapse, he changes the reader's assumptions about boarding-school headmasters. Headmasters are expected to personify order and propriety, dignity and tradition. Previous fictional headmasters had seemed ruthless or pretentious at times, but no author of American school literature had dared to present a headmaster who is criminally insane. A lust-crazed headmaster who preys upon a student—what could be more at odds with the conventions of boarding-school fiction? Hoyt becomes so unhinged that he causes the genre of *Good Times/Bad Times* to change from school fiction to horror. Suddenly, Kirkwood's novel displays familiar elements of Gothic literature: the setting filled with secrets and scandals; the unstoppable villain; the bewildered, persecuted victim; lurid images of confinement, madness, pursuit, vengeance, and doom.[10] Like Kirkwood's renderings of homoeroticism, his use of Gothic images reveals that boarding-school literature before *Good Times/Bad Times* had been quite predictable and that most authors of school novels had been playing it safe. Instead of putting his own stamp on narrative techniques used in earlier works,

4. Sexuality, Gothic Melodrama, and Boarding-School Fiction

Kirkwood demonstrates that school fiction has a great deal of undeveloped potential. This is not to say that *Good Times/Bad Times* is a literary tour de force. Kirkwood lacks Salinger's knack for true-to-life dialogue, Knowles's ability to write prose that shifts smoothly between urbanity and distress, and Auchincloss's aptitude for dramatizing the mores of Northeastern WASPs. In spite of its limitations, however, *Good Times/Bad Times* has played an important role in the development of American boarding-school literature. It is without question the most daring, iconoclastic novel the genre has produced.

5

"That was what made the school so useless": Anti-Prep Broadsides and A Good School

> *Robert Driscoll often assured himself that Dorset Academy was a good school; even so, there was a nagging qualification: if only it were more like a real school.*—Richard Yates, *A Good School*

This chapter examines several works in which the struggles of individual characters are linked to general indictments of boarding-school culture. The first part of the chapter discusses John Cheever's "Expelled" (1930), a short story that ridicules "the college-preparatory system," and four films—*Dead Poets Society* (1989), *School Ties* (1992), *Scent of a Woman* (1992), and *Outside Providence* (1999)—which also depict private academies in unflattering ways. The second part argues that Richard Yates's *A Good School* (1978) initially seems to present another anti-prep broadside. Dorset Academy has the veneer of an exclusive institution, but it turns out to be a weak imitation of Groton, Choate, and other famous New England schools. As one of Yates's characters points out, there was "something fanciful and even specious in the very beauty of the place—a prep school that might have been conceived in the studios of Walt Disney" (5). Dorset has "a wide reputation for accepting boys who, for any number of reasons, no other school would touch" (6). The faculty seems demoralized, and rumor has it that the school is bankrupt and likely to be shuttered. Later in the novel, Yates changes course, focusing the reader's attention on Dorset's

5. "That was what made the school so useless"

strengths instead of its failings.[1] Critics often describe Yates as a "merciless" writer, the kind of storyteller who creates naïve characters and then systematically demolishes their illusions. *A Good School* reveals a nostalgic side of Yates's imagination and stresses something that American school literature tends to overlook—the term "boarding school" does not necessarily signify exclusivity and prestige. The novel is built on a paradox: Dorset is a below-average school, but Yates's narrator William Grove thinks of his education there as an invaluable stroke of luck.

"It was meant to be an attack"

John Cheever withdrew from Thayer Academy, a boarding school in Braintree, Massachusetts, in 1928.[2] He returned the following year, but once again he dropped out. As an adult, Cheever claimed that he was kicked out of the school for smoking. Witness this exchange with John Hersey in *The New York Times Book Review*:

> "Your formal, or institutional, education was broken off when you were bounced from Thayer Academy at the age of 17. I wonder if you'd like to begin by telling us about that experience?"
> "I was delighted to be expelled from Thayer. It was not unreasonable on their part…"
> "What was the immediate cause of your expulsion?"
> "Smoking, an expulsion offense."
> "Who caught you? Were you caught with the crime blazing?"
> "I was caught by a teacher."
> "Was it exciting?"
> "It was intentional, John" [3].

Cheever repeated this personal myth so many times that he seems to have convinced himself that a cigarette break doomed his prep-school education. When Harvard University announced in 1978 that it was going to give him an honorary degree, for example, he wrote in his journal that "[t]o have been expelled from Thayer Academy for smoking and then to have been given [this honor] … seems to me a crowning example of the inestimable opportunities of the world in which I live and in which I pray generations will continue to live" (qtd. in Bailey, *Cheever: A Life*, 581). The truth about Cheever's departure from Thayer is that he dropped out, for the second time, after a school official urged him to do something about his abysmal grades.³ (In this respect, Cheever was a real-life Holden Caulfield. Like J. D. Salinger's boarding-school misfit, Cheever was warned repeatedly that he was in danger of being expelled, but did nothing to avoid what Holden calls "the ax.")

A few months later, Cheever submitted a short story titled "Expelled" to Malcolm Cowley, then an associate editor at *The New Republic*, who arranged for it to appear in the issue of October 1, 1930. *The New Republic* was one of the most left-leaning magazines in the country at the time and, as the note preceding "Expelled" illustrates, its editors welcomed the opportunity to introduce a young writer who slams a private boys' school and by extension the Northeastern WASP establishment:

> Teachers often write brilliant things about their pupils, but it is very seldom that pupils of preparatory-school age are able to return the compliment. Jon Cheever is an exception. Last spring he was expelled from an academy in Massachusetts at the end of his junior year. In the following sketches, written at the age of seventeen, he reproduces the atmosphere of an institution where education is served out dry in cakes ... ["Expelled," *The New Republic*, 171].

In addition to taking readers back to the beginning of Cheever's career as a writer—a time when he signed his work as "Jon" rather than "John"—this note clearly indicates that Cheever lied to *The New Republic* about his exit from Thayer. As the headmaster pointed out after "Expelled" hit the newsstands, Cheever "was not expelled from the Academy.... He left entirely on his own volition in the late spring season, presumably because of the added attraction of the May orchard blossoms, which he characterized [in the story] in his unique way" (qtd. in Bailey, *Cheever: A Life* 46). Despite many attempts by officials at Thayer to set the record straight, "Expelled" is often mislabeled as a work of nonfiction. In a recent article in *Vanity Fair*, for instance, James Wolcott notes that Cheever was "[f]irst published at the age of 18, with an account in *The New Republic* of being expelled from Thayer Academy" (76). Similarly, Lynne Waldeland writes (mistakenly) that Cheever's secondary-school education ended "when he was expelled from Thayer Academy" (17).

Cheever's deception notwithstanding, several prominent critics

5. "That was what made the school so useless"

have praised the virtues of "Expelled." John Updike observes that the story is "alarmingly mature ... with a touch of the uncanny, as the rare examples of literary precocity—Rimbaud, Chatterton, William Cullen Bryant, Henry Green—tend to be" (114). Blake Bailey calls it "an astonishing debut" (*Cheever: A Life* 47), and Charles McGrath argues that it is "one of the most assured and precocious debuts in all of American fiction—a signal, or it should have been, that the author was worth paying attention to" ("The First Suburbanite" MM36). Patrick Meanor points out that "Expelled" marks the first appearance of Cheever's dominant theme: "[It] became the first example of the single most important thematic pattern in all of Cheever's fiction: the fall. In a certain sense, most of Cheever's short stories and all of his novels are variations on this persistent theme; his work is obsessed with Edenic crises in every conceivable form. Many of the novels are concerned with the fall of a house—that is, a once-prosperous family that has fallen on hard times and whose major project is to regenerate an Edenic condition of innocent happiness; in short, to recreate a permanent paradise" (29). And James E. O'Hara concludes that "Expelled" displays some of the strongest features of Cheever's later fiction: "This first story demonstrates the remarkable gifts that, years later, would reappear in his best work: skillful pacing, sharp characterization and place description, and careful thematic development based on a clear narrative viewpoint" (3). (O'Hara goes on to suggest that the editors at *The New Republic* were probably more intrigued by the political implications of "Expelled" than by Cheever's literary ability: "Together he and Cowley had made a bold statement about the stultifying atmosphere of America's educational establishment. The application of the storyteller's talent made the statement into art of a sort, but not necessarily first-rate art. The distinction would have been of little concern to the *New Republic*; the story cut close enough to the bone of reality to interest its left-leaning readers" [3].)

The narrator of "Expelled," a young man named Charles, realizes he is on thin ice when the headmaster begins to speak to him in a genial way: "The first signs were [his] cordialities.... He was never nice to anybody unless he was a football star, or hadn't paid his tuition or was going to be expelled" (901). A few days later, the headmaster tells Charles that he is no longer welcome at the school:

"Well, Charles," he said, "some of the teachers say you aren't getting very good marks."

"Yes," I said, "that's true." I didn't care about the marks.

"But Charles," he said, "you know the scholastic standard of this school is very high and we have to drop people when their work becomes unsatisfactory." I told him I knew that also. Then he said a lot of things about the traditions, and the elms, and the magnificent military heritage from our West Point founder.

It was very nice outside of his room. He had his window pushed open halfway and one could see the lawns pulling down to the road behind the trees and the bushes. The gravy-colored curtains were too heavy to move about in the wind, but some papers shifted around on his desk. In a little while I got up and walked out. He turned and started to work again [901].[4]

After Charles describes his meeting with the headmaster, he spends the remainder of the story criticizing his former school. The trustees intend to build a bell tower instead of buying new books for the library because "no one would see the books" and visitors "would be able to see the tower five miles off when the leaves were off the trees" (902). Margaret Courtwright, an English teacher who frowns on James Joyce's representations of what she calls "sex reality," is revered at the school because "[h]er interpretation was the one accepted on college-board papers. That helped everyone a great deal. No one had to get a new interpretation" (904). Meanwhile, Laura Driscoll, the only teacher Charles respects, is fired for speaking out in defense of Sacco and Vanzetti. (This would have been particularly controversial at Thayer Academy because the suspected anarchists were sentenced to death for allegedly killing two men at a factory located a few miles from the school.) The headmaster tries to create the impression that Driscoll is leaving voluntarily, but she refuses to cooperate:

"Miss Driscoll," said the headmaster during her last chapel at the school, "has found it necessary to return to the West. In the few months that we have had her with us, she has been a staunch friend of the academy, a woman whom we all admire and love and who, we are sure, loves and admires the academy and its elms as we do. We are all sorry Miss Driscoll is leaving us..."

Then Laura got up, called him a damned liar, swore down the length of the platform and walked out of the building.

No one ever saw Laura Driscoll again. By the way everyone talked,

5. "That was what made the school so useless"

no one wanted to. That was all late in February. By March the school was quiet again. The new history teacher taught dates. Everyone carefully forgot about Laura Driscoll [908].

Driscoll never had a chance at the school, Charles concludes, because she "dragged history into the classroom, squirming and smelling of something bitter" (906). To keep her job, she would have had to imitate her older male colleagues, one of whom was notorious for spouting inane, condescending remarks like these: "You may be interested in the fact that a large percentage of this class was certified last year. I should like to have a larger number this year. Just think, boys: wouldn't it be fine if a very large number—a number larger than last year—was certified? Wouldn't that be fine? Well, there's no reason why we can't do it if we all cooperate and behave and don't ask too many questions" (906).

Later in the story, Charles expands his critique, arguing that his expulsion was practically inevitable, given the superficial values of the "college-preparatory system" and American society at large:

> Of course it was not the fault of the school. The headmaster and faculty were doing what they were supposed to do. It was just a preparatory school trying to please the colleges. A school that was doing everything the colleges asked it to do.
> It was not the fault of the school at all. It was the fault of the system—the non-educational system, the college-preparatory system. That was what made the school so useless.
> As a college-preparatory school it was a fine school. In five years they could make raw material look like college material. They could clothe it and breed it and make it say the right things when the colleges asked it to talk. That was its duty.
> They weren't prepared to educate anybody. They were members of a college-preparatory system. No one around there wanted to be educated. No sir.... Our country is the best country in the world. We are swimming in prosperity and our President is the best president in the world. We have larger apples and better cotton and faster and more beautiful machines. This makes us the greatest country in the world. Unemployment is a myth. Dissatisfaction is a fable. In preparatory school America is beautiful. It is the gem of the ocean and it is too bad. It is bad because people believe it all [909–10].

As this passage illustrates, Cheever's purpose in "Expelled" is to denounce a society and a "college-preparatory system" that have lost their way. Charles's school is crowded with pseudo-educators and students who want to learn just enough to win admission to exclusive universities. His grades, Charles insists, were beside the point. He was expelled because, like Laura Driscoll, he saw through the hypocrisies of the school and the "system." As Meanor observes, "Cheever transforms the expulsion into a 'felix culpa,' a 'happy fall' that saves the young protagonist from the life-denying ambience of educational institutions, which actually damage genuine creativity" (29). When a journalist referred to "Expelled" as a satirical story in a 1977 interview, Cheever took issue with that characterization: "Satire? It was meant to be an attack. You know there was a delegation of students from Thayer at the book fair today and they were saying things hadn't gotten any better, either" (Baum 142).

American school fiction has seldom presented this kind of root-and-branch attack on boarding-school culture.[5] As we have seen, the school narratives of F. Scott Fitzgerald, J. D. Salinger, John Knowles, et al. concentrate on disaffected students and hardly ever pass judgment on the schools they attend. The clearest echoes of Cheever's broadside can be heard in the American boarding-school films of the past twenty-five years. *Dead Poets Society* (1989; directed by Peter Weir, screenplay by Tom Shulman) depicts Welton Academy as an endlessly repressive, elitist institution. The school's opening-day assembly features a series of grandiose ceremonies, including a procession accompanied by bagpipes and the passing of a "Light of Knowledge" from the faculty to the boys in the first form. The headmaster boasts that Welton is the best preparatory school in the country and that seventy-five percent of its graduates "go on to the Ivy League." Several early scenes, moreover, cast the students at Welton as inmates in rep ties and penny loafers. In a stairwell, a school official scowls at a group of boys and says, "Slow down, you horrible phalanx of pubescence." Later on, a teacher snaps "Oh, shut up, will you?" during study hall and a housemaster shouts "Cut out that racket in there!" while making his rounds before lights-out.

John Keating, a Welton graduate who has returned to teach English, initially seems to challenge the school's ultra-conservative ethos. He orders his students to rip a chapter by a scholar named J. Evans Pritchard out of their textbooks, urges them to gain a new point of view by standing on his desk, and promotes originality and risk-taking. Keating's freewheeling personality makes a powerful impression on his students. One tries to become something resembling Norman Mailer's conception of the "White Negro," a grimace-inducing pose that involves an ersatz African nickname ("Nwanda"), a saxophone, and a beret.[6] Another makes a spectacle of his crush on a cheerleader from a local high school. A third disobeys his father by acting in a play and then stuns the school community by committing suicide after his father threatens to strike back by sending him to a military academy.

What most commentators have overlooked is that Keating's ability to shake up a staid boarding-school campus is linked to a number of less rebellious traits. He tells his students to avoid clichés, but some of his classroom rhetoric—"This is a battle and the casualties could be your hearts and souls.... Dare to strike out and find new ground"—is as trite as that of the old guard at the school. As David Orr points out, "in trying to avoid being a technique-obsessed pedant ... the teacher of poetry can easily become a slogan-spouting windbag.... Seen in this light, the text-ripping scene from *Dead Poets Society* doesn't show us a helpful new way of relating to poetry so much as the two standard, unhelpful approaches colliding" (14).[7] When Keating's students revive the Dead Poets Society, a mildly Bohemian club the teacher joined during his own schooldays, he advises them to think twice because "the present administration wouldn't look too favorably on that." When the student who calls himself "Nwanda" argues that it is time for Welton to become coeducational, Keating dismisses his activism as a "lame stunt." And when the school's authorities crack down, firing Keating and expelling "Nwanda," Keating obediently moves on. In their reviews of *Dead Poets Society*, Vincent Canby extolled the teacher's "assaults on the order of academe" (C8) and Desson Howe described the film as a "requiem for free-thinking" (43). These critics overstate Keating's commitment to reform. He experiments with "unorthodox teaching methods," but as soon as his employers object he agrees to stop disturbing the status quo. As Pauline Kael observed in *The New Yorker*, Keating "has no assertiveness ... and in emergencies he advises caution" (70).

School Ties (1992; directed by Robert Mandel, screenplay by Dick Wolf and Darryl Poniscan) also presents a forceful critique of a Northeastern prep school. David Greene, the movie's main character, is a Jewish teenager from a hardscrabble neighborhood in Scranton, Pennsylvania, but there is nothing particularly ethnic or coarse about him. To the contrary, several early scenes mark him as an All-American boy of the 1950s: a talented athlete, a tough kid unafraid to fight the leader of a biker gang, and an R&B fan partial to the Robins and Fats Domino. Having lost three consecutive football games to its rivals at a school called St. Luke's, St. Matthew's Academy of Cabot, Massachusetts recruits David to play quarterback and gives him a full scholarship for his senior year. This opportunity makes him the only Jewish student at an extremely old-fashioned Protestant school; therefore, taking his father's advice, David decides not to mention his religious affiliation to his new schoolmates. The young athlete is dazzled by St. Matthew's at first, but his excitement fades when he hears a string of anti–Semitic slurs.[8] One student brags that his record player was a bargain because he "Jewed down" the price. Another explains that it will be easy to snub the Jewish students at Harvard because "you don't have to room with them" and "they're not in the clubs." And when David sneaks into the chapel to pray on Rosh Hashanah, the headmaster, Dr. Bartram, barges in and says, "You people are very ... *determined*, aren't you? I seem to recall a blessing: 'Blessed are the meek, for they shall inherit the Earth.'" (The football coach at St. Matthew's does not appear to be a bigot, but it is not helpful when he asks David if he has any "diet problems.") In spite of these incidents, David makes friends easily, catches the eye of Sally Wheeler, an attractive student from a nearby girls' school, and excels on the football field. (It is probably not a coincidence that the number on David's jersey is 42, the same number Jackie Robinson wore when he broke the color barrier in Major League Baseball.)

All it takes to derail David's year at boarding school is one hostile, envious WASP. At a country-club dinner party, Charlie Dillon, a rich boy who expected to be St. Matthew's starting quarterback before David arrived, hears a St. Luke's graduate mention that David is Jewish. As soon as Dillon spreads this news (more specifically, he tells his classmates that David is a "lying, back-stabbing kike"), the football hero becomes a pariah.[9] David's roommate chides him for failing to disclose that he is a member of a despised minority:

5. "That was what made the school so useless"

"If it's no big deal, why didn't you just tell me in the first place? I'm your roommate."
"You never told me what religion *you* are."
"I'm Methodist."
"You're Methodist, and all the time I didn't know it."
"That's different."
"Oh, yeah? How's it different?"
"It just is. Jews are different. It's not like the difference between Methodists and Lutherans. I mean ... Jews ... everything about them is different."

Sally Wheeler calls David a liar and refuses to go out with him again. Someone scrawls a blood-red swastika and the words "Go Home Jew" on a sheet and hangs it in David's room. And when a teacher finds Charlie Dillon's crib notes on the floor after an exam, Dillon insists that it was David who cheated.[10] After the truth about Dillon's misconduct comes to light, David decides, in spite of the discrimination he has endured, to stick it out at St. Matthew's. "You used me for football," he tells Dr. Bartram. "I'll use you to get into Harvard." The film's closing shot shows David blending into a crowd of students, but he is no longer interested in fitting in. The students and faculty at St. Matthew's pay lip service to their "cherished honor code," but by the end of *School Ties* David realizes that he has seen more integrity in Scranton's factories and malt shops than he has at "the finest preparatory school in the nation."

Scent of a Woman (1992; directed by Martin Brest, screenplay by Bo Goldman) goes even further, depicting the Baird School as a corrupt institution in which a scholarship boy is shamefully mistreated. Charlie Simms's schoolmates chatter endlessly about the expensive vacations they have scheduled, and then one of them asks Charlie to join them at a ski resort, knowing that he will find the invitation humiliating. "What'd you do that for?" asks one of the classmates. "You know he's on aid." "On major holidays," his friend replies, "it's customary for the lord of the manor to offer drippings to the poor." Then the rich boys vandalize the headmaster's Jaguar and pressure Charlie to take part in their cover-up. When Charlie insists that he cannot identify the culprits, the headmaster applies the pressure of his Ivy League connections:

"The dean of admissions at Harvard and I have an arrangement. Along with the usual sheaf of applicants submitted by Baird, of which virtually—well, two thirds are guaranteed admittance, I add one name. Somebody who's a stand-out, and yet underprivileged. A student who cannot afford to pay the board and tuition in Cambridge. Do you know on whose behalf I drafted a memo this year?"
"No, sir."
"You. You, Mr. Simms. Now can you tell me who did it?"
"No, sir, I can't."
"You take the weekend to think about it, Mr. Simms!"

How can Charlie cope with this crowd of snobs and schemers? The answer, *Scent of a Woman* suggests, is that he needs the backing of his blind, alcoholic, misanthropic mentor Lt. Col. Frank Slade (U.S. Army, retired). Early in the film, Slade ridicules Charlie for attending a posh private academy:

"Giving me that old prep-school palaver? Baird School! Bunch of runny-nosed snots in tweed jackets, all studying to be George Bush!"
"I believe President Bush went to Andover, Colonel."
"You sharp-shootin' me, punk?"

In the climactic disciplinary-hearing scene, however, Slade rails against the hypocrisy of the "Baird men," ensuring that Charlie will remain on campus, immune to further harassment, until he graduates. More than any other recent film, *Scent of a Woman* suggests that the appearance of private academies can be misleading. Visually, Baird is the quintessential New England prep school, an elegant blend of manicured lawns, Ivy-covered walls, and stately academic buildings. By the end of the film, however, the audience can't help being disgusted by the entitled, self-inflating attitudes of virtually everyone who lives and works there.

The most incisive, non-formulaic prep-school movie of the past twenty years, strange to say, is *Outside Providence* (1999; directed by Michael Corrente, written by Corrente with Peter and Bobby Farrelly, the creators of *Dumb and Dumber* [1994], *There's Something About Mary* [1998], and other lowbrow comedies). *Outside Providence* contains a few raunchy sight gags and a few clichés about 1970s stoners, but it also makes a number of fresh observations about class, gender, and education at exclusive private academies. While driving home

5. "That was what made the school so useless"

from a disco, Tim Dunphy, a working-class teenager from Pawtucket, Rhode Island, gets stoned and crashes into a parked police cruiser. After Tim is arrested, one of his father's friends, a car dealer said to be "connected" to organized crime, persuades a judge to sentence Tim to one year of probation, on the condition that he will spend that year at Cornwall Academy, a prep school in western Connecticut, and graduate on time. (How did the car dealer come to have this kind of "pull" with the judge? Why Cornwall instead of a school in Rhode Island? Did the car dealer agree to pay for Tim's tuition, room, and board? The screenplay leaves these questions unaddressed, presenting Tim's improbable sentence as a fait accompli.) Tim's first impressions of Cornwall suggest that a scathing anti-prep broadside is underway. The headmaster, Dean Mort, is a fussy traditionalist, much like Dr. Thurmer in *The Catcher in the Rye*. During an assembly, Mort insists that his school has not been influenced in any way by the social upheaval of the late sixties and early seventies: "In the past ten years, other institutions of our ilk have chosen to 'liberalize' their curriculum. While these other institutions have grown to expect less from their students, we here at Cornwall expect *more*." Mr. Funderburk, Tim's housemaster, is a stern disciplinarian, much like Mr. Ludsbury in *A Separate Peace*. He recites a list of campus rules as soon as Tim steps off the bus from Pawtucket and metes out so many punishments that Cornwall begins to resemble a reform school for well-to-do juvenile delinquents. The school's abrasive atmosphere seems to rub off on its students. In two early scenes, for instance, an unpopular boy is tossed into a lake fully clothed and struck on the head by a perfectly aimed lacrosse ball.

After Corrente and the Farrellys make it clear that Cornwall can be just as unpleasant as Welton, St. Matthews, and Baird, however, they raise a number of issues seldom addressed in American prep-school narratives. First, in spite of Cornwall's faults, Tim's year there turns out to be a valuable opportunity. Unlike *School Ties*, *Outside Providence* does not romanticize its main character's working-class origins. At home, Tim has been immersed in two idiotic forms of American masculinity. His friends babble incessantly about alcohol, drugs, and the sexual adventures of Bunny Cote, supposedly the most promiscuous young woman at their high school. The card-table chatter of Tim's father and his cronies is equally crude and mindless, a stream of homophobic slurs and bitter complaints about the "Jew bastards" who put an end to the Nixon administration with "some lousy erased tapes." (One of Mr. Dunphy's friends points out that Bob Woodward and Carl Bernstein were "doing their job" and that Woodward is not Jewish, but the others pay no attention to him.) At Cornwall, Tim begins to see himself, his hometown, and his future in a new light. His girlfriend Jane Weston is so charming and intelligent that, for the first time, he values a young woman's friendship as much as her good looks.[11] Influenced by Jane and his roommate Irv Waltham, Tim even becomes vaguely interested in his schoolwork. He arrived at Cornwall expecting to go through the motions of his senior year and never set foot in a classroom again, but in the movie's final scene he tells his father and his younger brother that he intends to enroll at a junior college in the fall. That may not sound ambitious, but given Tim's prior indifference to education, it suggests that a genuine transformation is taking place. It would be going too far to suggest that Cornwall Academy makes a preppie out of Tim Dunphy, but the school does introduce him to possibilities which had never crossed his mind until he was forced to enroll.

Outside Providence also diverges from other prep-school movies by using stereotypical characters sparingly. Dean Mort is not a kindly Mr. Chips, but he is not a tyrant, either. His demeanor is always thoughtful and courteous and he is deeply saddened when one of Tim's friends in Pawtucket is killed in a traffic accident. *One* teacher at Cornwall is overbearing and *one* of Tim's peers there turns out to be a ruthless schemer. The movie does not suggest that these characters are typical products of "the college-preparatory system." Third, and perhaps most important, *Outside Providence* challenges the conventional opinion that prep schools are rarified enclaves that exclude and mystify outsiders. As Janet Maslin observes, Tim's transition from Pawtucket to Cornwall seems almost effortless: "[When he] arrives at the school carrying his belongings in a trash bag, it looks as if we're headed for another sociological skirmish among spoiled schoolboys and less privileged ones. But one of the most likable things about *Outside Providence* is its way of shrugging this off, letting [Tim] make friends easily, and just sending up the place's prim atmosphere" (E5). Similarly, Stephanie Zacharek notes that *Outside Providence* "is about class all

5. "That was what made the school so useless"

right ... [b]ut the movie is remarkable for the way it refuses to treat a lower-middle-class upbringing as a tragedy or as something to apologize for. [Tim] doesn't see his place in the social food chain as a roadblock to overcome: it's simply there, an unremarkable fact" (1). One of the film's most vivid depictions of the ties connecting wealthy and working-class young people is the scene in which Tim and Jane exchange Christmas presents. Tim gives Jane a pair of roach clips. She is delighted. After all, the 1970s drug culture was omnipresent: tough kids from Rhode Island liked to get high, and so did Virginia horse-country preppies on their way to Ivy League universities. Jane gives Tim an 8-track tape of Bruce Springsteen's debut album *Greetings from Asbury Park, N.J.* He is delighted. After all, before Springsteen became a major star, he was a cult artist whose audience cut across class boundaries. The gifts, that is to say, reflect the characters' shared interests, not the fact that one is a child of the upper middle class and the other was raised in a post-industrial wasteland.

All of these films stress that adults and adolescents view boarding schools in radically different ways. The parents, faculty, administrators, and other adults in *Dead Poets Society, School Ties, Scent of a Woman* and *Outside Providence* are great believers in the prep-school myth. Time and again, they tell young preppies that they are some of the luckiest young men in the country. Their schools are superb. They will have the inside track when they apply to exclusive colleges. They are being groomed to become rich and successful, so they must take advantage of the opportunities provided by their schools. These assumptions are not necessarily wrong, but they turn out to be simplistic and naïve. The adult characters idealize prep-school life because they see it from a distance. The student characters see their schools differently because they do not have the luxury of contemplating their presumably bright futures. They have to grapple, in the present, with bigotry, snobbery, hypercompetitive schoolmates, sadistic teachers, cheating scandals, and all of the other dangers and drawbacks of prep-school life. These issues, the films suggest, give rise to a role reversal: while the adults in prep-school movies tend to be idealists, the adolescents are pragmatists whose assumptions about their schools are based on firsthand experience. Only one adolescent character in these films, Charlie Dillon, the most corrupt student in *School Ties*, speaks explicitly about the prep-school myth. He tells David Greene that he *hopes* his education at St. Matthew's will pave the way toward a rewarding, prosperous future, but then he concedes that only time will tell: "Good grades, the right schools, the right colleges, the right connections—those are the keys to the kingdom. None of us goes off and lives by his wits. We do the things they tell us to do, and then they give us the good life. I goddamn hope we like it when we get it."

The Death Knell of the School

William Grove, the main character in Richard Yates's *A Good School*, attends Dorset Academy because of a pushy stranger and a tuition discount. In 1941, Grove recalls, his mother taught a weekly sculpture class at her apartment in Greenwich Village. One of the students, "a rich girl of exceptional beauty and charm named Jane," invited the Groves to her wedding and William was dazzled by the event:

> It was a real Society wedding, held outdoors on Jane's parents' enormous lawn in Westchester County, and we'd never seen anything like it. The groom was almost as stunning as the bride, a young naval officer in a flawless white uniform with a choker collar and stiff black-and-gold epaulets. There was an orchestra, there was a dance floor on a specially-built platform trimmed with white canvas, and there were what seemed hundreds of lovely girls who danced with their partners as soon as Jane and her naval officer had used his fiercely gleaming sword to cut the cake [3].

One of the other wedding guests sees William gazing at the orchestra and the couples on the dance floor and takes it on herself to map out his secondary education:

> "Is this boy in school?" a woman's harsh voice inquired.
> "Well, actually," my mother said, "I've been trying to think of a school for him, but there are so many schools and it's all so confusing I really—"
> "Dorset Academy," the woman said ... "It's the only school in the East that understands boys. My boy loved it.... Dorset Academy, Dorset, Connecticut. Don't forget it. Write it down. You'll never be sorry" [4].

Mrs. Grove contacts Dorset, and within a few days the headmaster stops by to tell her more about the school. She is impressed by Mr. Knoedler's

5. "That was what made the school so useless"

polished manners, but confesses that she and her ex-husband cannot afford Dorset's tuition fees. Not to worry, Knoedler replies. Would she reconsider if he reduced the fees by fifty percent? Mrs. Grove accepts the offer, and in the fall semester William enrolls in the fourth form. All of these details, Blake Bailey explains in *A Tragic Honesty: The Life and Work of Richard Yates* (2003), were drawn from Yates's past. His mother was in fact invited to a society wedding, where "an overbearing grande dame insisted that [she] look into [a boarding school called] Avon Old Farms." Avon's headmaster responded to Mrs. Yates's letter of inquiry with a "personal visit" and "offer[ed] her on the spot a scholarship for half the—rather exorbitant—tuition" (45). When *A Good School* was published in 1978, "the reactions of Yates's former schoolmates and teachers to 'this obvious *roman-à-clef* ranged from 'apoplectic' to 'philosophic and amused.' In fact the latter was far more the norm ... and naturally such reactions depended on the reader's sense of humor as well as how lightly one got off" (48–49).

At first glance, Dorset appears to be the real thing—a proper, well-appointed New England boarding school:

> Dorset Academy lay miles from any town in northern Connecticut. It had been built and founded in the nineteen-twenties by an eccentric lady millionaire named Abigail Church Hooper, often quoted as having said her life's ambition was to establish a school "for the sons of the gentry," and she had spared no expense. All of its buildings were of thick, dark red stone in what we were told was "Cotswold" architecture, with gabled slate roofs whose timbers had intentionally been installed when the wood was young so that in aging they would warp and sag in interesting ways. Four long classroom-and-dormitory buildings formed a lovely quadrangle, three stories high and enclosing many big trees. Beyond it, along curving flagstone walks, lay an attractive assortment of other buildings large and small, each with its sagging roofline and its display of deep, expensive lead-casement windows, and there were rich lawns [5].

In spite of its superficial elegance, however, Dorset proves disappointing in any number of ways, "a striving entity that isn't quite making it" (Castronovo and Goldleaf 82).[12] Mrs. Hooper had intended to double the size of the school by building a second quadrangle, but she changed her mind after foundations had been set in place: "They were like long, low ruins of an ancient place, those unfinished foundations;

they jarred your sense of symmetry; they cluttered the view on your way to the infirmary, or over to the science building.... And at night, if you weren't careful, you could stumble over the masonry" (44). This abandoned project marked the onset of the school's chronic financial problems. The enrollment is sparse: 125 boys spread over six forms. (The faculty and other school officials try to turn this problem into a selling point by insisting that the small number of students ensures that "each boy gets more personal attention" [5].) Knoedler spends half of each year traveling to the homes of potential students to deliver the sales pitch he used to reel in Mrs. Grove. Alarmed by Dorset's budget shortfalls, the board of trustees urges the faculty to accept a temporary pay cut. They refuse, and that decision sounds the death knell of the school:

> "Like all private schools, we rely on tuition as our primary source of income," Knoedler said. "In the past, from time to time, we've been able to draw on funds made available by Mrs. Hooper's foundation, but that source is closed to us now.... With a small enrollment, and with many of the boys paying half tuition, we can't begin to meet our costs. We've been operating at a deficit for some years, and we've reached a point of crisis."
>
> "I met with the board of trustees last week, and a suggestion was made which I'll pass along to you now. If each member of the faculty were to accept a voluntary cut in salary as a temporary measure—oh, perhaps twenty-five percent—we might well be able to remain solvent."
>
> And they turned him down.... The refusal was unanimous.
>
> "All right, gentlemen," Knoedler said, "I've presented the board's recommendation and I've noted your response.... I'll keep you informed on any new developments" [97–98].

When Miss Hooper withdraws her financial support once and for all, the faculty scramble for new teaching jobs and the parents of Dorset's remaining students regret having entrusted their sons to a school that has failed "like some sleazy little commercial venture" (169). In an episode brimming with dark comedy, Dorset's former benefactor invites the boys in the school's last graduating class to her mansion for tea and startles them by blaming the school's downfall on "your man Knoedler" and insisting that World War II is the latest phase of President Roosevelt's clandestine plot "to turn us all into Communists and Negroes" (164). Bailey observes that Mrs. Theodate Pope Riddle, the

5. "That was what made the school so useless"

real-life model for Miss Hooper, was "the very tissue of which ... [local legends] are made: though whacked on the head by a heavy beam and given up for dead, [she] survived the sinking of the Lusitania and went on to become Connecticut's first female architect." Mrs. Riddle designed Avon "in the English Cotswold style, and insisted it be built using red sandstone from local quarries. She further insisted, with bizarre but rather endearing fanaticism, that the five hundred or so construction workers restrict themselves to the use of seventeenth-century tools ... and even to 'work by rule of thumb and to judge all verticals by eye.' When she discovered a worker using a modern level and plumb rule, Mrs. Riddle became furious and sacked the lot of them" (*A Tragic Honesty* 45–46). In spite of Mrs. Riddle's eccentricities, Bailey continues, Avon Old Farms proved ahead of its time: "The intolerance for misfits so commonplace at such bastions as St. Paul's, Andover, and Exeter was anathema to the arch-progressive Avon, which was innovative in a number of ways. Seventy-five years ago there was an on-site psychologist to commiserate with some of the quirkier students, as well as a remedial reading program instituted by Harvard-trained specialists. Indeed, Avon's remarkable success with both the quirky and dyslexic was its greatest claim to fame, and nowadays on-site psychologists and remediation programs are de rigueur at all but the most benighted schools" (*A Tragic Honesty* 46).

The teachers at Dorset seem well-meaning but demoralized. Jack Draper brews liquor in the chemistry lab and drinks heavily to avoid thinking about his wife Alice's poorly concealed affair with a French teacher named Jean-Paul La Prade. (Draper's drinking problem is especially disturbing because he is "a frail man so crippled by polio in all four limbs that he [can] barely walk or hold a pencil" [11].) Dismayed by his mediocre surroundings, Edgar Stone, a Harvard graduate with a Ph.D., becomes virtually silent, withdrawing from his family, his colleagues, and his students. Robert Driscoll, an English teacher, seems relatively self-confident and satisfied with his career, but even he can't help noticing the ways Dorset fails to measure up to his alma mater (Deerfield Academy) and the school at which he started his teaching career. Most of Dorset's students also seem troubled. John Haskell suffers a nervous breakdown and runs away from the school. When Knoedler and Driscoll track him down on a country road and take him to his mother's house, she blames Dorset for her son's distress and accuses Knoedler of making prudish remarks about her relationship with a riding instructor:

> "Could we start at the beginning, please, Mr. Knoedler?" she said, and she seated herself in a way that emphasized the swing and rustle of her full skirt. "Can you tell me what's been going on in that romantic-looking little school of yours?"
>
> Knoedler cleared his throat. "Well, John's been under a good deal of pressure lately, Mrs. Atwood," he began, "and he's always been a high-strung boy, as you know..."
>
> Then suddenly Mrs. Atwood got up, piqued by something Knoedler had said ... and walked away to the mantelpiece, where she whirled to face him again.
>
> "It strikes me, Mr. Knoedler," she said, "that you people run a pretty funny little school. What do you *do* to the kids there? What do they do to each other? I send you a great deal of money to prepare my son for college and he comes home looking crucified, and all you can do is sit around making little innuendos about my private life."
>
> "I was aware of no innuendos, Mrs. Atwood," Knoedler said, blushing.
> "I certainly meant nothing of the sort, and I—"
> "Oh, come off it, Knoedler" [71].

Grove is tormented by schoolmates and disappoints his parents by failing most of his classes. Sixteen-year-old Terry Flynn "was only in the second form—he was still learning to read—and so his classmates were not his contemporaries" (10). Bucky Ward's moods veer from boyish playfulness to explosions of rage: "'*Things!*' he said. 'Christ, Grove, do you ever get so you can't stand *things*? *O*bjects? That cup. This school. Clothes. Cars. All the God damn senseless *things* in the world. You oughta see my family's house. Oh, it's very nice and it's very big and it cost my father a hell of a lot of money, but I can never make him understand it's just another *thing*'" (88). Bobby Driscoll is bullied in his dorm and reprimanded by his father when tries to use his parents' house as a safe haven. Most of Mrs. Atwood's allegations are unfounded, but her suspicion that there is something cruel about the campus culture at Dorset is right on target. Early in the novel, a student entertains several classmates with fresh gossip about Draper's alcoholism: "Mac-Kenzie had to go over to the lab last night to get a book or some damn thing, and when he turned on the lights there's Draper on the floor, flat on his back, waving his arms and legs around in the air like some—

5. "That was what made the school so useless"

you know, like some bug tryna turn himself over? So MacKenzie gets down and picks him up ... and this terrific smell of alcohol hits him: Draper was *plastered*!" (11). Later on, the Dorset boys can hardly contain their homophobic glee when they realize that an upperclassman has spent several hours locked in his room with a younger student:

> "Weaver's got a little kid in there with him," somebody said. "Little kid from Two building."
> Then Pete Giroux went up with a bar of soap in his hand and wrote "HOMO" across Weaver's door. All the dormitory doors were made of dark wood, finely and deeply grooved; it would be impossible to wash the lettering out of those grooves....
> "Come on outa there, Weaver," Pete Giroux called like a cop in the movies, "or we're coming inta get ya." Another boy was crouched and working with a jackknife at the wooden bolt of the door.
> It opened suddenly and very briefly, just enough to let the little kid out into the hall. He stood there blinking in his rumpled dinner clothes, trying to look as if he didn't know what this was all about. He was twelve or thirteen...
> "Arright," Giroux told him, "getcher ass outa here, punk. Fast."
> Then they concentrated on "getting" Henry Weaver, though there was no clear plan for what to do when they got him [56].

Yates's schoolboys also draw some kind of warped amusement from a hazing ritual in which they tear off a schoolmate's clothes and masturbate him, supposedly to prove that he is gay. Grove endures this mistreatment during his first year at Dorset and, near the end of the novel, Robert Driscoll hears a commotion in a dorm room, hurries in to see what the boys are up to, and finds that the latest victim is his son. After he chases away the perpetrators, Driscoll assures Bobby that the incident was nothing to worry about: "This doesn't matter. It's just a dumb little thing that happens in prep schools.... It was you this time and it'll be somebody else another time. It's just a dumb little prep school thing and it doesn't matter" (150–51). Driscoll's assertion that this kind of abuse is not uncommon in prep schools helps to clarify a puzzling moment in *The Catcher in the Rye*. When Holden Caulfield's sister Phoebe asks if he can name one thing that he likes, his thoughts turn to a former schoolmate:

> There was this one boy at Elkton Hills, named James Castle, that wouldn't take back something he said about this very conceited boy, Phil Sta-

bile.... So Stabile with about six other dirty bastards, went down to James Castle's room and went in and locked the goddam door and ... started in on him. I won't even tell you what they did to him—it's too repulsive—but he *still* wouldn't take it back, old James Castle.... Finally, what he did, instead of taking back what he said, he jumped out the window. I was in the *shower* and all, and even *I* could hear him land outside [220–21].

As Edwin Haviland Miller argues, Holden's memories of this incident are a terrible additional burden for a teenager still mourning the death of his younger brother: "A few years earlier, Jimmy Castle, a classmate, was so tortured and brutalized, presumably genitally, by a bunch of students that he leaped from the window, wearing Holden's turtleneck sweater. As though Holden is not sufficiently burdened with his unresolved grief for Allie, he has had to cope with this tie to an unfortunate classmate" (136). Holden's self-censored account of Castle's death should seem familiar to anyone who has also read *A Good School*. Like Castle, William Grove and Bobby Driscoll are assaulted by groups of six boys who "start in" on their victims in a "repulsive" way. Salinger avoids going into detail about the actions that led to Castle's death, but by the late 1970s, Yates evidently assumed that readers could tolerate a description of this "thing that happens in prep schools."

In "The Lost World of Richard Yates" (1999), an essay that surveys Yates's career and laments his posthumous decline into all-books-out-of-print obscurity, Stewart O'Nan concludes that what distinguishes Yates from other novelists of his era is "the bleakness of his vision," the "merciless" way he exposes his characters' faults and misfortunes:

> As Greek tragedy turns around its characters' fatal flaws, so does Yates's fiction. The depth and breadth of characterization is much fuller, of course, but the end result is the same: the characters earn their downfall, seem fated to it. It's this merciless limning of his people that makes Yates unique and the process of reading his work so affecting (some would say terrifying). We recognize the disappointments and miscalculations his characters suffer from our own less-than-heroic lives. And Yates refuses to spoon-feed us the usual redeeming, life-affirming plot twist that makes everything better. No comedy dilutes the situation. When it's time to face the worst, there's no evasion whatsoever, no softening of the blows.... What is distinctive about [Yates's fiction] ... is not merely the bleakness of his vision, but how that vision adheres not to war or some other horror but to the aspirations of everyday Americans [6].

Similarly, Richard Price observes that Yates seemed unwilling throughout his career to soften "the destinies of his characters—the slow motion train wreck of the lives to come, the soul-killing realizations that will invariably be their lot" (ix). As David Castronovo and Steven Goldleaf point out, this emphasis on crushing disappointment separates Yates's narratives from those of the American novelist he respected the most: "All his life Yates admired F. Scott Fitzgerald: the green light at the end of the dock in *The Great Gatsby*, the promise of something glimmering and special just ahead, is one of his master themes; and yet Yates never seems to submit to the glamour and joy of American promise. In his novels and stories he subtracts most of the romance from his people's lives, rewriting Fitzgerald's winter dreams of love and social ambition in a minor key. Yates's people are almost always strugglers on their way to jobs in business rather than golden people at the country club" (6–7). In the opening pages of Yates's novel *Revolutionary Road* (1961), April Wheeler's belief that she has what it takes to become a successful actress is obliterated. Her husband Frank's notion that he is destined to become some sort of artist or intellectual proves sturdier, but eventually he is humbled, too. Throughout the novel, Yates's treatment of the Wheelers seems akin to a police interrogation. April wants to deny that she has become an ordinary suburban housewife and Frank wants to deny that he has become an ordinary corporate drone, but Yates puts so much pressure on their delusions that they are eventually forced to confess. Similarly, in *The Easter Parade* (1976), Mrs. Pookie Grimes and her daughters cling to the hope that they will become rich and carefree in the future, but Yates's plot slowly grinds away their optimism, accentuating "the depths to which people deceive themselves into thinking they're somehow special, set apart from the herd" (Bailey, *A Tragic Honesty*, 127). "The novel opens," O'Nan explains, "with the simplicity of a folktale: 'Neither of the Grimes sisters would have a happy life, and looking back it always seemed that the trouble began with their parents' divorce.'... Pookie drinks and rarely works, so the family is short of money; still she believes they're special, and that her two girls will turn out to be something.... They don't. As the opening line promises, their lives are unhappy, their promise chronically unfulfilled" (11).

Yates's treatment of his characters in *A Good School* is uncharacteristically gentle, it seems to me, because few of them test positive for self-deception. Instead of daydreaming about future triumphs, Yates's students and teachers busy themselves with a day-to-day struggle to get by. Several critics have argued that Yates wasted his exquisite craftsmanship on shopworn subject matter. *Revolutionary Road*'s meditations on the spiritual poverty of 1950s suburbs and white-collar offices, for example, were hardly groundbreaking in light of the work of sociologists such as David Reisman and C. Wright Mills and novels such as Sloan Wilson's *The Man in the Gray Flannel Suit* (1955). (Bailey notes that two reviewers "took the line that [*Revolutionary Road*] must be negligible because it dealt with the tired subject of suburban discontent: 'No amount of contrived symbolism can hide what has become a hackneyed theme,' wrote R. D. Spector in the *New York Herald Tribune*, and W. E. Preece of the *Chicago Tribune* went further, claiming the book reads like a 'parody of all the ... type-cast novels that went before it'" [*A Tragic Honesty* 228].) Similarly, Yates's *A Special Providence* (1969) was hardly the first novel about a World War II veteran who faces an uncertain future when he returns to the United States.

A similar charge could be leveled at *A Good School*: after *A Separate Peace* and *The Rector of Justin*, couldn't Yates have chosen a less familiar setting than a Northeastern prep school in the early 1940s? That is a reasonable question, but Yates refreshes his subject matter by challenging the prep-school myth more directly than any previous American novelist had done. Few readers will mistake Dorset's students and teachers for the prep-school elite. Grove is a wretched character at first, a slovenly, unpopular boy who feels so humiliated after he endures the hazing ritual also inflicted on Bobby Driscoll and Salinger's James Castle that he wonders "how he [is] going to live the rest of his life" (27). By the end of the novel, however, Grove bounces back through sheer perseverance. He wins an essay-writing contest and joins the staff of the school newspaper. And during his senior year, he charms a young woman named Polly Clark at a dance and then decides to end their flirtation, partly to quit while ahead and partly to spare the feelings of his friend Bucky Ward, who had invited Polly to Dorset and was hurt by her interest in Grove. The story of Grove's boarding-school education contains no triumphs or transformations, but Yates makes it clear that his accidental preppie has rolled with the punches,

5. "That was what made the school so useless"

survived the worst days of an extremely difficult adolescence, and taken a few steps toward a future career as a writer. Throughout most of the novel, the title *A Good School* seems sardonic, but in the closing chapter, Grove insists that it means just what it says: "If my father had lived I would certainly have thanked him for paying my way through Dorset Academy. I know he never trusted the place, and for that reason I would have persisted if he shrugged off my thanks. I might even have told him—and this would have been only a slight exaggeration—that in ways still important to me it *was* a good school" (178). Grove rises, in other words, while Dorset falls. As Mary Jean DeMarr and Jane Bakerman observe, Yates contrasts "the development of his protagonist with the disintegration of the prep school that forms him" (213).

Jack Draper's struggles also highlight the potential rewards of fighting through adversity. The chemistry teacher could hardly be a more wretched figure early in the novel: an alcoholic crippled by polio, betrayed by his wife, and mocked by his students. In what may be the most painful moment in a novel rife with emotional distress, Draper cannot avoid joining the school community in a standing ovation for his wife's lover:

> "One of our masters and friends, [the headmaster] announced, "has volunteered to serve his adopted nation. Mr. Jean-Paul La Prade today accepts a commission as captain in the United States Army. I congratulate him personally, as I know we all will, and I know we'll all wish him well" …
>
> This was ridiculous. La Prade had to rise from the seated faculty and stand in a sea of applause while a hundred and twenty-five pink young faces came swiveling around to smile at him over the backs of chairs… [T]he worst part, the awful part, was that it brought a quick warm swelling to the walls of his throat. My, God, he thought, my God, I'm going to cry. What saved him, as he crouched and turned briefly right and left to acknowledge the clapping of his colleagues on either side, was a glimpse of Jack Draper's pale withered hands trying to clap along with the others, probably making no sound [92].

This humiliating experience, made especially painful by Yates's decision to present it from La Prade's point of view, nearly destroys Draper. After La Prade's departure, Draper locks himself in the chemistry lab and tries to hang himself, but the exertion of climbing onto a table leaves him too fatigued to continue. Draper's anguish is extreme and some of his reactions to it make matters worse, yet he endures and eventually improves his circumstances the same way Grove does: by resisting the temptation to give up. When Mr. Knoedler announces that Dorset is going out of business, Draper begins to search for a new teaching job. His wife complains that his refusal to conceal his disability in his application letters is self-defeating, but on second thought she is moved by his integrity, which she describes as "[t]he way you sort of—carry on; the really gallant way you face each day in this awful, awful little place..." (161). Alice Draper is an unsympathetic character in many ways, but Yates chooses her to convey the only definition of heroism that appears in his fiction: the capacity to accept disappointments and limitations and continue to "face each day" in spite of them. John Skow's review of *A Good School* is insightful for the most part, but he fails to recognize that for all of its dark moments, it is probably Yates's most hopeful, affirmative book. Instead of highlighting the hard-won survival of Grove, Draper, and other characters, Skow chides Yates for failing to look past his characters' isolation and self-pity: "The reader senses an insufficiency.... Staring unflinchingly at bad nerves and loneliness is admirable, but fearing to look at any other sort of human condition is not, and the cautiousness of Yates's writing comes very close to fear" (84). David Castronovo and Steven Goldleaf describe *A Good School* more accurately in their 1996 study of Yates's fiction: "Few novels about prep school life expose gentlemanly authority and show affection for it at the same time. Such ambivalence diminishes the satiric force of [*A Good School*], making it a complex, nuanced treatment of class rather than an indictment or expose. Most of the 'funny little' places and people in [Yates's fiction] are less than likable; but Dorset generates nostalgia and affection" (81). Similarly, Martin Naparsteck writes that "[o]ver and over in *A Good School*, far more than in any other work by Yates, there is a sense that despite the inevitability of sadness there is hope that things can turn out better" (109).

Dorset Academy has little in common with the "gorgeous world" of privileged students, distinguished teachers, and memorable sporting events that John Knowles recalls in "A Special Time, A Special School," his essay about the years he spent at Phillips Exeter Academy. (See Chapter 2 for a discussion of this essay.) Indeed, many of Yates's characters seem embarrassed by Dorset. Edgar Stone can hardly bear to work at such a down-at-the-heels institution. Robert Driscoll is baffled and annoyed by Miss Hooper's decision to limit the school's athletic program to intramural sports: "For one thing, whoever heard of a school that didn't field varsity teams in competition with other schools? Wasn't that the very heart of prep school life?" (31). Mr. Gold, the manager of the school's print shop, "despise[s] all Dorset boys on principle" because he assumes that they are "rich, spoiled little snot-noses" (53). Conversely, when several students from Dorset travel to a private academy for girls to take their College Board exams, their female counterparts laugh at them because they know Dorset is a flimsy imitation of New England's most exclusive private boys' schools. The only contrarian who seems inclined to defend Dorset is its creator. Yates does not depict the school as a refuge from "the real world"—it *is* the real world, a setting fraught with all of the hardships and disappointments he stressed throughout his career. *A Good School* is no place to search for privilege and glamour. The novel holds that it is impossible to distance yourself from the human condition, as defined by Richard Yates, by spending time on a prep-school campus with flagstone walks, interesting architecture, and a lovely quadrangle.

6

Isolation and Conflict in Tea and Sympathy *and* Peace Breaks Out

Because he's an off-horse, you and the rest of them are only too glad to put two and two together and get a false answer ... anything which will let you go on and persecute a boy whom you basically don't like.—Robert Anderson, *Tea and Sympathy*

In the decade after World War II, the most popular young men at American boarding schools earned respectable grades, but did not seem bookish. They played for school teams, but did not say much about their athletic skills. They were outgoing, but their friendliness had limits. If a student expressed deep feelings in front of his schoolmates, for example, he was sure to provoke no end of mockery. In short, prep-school students expected their peers to be self-confident and accomplished, but always in an understated way.[1] What happened when students did not meet this expectation? That's the question posed in Robert Anderson's play *Tea and Sympathy* (1953) and in *Peace Breaks Out* (1981), John Knowles's second school novel. In both works, students at Northeastern boarding schools conclude that one of their peers is an "off-horse," a misfit who must be put in his place. This kind of hazing takes place at all sorts of schools, but Anderson and Knowles suggest that it can be especially destructive at private academies. First of all, because most prep schools are self-isolating communities in small, out-of-the-way towns, it does not take long for conflicts that arise on their campuses to spin out of control. Secondly, Anderson and Knowles highlight the emotional volatility of young men at boys' schools. These students are teenagers who have been sent away from their homes. Their opportunities to stay in touch with people and events outside of their schools are strictly limited. Day after day, their attention is focused on the same schoolmates, classes, and sports. For these reasons, their suspicion and resentment flare up very quickly. Thus, unlike Knowles's *A Separate Peace* (1959), Richard Yates's *A Good School* (1978), and other American school narratives, *Tea and Sympathy* and *Peace Breaks Out* are not primarily concerned with the inner lives of adolescents. Instead, they investigate the persecution of unpopular students at remote, cloistered boarding schools.

Regular Fellows

In 1910, Woodrow Wilson delivered a speech at Lawrenceville's centennial celebration. "A great school like this," Wilson said, "does not stop with what it does in the class room; it organizes athletics and sports of every kind, it organizes *life* from morning to night" (qtd. in Hicks 528). Endicott Peabody, the founder of the Groton School, undoubtedly would have agreed. In fact, he insisted that his school's commitment to organizing young men's lives was the secret of its success:

> [Peabody's] major educational precept was that every minute of a boy's waking hours must be filled with study, religious devotions, or strenuous exercise. Above all, the slightest opportunity for that insidious form of idleness known as loafing must be avoided like the plague. "The curse of American school life is loafing. The tone of loafers is always low.... The best thing is for a boy to work hard ... to play hard ... and then, when the end of the day has come, to be so tired that he wants to go to bed and go to sleep. This is the healthy and good way for a boy to live" [Kintrea 98].

To manage "every minute of a boy's waking hours," it is necessary for educators to cut students off from everyday life away from their schools. In the late 1800s and early 1900s, that was a cornerstone of American boarding-school culture. Private academies were deliberately set apart from American society at large. They were designed to help privileged young men avoid the distractions and temptations they would find in New York, Boston, and other metropolitan areas. Distance young men from drinking, gambling, and promiscuity, focus their attention on academics and sports, and then you can provide the around-the-clock supervision endorsed by Wilson and Peabody. When wealthy parents heard about the mode of education offered by the era's "great headmasters," they began to send their sons to boarding schools in large numbers. As James McLachlan observes, most of these parents were "well-born city dwellers who were as concerned about the corrupting and enervating effects of urban life ... as they were about the lack of scholarship and moral direction in [other schools]" (7).[2] David V. Hicks, a former headmaster of St. Paul's School, explains that Northeastern boarding schools promised "more than a rustic retreat from the crassness and materialism of the Gilded Age," but they all began with the assumption that to provide a first-rate education, it is necessary to disconnect students from "the popular mainstream culture of adolescent America" (530). (Hicks goes on to say that it is practically impossible to set private academies apart from the mainstream today: "[T]he sprawling of suburbia and the amazing expansion of America's highway system after World War II conspired against the isolation of [boarding schools], and the contemporary revolution in technology and telecommunications threatens to complete their integration into the larger society. Television, cable, E-mail, and now the Internet prevent these schools, even if they wanted to, from forming a culture that is walled off" [530].)

The proponents of boarding-school education saw its advantages very clearly, but they do not seem to have given much thought to its potential costs. By placing schools in rural villages, the founders of the nation's oldest prep schools created highly secluded and highly conformist institutions. At their schools, young men were trained to dress, speak, and behave in certain ways. Nonconformity was a dangerous business; students who did not fit in ran a high risk of being mistreated by peers and disciplined by faculty. American school literature has repeatedly highlighted this feature of prep-school life. It insists that to attend a private academy is to be watched closely and judged rigorously. Few student characters in the novels, short stories, and films discussed in this book are widely praised and respected. Some are more talented or well-liked than others, but I cannot think of one who is regarded as an exemplary product of what John Cheever called "the college-preparatory system." In *The Catcher in the Rye* (1951), Holden Caulfield's roommate Ward Stradlater is one of the best athletes at Pencey Prep and apparently something of a ladies' man, but J. D. Salinger also stresses that Stradlater is a poor student who gets by in part by cheating. Just before Holden leaves Pencey, for instance, Stradlater says that he is too busy to work on an English composition and asks Holden to be "a buddy" and write it for him (37). Similarly, Finny in Knowles's *A Separate Peace* and Terry Flynn in Yates's *A Good School* are outstanding on the playing fields but well below average in their classes. (Gene Forrester describes Finny's grades as a "procession of D's in every subject" [53] and Terry, who flunked out of three other boarding schools before he enrolled at Dorset Academy, is "still learning to read" [10] at the age of sixteen.) The roster of student characters who are disparaged in American prep-school narratives, on the other hand, seems endless. Some fictional preppies are criticized for being too stylish and well-groomed; others because they are regarded as slobs. Some are criticized because they are not athletic; others because they are said to be dumb jocks. Students in these works are criticized for getting low grades and for being "grinds." Some lose the respect of their peers because they are willing to fall in line and take orders; others because they are stubborn and independent. Students are censured for wearing unusual clothes, for having unusual hobbies, for being cruel, for being naïve, for being cynical, for being humorless, for being effete, for being unsophisticated, for being reckless, and for being cowardly. In short, American school fiction suggests that just about any trait that is considered out of the ordinary is enough to provoke ridicule and suspicion on prep-school campuses. This phenomenon gives rise to a striking contradiction: private academies are frequently called elite, but individual students at those schools are rarely treated as though they were members of "the elite." To the contrary, they are constantly evaluated, constantly expected to prove that they have what it takes to fit in and measure up.[3] Outsiders tend to assume that students at boarding schools are encouraged to feel superior to their contemporaries at less prestigious institutions; insiders, by contrast, tend to stress the ways in which boarding-school culture forces young people to face their limitations and do something to correct—or at least to conceal—them.

This culture of judgment and conformity helps to explain the persecution suffered by Tom Lee, the main character in Robert Anderson's *Tea and Sympathy*.[4] The play is often labeled as an attack on anti-gay prejudice at American prep schools in the 1950s, but that description is only partially accurate. Tom, a 17-year-old junior at an unnamed private academy in New England, is not gay. The audience knows from Act I that he is in love with Laura Reynolds, the wife of his housemaster, and the play ends just before Laura, who has decided to end her marriage, sleeps with Tom in his dorm room. ("Years from now," she tells him, "when you talk about this ... and you will ... be kind" [182].) A teacher named David Harris is summoned to the dean's office after he is accused of seducing Tom, but Anderson does not make Harris's sexual orientation entirely clear.[5] Thus, if *Tea and Sympathy* is an indictment of homophobia, it is a curiously indirect indictment that decries prejudice against gay men and boys without presenting a single openly gay character. The primary target of Anderson's critique, it seems to me, is the judgmental culture at American boarding schools.

The most startling aspect of *Tea and Sympathy*, from today's perspective, is how little evidence is required to convince Tom's father, his schoolmates, and his housemaster that he is gay. He prefers not to get his hair cut as short as most of his schoolmates do. He spends an afternoon at a beach known as "the dunes" with David Harris. (In what is arguably the least convincing moment in the play, Tom insists that he cannot understand, even after Harris is interrogated by the dean about swimming and sunbathing in the nude with a student, why the teacher fears that he is in danger of losing his job.) Tom plays tennis instead of football, hockey, or some other rugged team sport. He refuses to join a group of schoolmates when they peek through his dorm-room window at a teacher's wife while she nurses her baby. He has second thoughts after he decides to prove he is straight by going out with an allegedly promiscuous woman. He likes to play folk songs on the guitar. He has acted in several school plays, and because the school is not coeducational he has performed in costume as Lady Macbeth, Lady Teazle in Richard Brinsley Sheridan's *The School for Scandal*, and other female characters.

The school community takes these facts as indisputable proof that Tom is a "fairy," and his persecution begins. When Bill Reynolds, the housemaster, hears about the incident at the dunes, he does not ask Tom for his side of the story. Instead, he concludes that Tom has been having an affair with Harris and must be expelled immediately, for his own sake and the sake of the school. "Tom's always been an off-horse," Reynolds tells his wife. "And now it's quite obvious why. If he's kicked out, maybe it'll bring him to his senses. But he won't change if nothing's done about it" (48). When Laura Reynolds replies that it would be unreasonable to expel a student without investigating the charges against him, Bill scoffs, insisting that there is plenty of evidence supporting the charges and that women do not understand "queers":

> "[Y]ou watch, now that it's out in the open. Look at the way he walks, the way he sometimes stands."
> "Oh, Bill!"
> "All right, so a woman doesn't notice these things. But a man knows a queer when he sees one" [48].

The housemaster's attitudes are repugnant, but he expresses them without hesitation because they were commonplace at private academies in the World War II era. As Gore Vidal, a graduate of Phillips Exeter Academy, recalls in *Palimpsest* (1995), "[t]he American hysteria about homosexuality was so extreme in [the 1940s] that friendships between boys were deliberately discouraged, a cruel and counterproductive thing to do in an all-male environment" (87). In light of the remarks about homosexuality made by school officials in Vidal's "The Zenner Trophy" (1950), Louis Auchincloss's *The Rector of Justin* (1964), and James Kirkwood's *Good Times/Bad Times* (1968), moreover, Bill Reynolds's reactions to the rumors about Harris and Tom seem all too predictable. (See Chapters 3 and 4 for discussions of these works.)

The reactions of Tom's peers, who had considered him the most effeminate boy at school long before rumors about his relationship with Harris started to circulate, are equally mindless and mean-spirited. They exit the shower room in the gym *en masse* when Tom walks in. They call him "Gracie" and ask which one of his boyfriends is going to take him to an upcoming dance. A particularly homophobic student named Ralph insists that he is going to lock the door of his dorm room at night as long as he and Tom are living under the same roof and slaps Tom across the face, drawing blood, when Tom tells him to stop staring through binoculars at the woman nursing her infant next door. "Maybe if it was Dr. Morrison instead of Mrs. Morrison," Ralph says, "he'd be more interested" (39). Then Ralph turns his hostility toward Tom's roommate Al, asking how he can stand rooming with a "queer." Al does not believe that Tom is gay but, under pressure from Ralph, his father, and his friends on the school's baseball team, he decides to find another roommate and move to another house on campus.

Tom's situation becomes even more painful when his father, an alumnus of the school who has become a business executive in Boston, lines up with the bigots and bullies. Herb Lee rushes to the school when he hears the rumors about Tom and Mr. Harris, worried that his son's reputation (and by extension his own) may be damaged beyond repair. "What's happened?" he asks Bill Reynolds. "Why isn't my boy a regular fellow? He's had every chance to be since he was knee-high to a grasshopper—boys' camps every summer, boarding schools.... He's always been with men and boys. Why doesn't some of it rub off?" (59–60). When Laura Reynolds insists that Tom *is* a "regular fellow," even though she dislikes the term, and points out that he is the best tennis player at the school, Herb is not convinced. "[Tom] doesn't even play tennis like a regular fellow," he replies. "No hard drives and cannonball serves. He's a cut artist. He can put more damn twists on that ball" (60). (Evidently, Herb is disappointed that Tom plays tennis because he had no athletic ability as a young man and was hoping to experience varsity football through his son. As Bill Reynolds explains, "[Herb] was Graduate Manager of the team when I was a sophomore in college. He was always the manager of the teams, and he really wanted his son to be there in the center of the picture" [46].) Then Herb explains that he has recently gotten to know a young man who seems far more masculine and promising than Tom:

> I *want* to be proud of [Tom]. My God, that's why I had him in the first place. That's why I took him from his mother when we split up, but.... Look, this is a terrible thing to say, but you know the scholarships the University Club sponsors for needy kids.... Well, I contribute pretty heavily to it, and I happened to latch on to one of the kids we help—an orphan. I sort of talk to him like a father, go up to see him at his school once in a while, and that kid listens to me ... and you know what, he's shaping up better than my own son [61].

6. Isolation and Conflict

After Herb explains that his University Club protégée, unlike his son, is a "regular fellow," he launches a campaign to improve Tom's reputation. Several faculty members suggest that Tom would probably be "more comfortable" if he transferred to another school, but Herb argues that to change his accusers' minds Tom must "stick it out" (62). He will have to put up with some "kidding" from his schoolmates, of course, but that will toughen him up and help him "prove to them he's … well, manly. It may be the thing that brings him to his senses" (63).

Tom does his best to take his father's advice. He stays at the school, suffers the slings and arrows of prep-school unpopularity, and tries to demonstrate that he is "manly" by going out with Ellie Martin, a townie waitress with a reputation for promiscuity, but the plan backfires. When Tom is threatened with expulsion for leaving the school without permission, Herb looks forward to congratulating his son. He assumes that the scandal involving Ellie Martin will put an end to the rumors about Tom's sexual orientation because expulsion for sneaking off to see a woman is "so much more normal" (158) than expulsion for swimming and sunbathing in the nude with a male teacher. "[B]eing kicked out for a thing like this," he explains, "while not exactly desirable, is still not so serious. It's sort of one of the calculated risks of being a man" (160). Moments later, however, Herb learns that the incident at Ellie Martin's apartment has only made matters worse. Tom arrived there determined to lose his virginity, but he could not force himself to go through it. Because he is in love with Laura Reynolds, he pulled away from Ellie at the last moment, burst into tears, and threatened to stab himself with a kitchen knife. When Herb hears the truth, he shows no interest in comforting his traumatized son. Instead, his first impulse is to cover up Tom's failed attempt to prove to the school community that he is "normal." "Does everyone know this?" Herb asks. "Maybe there's some way of getting to this girl so she won't spread the story" (161, 163). (In several passages, Herb responds to Tom's alleged homosexuality as if it were a contagious disease. Herb is obviously more comfortable spending time with Bill Reynolds than with his son, for example, and when Tom tries to kiss his father on the cheek, the stage directions indicate that Herb "holds him off with a firm handshake" [66].)

Throughout *Tea and Sympathy*, Anderson suggests that Herb Lee's efforts to repair Tom's reputation were doomed from the start. The play is oddly static: Tom is generally regarded as a "fairy" when the curtain rises and he is still regarded that way when it falls. Laura Reynolds and Tom's roommate Al know that Tom is straight, but everyone else at the school seems to believe the opposite. None of Anderson's characters changes his or her mind. Tom rolls with the punches and is sexually initiated by the woman he loves, but his triumph over his unpleasant circumstances is never disclosed to the community. Laura intends to leave the school forever, and the audience knows that Tom will not mention, let alone brag about, his tryst with her. Among other things, *Tea and Sympathy* underscores the difficulty of proving a negative proposition in a remote, cloistered environment.[6] After rumors about Tom's sexuality circulate on campus, everything about him, from his musical taste to the way he walks, is interpreted as evidence substantiating the rumors. By contrast, no one suspects that Bill Reynolds, a graduate of the school and a teacher with a solid reputation as a "regular fellow," may not be as straight as he seems. Reynolds has been married to a beautiful former stage actress for less than a year, yet he spends most of his free time hiking and organizing sporting events with teenage boys. When the school puts on a dance, Tom offers to escort Laura because he knows that her husband will be out of town with his all-male entourage. When Laura approaches Bill to kiss him early in the play, he turns away awkwardly, muttering something about having to make a phone call. And when Bill finds out that Laura has been planning a romantic summer vacation in Canada, he vetoes the idea because has invited several students to join him and Laura at a lodge in Maine. Early in the play, Laura patiently tolerates Bill's habit of surrounding himself with boys, but when Bill joins the crowd of prep-school males persecuting Tom Lee, she lets her husband know that she is worried about his obvious reluctance to spend time alone with her and his "almost compulsive" habits in the bedroom:

> LAURA: Oh, Bill, we so rarely touch any more. I keep feeling I'm losing contact with you. Don't you feel that? ... I know, you've got to go, but it's just that, I don't know, we don't touch any more.... A tension seems to grow between us ... and then when we do ... touch ... it's a violent thing ... almost a compulsive thing. (BILL is uncomfortable at this accurate description of their relationship. He

6. Isolation and Conflict

sits troubled. She puts her arms around his neck and embraces him, bending over him.) You don't feel it? You don't feel yourself holding away from me until it becomes overpowering? There's no growing together any more ... no quiet times, just holding hands, the feeling of closeness, like it was in Italy. Now it's long separations and then this almost brutal coming together and ...

BILL: For God's sake, Laura, what are you talking about? (He rises and goes to his desk.) It can't always be a honeymoon [112].

Laura's patience runs out when she hears about Tom's evening with Ellie Martin and his talk of suicide. Outraged by the role her husband has played in the young man's ordeal, she tells Bill that Tom is "more of a man" than he is and that he has refused to help the outcast because Tom represents "the thing you fear in yourself" (173, 175).[7] Bill, the "manly" prep-school teacher who hopes to become the school's headmaster one day, nearly hits Laura, but he stifles that impulse, ridicules her for "mothering that fairy" (175), and says that it is time for her to leave the school. Laura does not argue with him. "When I'm gone," she says, "it will probably be agreed by all that I was an off-horse too, and didn't really belong to the clan, and it's good riddance" (172).

Throughout *Tea and Sympathy*, Anderson uses Laura's perspective as an outsider to illustrate that day-to-day life at an isolated boarding school can give rise to a kind of ethical confusion. Bill, the dean, other members of the faculty, the students, and Herb Lee jump to conclusions about Tom's sexual orientation because they are prep-school men. They have been trained to respect a certain type of "manliness" and to mistrust the "off-horses" who diverge from it. Thus, when they notice the ways in which Tom does not conform with the masculine ideal endorsed by 1950s boarding-school culture (he sings French ballads, prefers not to get a crew-cut, and so on), they assume that he must be gay. With the exception of Tom's roommate Al, not a single male character considers the possibility that Tom may be misunderstood. Why are his teachers and schoolmates so eager to judge and ostracize him? The answer, it seems, is that they are fearful. They know that they are being watched closely, too. They know that they are expected to measure up to the boarding-school masculine ideal, and that every failure, large or small, is going to be noticed. Laura, on the other hand, has been married to a boarding-school teacher for less than year, so her judgment is not influenced by the school's traditions and values. She has observed all sorts of men on and off of New England campuses and could not care less about boarding-school assumptions about what it takes to be "manly."

Laura's point of view enables her to see the other characters in the play very clearly. When David Harris is accused of having an affair with Tom, she is the only person on campus who seems to notice that the evidence against Harris is almost non-existent. When Bill insists that he wants to see Tom kicked out of school, Laura recognizes that the pariah reminds Bill of his own unhappiness when he was a lonely prep-school student. When Lilly Sears, the wife of another faculty member, claims that the pent-up male sexual energy at the school gives her "the willies" (5), Laura sees that Lilly enjoys playing the role of prep-school sex symbol. Lilly pretends to be annoyed by the attention she receives from students—"All the boys talk about me. They have me in and out of bed with every single master in the school" (8)—but Laura doesn't buy it. It is obvious to her that Lilly feels so deprived of the attention of men that she relishes the attention of boys. Most of all, Laura's impressions of Tom are infinitely more perceptive than those of the prep-school crowd. She understands right away that Tom is straight, but desperately lonely. His mother is alive, but he has not seen her in years. (Anderson does not go into detail about the end of the Lees' marriage, but the facts he does provide suggest that Herb was awarded full custody of Tom after he proved that his wife had been unfaithful.) Disappointed by his son's interests in singing, tennis, and other supposedly "unmanly" activities, Herb sends him away year-round to boarding schools and summer camps. Unlike everyone else who hears the story of Tom's "date" with Ellie Martin, moreover, Laura recognizes that sexual orientation had nothing to do with the incident. Tom did not go through with it because he was too sensitive, and too infatuated with Laura, to believe in "such a test" (179). In other words, Laura sees that the school's cloistered environment has caused Bill, Lilly, and other characters to lose touch with reality. She presents an insightful critique of boarding-school culture, but Anderson casts her as a modern-day Cassandra. Her conclusions are correct time and again, but no one except for Tom takes her conclusions seriously. To the contrary, she is told repeatedly that her judgment misses the mark because she does not know enough about prep schools and the young men who attend them.

Tea and Sympathy exposes the cruelty and stupidity of homophobia, to be sure, but its central message is that the culture of conformity at American boarding schools is mindless and destructive. Despite the long list of characters who preach the virtues of "manliness" in the play, the school community Anderson imagines is filled with cowardice. Bill Reynolds married Laura and labels Tom as an "off-horse" to deflect questions about his own sexuality. Tom's roommate Al, an athlete and a "regular guy," believes that Tom is straight, but when the going gets tough he does nothing to support his embattled roommate. Quite the opposite: when Tom asks Al why the other students are treating him so badly, Al replies (echoing Bill Reynolds's earlier remarks) that Tom should try not to stand and walk like a "fairy." Ralph and the rest of the students bully Tom because they want to demonstrate that they are members of the "manly" tribe that loathes "fairies." Anderson suggests, moreover, that the boarding-school masculine ideal is not all that impressive in the first place. Privileged teenagers who do well in their classes, dress in blazers, flannel pants, and penny loafers, and exude a certain low-key self-confidence are exceptionally "manly?" Try to explain that in a Marine Corps barracks or a fire house.

A Little Schoolboy Tempest

In the first chapter of John Knowles's *Peace Breaks Out*,[8] a World War II veteran named Pete Hallam joins the faculty at the Devon School. Hallam, a 1937 graduate of Devon, does not intend to make teaching his career. He returns to his old school because he wants to readjust to civilian life in a familiar, comfortable setting. Hallam suffered a great deal during the war. His youngest brother and three of his former Dartmouth hockey teammates were killed in action. Two men in his company had nervous breakdowns. He was wounded by shrapnel and held for several months as a prisoner of war in Italy. Then his wife filed for divorce while he was still overseas. Hallam rarely speaks about the war, in part because he is plagued by nightmares and flashbacks:

> These kids at school here now will never go through what we went through.... We are the last to have to pass though that. It will never happen again. It won't because it can't.
> Monte Cassino Abbey, one of the great sanctuaries of European culture, pulverized by American bombers as he watched ... dead children lying beside a road ... skeletal, haunted wraiths in the prison camp ... Corporal Bergland's head abruptly transformed into a kind of bloody mush [13–14].

Hallam comes back to Devon hoping that a year or two of teaching will improve his physical and mental health and help him to decide what he wants to do with the rest of his life. During his years in the army, the school was a "close-held memory of peacetime ... [that] stood in his infantryman's recollection as untainted and unthreatened and reassuring, a valued part of his past" (1). And when Hallam returns, the campus, the village of Devon, and the pastoral landscapes surrounding it are so serene that they seem artificial, like scenery on a stage. "Is that really the Chapel over there where I sat every morning for four years," he asks one of his former teachers, "or is it cardboard? Are the bells really still in that tower, and do they still ring? It's a little hard to believe somehow" (8).[9] The great irony of *Peace Breaks Out* is that Devon lets Pete Hallam down. Instead of providing an "untainted and unthreatened" setting for recuperation, the school turns out to be rife with suspicion and conflict. Life in the military was "a mess" (38), but its dangers were obvious and universally understood. The dangers of life at a boarding school, Hallam discovers, are far more subtle. To put it another way, the young veteran learns the lesson Richard Yates emphasizes in *A Good School*: private academies may appear to offer a refuge from "the real world," but for many students and teachers that is an illusion.

Why does Devon fail to provide the peace and quiet Hallam expected to find? Several characters in *Peace Breaks Out* argue that the students there are on edge because they "missed out" on the excitement and adventure of World War II. The day Hallam moves into his faculty apartment, one of his new colleagues, a Latin instructor named Roscoe Latch, tells him that the young men at Devon have changed significantly as a consequence of the war:

> You're going to find the students rather different from your day, you know.... Rather more serious, funnily enough, a bit "traumatized," in

the cant psychiatric word, by the war they have just missed becoming involved in. The world has been an amazing and stupefying and extremely dangerous place all through their adolescence and it has left its brand on them. They're not as happy-go-lucky as you boys were, Depression or no Depression. They're tougher, somehow.... I believe they feel that anything, anything at all, may possibly happen to them in their lives after all that. The sky's the limit, and so is hell [9].

Nick Blackburn, a student in Hallam's American history class, says that although he and his peers in the Class of 1946 did not serve in the armed forces, the war filled them with aggression, guilt, and fear that did not go away after Germany and Japan surrendered. "There was a violence lying around," he thinks, "like unexploded shells, hand grenades which anybody in a rage might blindly hurl, left over from the incredibly abrupt end of the war, just last August" (31). Later on, Nick tells his brother Tug that he envies the young Americans who served: "Now that the war's over I'm beginning to miss it.... I'm beginning to—well, we missed something, we missed it. The big drama of the century. We missed getting sent to some strange part of the world and doing some strange thing there, like being a frogman and swimming underwater into Tokyo Harbor and attaching a mine to a Jap battleship" (46–47). Wexford, the editor of the school newspaper and by far the most pretentious student at Devon, articulates a broader version of this theory. He argues that the United States as a whole has become troubled because, unlike so many other countries, it was not "cleansed" by the war's destructive power:

> Curious feeling ... missing the great drama *de nos jours* just by a hair, by being one year too young. I guess we'll always be sort of a new Lost Generation because of that.... What I'm talking about has been called "the dark night of the soul." Suffering. That's how people are purified. John the Baptist in the Desert. Christ in Gethsemane. The Jews during their Captivity. You see, it happens to whole people too, nations, not just individuals.... I'm saying something very simple ... the U.S. of A. is still full of poisons because we weren't defeated or occupied or even bombed in the war. So we've got all the crust of selfishness on us, we're greedy, hypocrites, *lechers*, because our vices didn't get bled and scraped and blasted away by the war [32, 33, 36].

Knowles also makes it clear that the students at Devon are emotionally volatile because they spend day after day cooped up on a boarding-school campus. Early in the novel, a young man insists that he and his peers know nothing about the national problems of the day because they are "[b]uried up here in the sticks" (30). During a ski trip, Nick Blackburn says that he dreads returning to Devon and its ultra-predictable routines: "[It] all starts again tomorrow, doesn't it? Physics. Latin. Chapel. Gym. Prune whip. Lights-out. Ugh" (52). For the "great headmasters" of the early twentieth century, this kind of schedule was nothing less than "the healthy and good way for a boy to live" (Kintrea 98). For Nick, it is drudgery that will continue, completely unchanged, until he graduates. The students at Devon are under pressure to move on to exclusive universities and prestigious careers. They live under the boarding-school code of judgment and conformity that Robert Anderson exposes in *Tea and Sympathy*. Above all, they are cut off from what David V. Hicks calls "the popular mainstream culture of adolescent America" (530). Early in *Peace Breaks Out*, the narrator explains just how tightly controlled daily life at Devon was in the late 1940s:

> [T]here were just two outlets for energy available to the students: study and sports. Out on the fringes were extracurricular activities and religion, but the two great avenues lying foursquare in the student's path were his books and his team. Students were forbidden to go to the movie house in town. They could listen to a radio only in [basement rooms in their dorms] and only for a short period. They could not leave this isolated New England village without special permission, they were of course not allowed to own any vehicle more sophisticated than a bicycle, any student caught using any alcoholic beverage was immediately expelled, and God only knew what would happen if any sexual experimentation was discovered.
>
> There were no rules at Devon, ran the standard conundrum explaining suitable behavior in the school, until they were broken [39].

The students in *Peace Breaks Out* respond to the school's inflexible routines by growing restless and looking for trouble. Their chronic sense of boredom and irritation seems normal at first, but it rises steadily until it produces hatred, persecution, scandal, and a case of involuntary manslaughter. (In this respect, *Peace Breaks Out* resembles Spike Lee's 1989 film *Do the Right Thing*, another work in which the anger of a large cast of characters continues to escalate until it boils over, resulting in the death of an abrasive young man.) The chain of

6. Isolation and Conflict

events leading to the tragedy at Devon can be traced back to Pete Hallam's first class meeting. Hallam begins the discussion in what he thinks is a harmless way: he asks the students to summarize their views of American history, from the colonial period to the present. Eric Hochschwender, a "rigid, blond, blue-eyed young man ... with a sharp-cut face and head and a disdainful manner" (15), replies that the United States has become rich and powerful even though it has always been a "mongrel country" populated to a large extent by "inferior" racial and ethnic groups:

> "American History is just the sum of what the American people make it, that's obvious to anyone. When you get a country like this, made up of the decayed remnants of the aborigines, and then add—"
>
> "You mean the American Indians," interrupted Pete, eying him.
>
> "That's right," replied Hochschwender condescendingly, as though it were possible that what he was saying might turn out to be over this teacher's head. "Do you want me to go on?" he inquired.
>
> "Go on."
>
> "Mix the decayed remnants of the aborigines with a lot of flotsam from England, religious fanatics here in New England, bankrupt aristocrats and indentured servants in the South, then add new floods of rejects from Europe, the dregs of inferior places like Ireland and Italy and the Slav countries, pour on a few million savages from Africa, and what do you expect? A mongrel country getting bigger and bigger and winning wars because the land they've got is so rich in resources that they can defeat superior countries" [18].

Everyone in the room is offended by this harangue. Hallam insists that he will not put up with "sniping" and "racial cracks" (19). "This is a school," he continues, "and all opinions can be expressed, but when they're *that* discredited they won't be allowed to stand" (19). Cotty Donaldson, the captain of Devon's football team, complains that "the description of this country we've just heard is a bunch of Fascist crap!" (19). Wexford attacks Hochschwender personally, asking if he cribbed his ideas from Hitler's *Mein Kampf*. Then Hochschwender strikes back, arguing that Wexford has ruined the school newspaper and ought to be "impeached": "People have been talking about all the freedom in this country, free press and all. But the paper here isn't just slanted and biased, it's plain stupid. It's an illiterate paper.... Isn't there some way an editor can be replaced? ... This is a democracy here, as everybody keeps insisting. Can't we have a plebiscite? Can't we vote on keeping Waxwork here or replacing him?" (20–21).

Hallam notices right away that the mutual hatred expressed by Hochschwender and Wexford goes beyond ordinary teenage rivalries. When Hochschwender speaks, the teacher observes, Wexford's face is "a study in contained—contained *something*—rage? vengefulness? mortification? scorn? Pete didn't like the look. This class was going to take some handling" (22). Hallam, a well-liked student-athlete during his own schooldays, knows exactly what is required to become popular at schools like Devon, and it is obvious to him that Hochschwender and Wexford do not have what it takes.[10] In a community that prefers a "pleasant, easy, laughing attitude" (15), these young men are unpleasant, confrontational, and humorless. In a community that prefers dignified, understated language, Hochshwender calls Irish-Americans "Micks" and "mackerel snappers" and Wexford calls Germans "Huns" and "Krauts." Moreover, the young men deviate from the boarding-school ideal because they are two of the least athletic young men at Devon. Hochschwender's heart was weakened by rheumatic fever when he was eleven years old, so his exercise is limited to gently rowing a scull on the Devon River. Wexford pretends to be a golfer, but he is hardly ever seen on the course. Instead, he tends to play a hole or two and then sneak away through the woods so he can spend the rest of the afternoon reading Gibbon, Proust, or Nietzsche and playing classical music on a baby grand piano. "Virtually alone among Devon boys," the narrator says, "Wexford was sallow—a lounge lizard, bookworm, pianist, smoker, palaverer, debater, away-from-school drinker, and rumor had it secret drinker at the school as well" (54).

Still angry about the conflict in Hallam's class, Wexford tells a group of schoolmates that Hochschwender is "a Nazi sympathizer" and "the worst menace to the Devon School, the Devon spirit" (40, 42). Hallam tells the young men to stop provoking each other, but his warning does not "stem the swelling animus between these two bright, articulate, and somehow precociously bitter students" (62). Because he got along well with his peers at Devon, Hallam is fascinated by the "almost incendiary" hostility between Hochschwender and Wexford:

> They hated each other. But also and simultaneously they seemed to hate something about themselves. There was a curious, fundamental

6. Isolation and Conflict

similarity between them which made their mutual aversion almost incendiary.

For a while Pete secretly found this enmity rather entertaining; he thought it made meetings of the class more stimulating; the atmosphere sometimes fairly crackled with animosity.... But a little further into the fall term he began to sense an intensity coming into their exchanges which sounded almost hysterical around the edges, something unhealthy and possibly uncontrollable.

He was going to have to do something about it [62–63].

Hallam mentions the conflict to the students' faculty advisors, but neither official seems to take his concerns seriously. Then Hallam decides that it is up to him to intervene and "defuse the situation" (63). He knows he is the most inexperienced faculty member at Devon, but after all, he tells himself, this is a dispute between two teenagers at a New England prep school. If he could endure shrapnel wounds and a POW camp, surely he can manage two arrogant kids. He summons Hochschwender and Wexford to his apartment in Pembroke House, gives them glasses of ginger ale, insists that their "gut-hatred" has gone too far, and urges them to "talk it out" (63–64). Hochschwender argues that he has been engaging in free speech, exercising one of the rights Hallam and his fellow veterans fought to defend. Then Wexford throws gasoline on the fire. He calls Hochschwender a traitor and a Nazi and insists that he has the right to oppose "nakedly Fascist viewpoints" (64) whenever and wherever he encounters them. Recognizing that he has failed to "bring off any truce or even barest mutual tolerance" (65), Hallam cuts the meeting short. He tells the students to be more civil to each other and says that they will be punished severely if their verbal clashes lead to a fistfight. Hallam feels slightly disappointed after the meeting, but at the same time he is amused by the young men's overreactions and his own inability to get the job done as a mediator. What he does not understand is that his failure to "defuse" the rivalry was a crucial missed opportunity. The conflict will soon become more than a string of insults: Wexford is going to orchestrate a witch hunt and Hochschwender is going to die.

Throughout the novel, Hallam's thinking is marked by an unresolved contradiction. On the one hand, his students' hot tempers suggest to him that "violence in people was ceaseless and eternal and everywhere" (103). On the other hand, as a war-scarred, divorced man in his late twenties, he finds it impossible to believe that the wrath of two teenagers is a serious matter. During Christmas vacation, for example, he muses that young men like Hochschwender and Wexford pretend to be self-confident, but in fact they are "babes in the woods ... self-ignorant and confused, at best very partial semi-adults, saying in effect: I'm completely sound and normal and a total human being and aware of everything about myself, while in reality they were most of them cross-eyed with confusion about themselves, insecure as a house on stilts in a hurricane, pretending manfully, or almost manfully, that they were not stumbling blindfolded into the pitfalls of their futures" (71–72).

Not long after the meeting with Hallam, Hochschwender sends a letter to the school newspaper in which he insists that mandatory attendance in Devon's chapel should be abolished. The letter is a ruse. Hochschwender has nothing against chapel services; his purpose is to expose Wexford and other students at Devon as hypocrites who claim to be patriotic while opposing civil liberties. "I wanted to smoke Wexford," Hochschwender tells his roommate, "and I've done it. *Now* you'll see intolerance, American style" (69). The plan succeeds at first. Wexford writes an editorial denouncing Hochschwender's letter as "'godless' and 'corrupting' and 'the thin edge of the wedge' and 'a vicious attempt to undermine the foundations of the school'" (69).[11] Then Hochschwender finds that some of his peers have expressed their "intolerance, American-style" by destroying his bicycle and scattering its parts around his dorm room. Hochschwender responds to these reprisals by intensifying his hateful rhetoric about the United States:

> In [Hallam's] class he exhibited to the hilt his arrogance, his amazing capacity for and apparent pleasure in offending everyone in sight. "Well of course the Civil War was just the North wanting to take over the South's markets. They didn't give a damn about the niggers." "Everybody knows that America was colonized by tramps and criminals, the scum of Europe." At least two members of the class had ancestors who had come over on the *Mayflower*. "The Nazis learned genocide from America, of course, what you did with your Indians." It was characteristic of him to refer to Americans as "you." Hochschwender's family had been in Wisconsin for several generations [72].

6. Isolation and Conflict

Hallam worries that the tensions in his history class have gone too far—"Could an obnoxious, phony, Hitlerian poseur ... be expelled, simply for being obnoxious? Could he be hounded out by the others? Was that to be permitted?"—but then he concludes, once again, that he is letting a "little schoolboy tempest grow all out of proportion in his imagination" (75).

In the spring semester, the teacher is relieved to discover that the most popular students at Devon have started to poke fun at Hochschwender, Wexford, and their feud:

> The Boys were turning the whole potentially explosive issue into a joke. Thank God a boy had a sense of humor. Without that, schools such as Devon would blow apart.... Pete Hallam concluded that there was nothing to worry about at the Devon School. It had survived the Articles of Confederation, Citizen Genet, the burning of the White House, the Know-Nothings, Fort Sumpter, Custer's Last Stand, the sinking of the Maine, Henry Ford, poison gas, Carry Nation, the New Deal, Hitler, and it was going to go on surviving [79, 81].

This proves to be wishful thinking. The beginning of the "tempest" at Devon is insignificant compared to the events to come. The endgame begins when Wexford suggests that his class should place a stained-glass memorial window behind the altar in the chapel to honor Devon's graduates who died in World War II. The school community is moved by this gesture, but Hallam worries that the window is based on a shallow, sentimental view of military service: "There was a lack of pain, and a void where monumental irritation ought to be. The very beauty of the window, totally at odds with the abject physical ugliness of military life, was a lie. This window depicted something graceful and exalted and clean and beautiful. It was as though a tornado were portrayed as lively, quicksand as sport" (116). After the window is unveiled, Wexford sneaks into the chapel late at night and smashes it, knowing that his schoolmates will assume that Hochschwender, the Nazi apologist who calls the United States a "mongrel" nation founded by "the scum of Europe," was the culprit.

The school community is stunned by this act of vandalism, but Hochschwender does not allow it to interfere with his routines. Instead, he takes his scull out on the Devon River and muses about what he regards as the unappreciated virtues of the Third Reich:

Well, there *were* certain favorable things to be said about Nazi Germany. Hitler had ended the Depression and the unemployment there, hadn't he? He'd built the superb system of *Autobahns*, the envy of the world. He'd made it possible for his country to lead the world in jet planes, rocketry. Eric had always been fascinated by scientific and engineering advances....

As for all the hatred of Hitler, tales of his persecution of the Jews and Gypsies and Poles and the Catholic Church and the Protestant churches, of sexual deviants and just about anybody who didn't suit him, well all that was just based on rumor. The newsreels of the piled bodies in concentration camps? Faked [152, 153].

Enjoying a beautiful spring afternoon, the Holocaust denier congratulates himself for bringing freedom of speech to an old-fashioned school in a "rural backwater" (153). He thinks of the students at Devon, except for himself and Wexford, as "little everyday conformists" (153). He rows past a tree that leans out over the river and recalls, in *Peace Breaks Out*'s only direct reference to Knowles's previous school novel, that it was the place where "that legendary Devon athlete had been injured a couple of summers ago, and had later died" (154).

Hochschwender's daydream ends when Cotty Donaldson, the varsity football captain, and three other athletes from Pembroke House approach in two canoes and demand to speak with him. Hochschwender refuses, and they threaten to beat him with one of his oars. They accuse him of smashing the memorial window and pressure him to confess. Then they shove his head underwater until he turns "bluish-white" and faints (157). The accusers carry Hochschwender to Devon's infirmary, but it is too late. He briefly regains consciousness, but then Dr. Stanpole announces that he is dead: "'His heart just wasn't strong enough. We couldn't quite make it. Tried. Just couldn't quite make it.' He let out a long breath. 'How sudden a death can be, a light going out'" (163–64). Hallam suspects that Wexford deliberately provoked the crisis by destroying the memorial window and does not believe Donaldson and his friends when they claim that they found Hochschwender unconscious in his scull, but he finds little evidence to support his suspicions. The perpetrators get away with everything. In fact, at Commencement Donaldson gives a speech about "service to others" and Wexford is given a special award "for organizing the unique and imaginative tribute to the young men Devon gave to the war" (190).

6. Isolation and Conflict

In some respects, *Peace Breaks Out* echoes *Tea and Sympathy*. Hochschwender and Wexford are arrogant and obnoxious, to be sure, but Knowles's deeper point is that there is something dysfunctional about American boarding-school culture. The community at Devon could have discouraged the antagonism between the two young men, but instead it allowed their feud to escalate until became uncontrollable. Throughout the novel, characters at Devon choose sides and try to take part in the conflict. When Hochschwender spouts "incendiary" political rhetoric, his peers attack him personally instead of taking issue with his arguments. When Hochschwender submits his letter to the *Devonian*, the community could have ignored his intentionally misleading pose as a dissident far too sophisticated to sit through chapel services. Instead, it turns his letter into a cause célèbre. As the narrator explains, "[The] letter by itself might have caused a flurry and been forgotten. But combined with [Wexford's] inciting editorial and others following it up, and a brace of offensive, arrogant letters from Hochschwender, the flame was whipped into a conflagration, faculty and alumni began to be sucked in, and the school seemed suddenly to be stumbling toward a major conflict" (69). Hochschwender and Wexford were the initial combatants, that is to say, but their battle progressed from "flurry" to "conflagration" because they were joined by schoolmates, teachers, and graduates. Hallam appears to be the only person at Devon who recognizes that the controversy is potentially dangerous. He notices that it has permeated the school, "seeping like escaping gas along the corridors, insinuating itself into … classrooms, drifting over faculty dinners" (75), but, as we have seen, he ultimately finds the conflict too trivial to hold his attention.

Throughout *Peace Breaks Out*, Knowles's characters seem far more frightened and restless than the denizens of a New England prep school campus ought to be. The students grumble repeatedly that they were unfortunate to "miss out" on a war that left more than fifty million dead. The faculty, meanwhile, seem intimidated by the students under their supervision and do everything they can to avoid them. The narrator observes, for example, that in the dining hall "the Masters and their wives and children [sat] at circular tables in the four corners, isolating themselves as much as possible from this horde of teenage boys filling the rest of the room" (29). Similarly, the reader learns that in Devon's dormitories the masters "inhabited ground-floor apartments and maintained a simmering truce with the students" (44). This is not what the "great headmasters" had in mind. The traditions of New England boarding-school education hold that students are supposed to devote every hour of every day to working hard and playing hard. In *Peace Breaks Out*, they spend countless hours following the Hochschwender/Wexford dispute as if it were a precursor of reality television. Prep-school tradition also holds that students must be kept under twenty-four hour adult supervision. In *Peace Breaks Out*, the adults on campus keep their distance from the "horde of teenage boys" whenever possible.

At Devon, Hochschwender and Wexford are regarded as firebrands, but that turns out to be a misconception. It would be more accurate to say that they resemble Jules Griscam in Louis Auchincloss's *The Rector of Justin* (1964): privileged young men posing as fearless rebels. They are considered dangerous only because they are slightly more dangerous than their polite, soft-spoken peers. As Knowles suggests throughout *Peace Breaks Out*, Hochschwender is not a genuine American Nazi; he is an earnest schoolboy who happens to be insufferable when he talks about history and politics. Like countless adolescents in Knowles's time and our own, he seems to be repeating dogma he learned at home to anyone who will listen. And like Radio Raheem, the character choked to death by a police officer in *Do the Right Thing*, Hochschwender is a loud, deliberately unpleasant young man who deserves to be shunned or told to keep his bitterness to himself, not to be assaulted with deadly force.

Wexford is also misunderstood by the community at Devon. He is not a boarding-school Machiavelli; he is simply an arrogant teenager with a knack for stirring up controversy. Early in the novel, Knowles stresses that Wexford has an extremely high opinion of himself. Near the end of a long interior monologue, the high-school newspaper editor fantasizes about a glorious future in which he will rise above the mediocre souls in his family and at his school:

> Just as he was probably the most notable member of this class at Devon, and perhaps in the whole student body—notable in the literal sense of the word: someone who was always noted, noticed—so he would be in the great world beyond it later.

6. Isolation and Conflict

> I'm going to be famous, Wexford decided, sitting by the fire opposite Father. There's no doubt about it.
>
> For some reason, the family characteristics were not his characteristics, his strengths, not at all. They were serene and leisurely and secure. He was driven. His own private sense of insecurity and urgency would make him famous, influential. He *had* to be superior, show it, prove it, shove it down other people's throats. He could not brook people who acted as though they were his equals. He did not have friends, he had followers [60–61].

When Wexford is not causing trouble at Devon, however, he shows no ability to live up to his delusions of grandeur. At his parents' vacation home on Cape Cod, he sits quietly while his father holds forth about education, journalism, politics, and money. In this episode, Wexford does not seem "notable" or "superior" at all. Quite the opposite: he hardly gets a word in, and when he does his father points out all of his mistakes and limitations.

Wexford seems even more overmatched during a weekend trip to Boston. On a Saturday night, he sits alone at a bar, sipping Scotch and enjoying "the special pleasure of sitting back silently to contemplate the follies of those around him" (78). Wexford's sense of superiority falls to pieces, however, when he is propositioned by Jenny and Brian, a young married couple. "'You want to come over?' Jenny asks. 'Come on. We can talk about it all there ... talk about it ... or,' a quick grin, 'whatever else we want to do ... all three of us ... or you and me ... or,' she finished airily, 'you and him.'" (86). Wexford, the would-be sophisticate who tells himself that he collects "followers" instead of friends, is stunned by Jenny's directness and utter lack of embarrassment. He mutters that he is waiting to meet a date. He gets up to leave and thanks Jenny for the invitation, "writh[ing] inwardly on hearing these idiotic words" (86). Then he rushes through the crowd and out of the bar, humiliated by the offer and the way Jenny stared at him while he ran away:

> What did they *mean* by coming up to him like that! What did they take him for, some kind of male prostitute?
>
> A woman full of sexual aggression and her fairy husband, two utter strangers, try to drag him back to their apartment for some kind, or all kinds, of sex. He was shaking, he was enraged to find; it was all an uncontrollable—something, an uncontrollable challenge. *He* was supposed to

issue the challenges.... He was not ready for them or it or any variation or combination of possibilities like that, not here and not yet and not now and maybe never; it was mortifying and sickeningly exciting and an abasement and it shook his hold on himself [87].

The next day, Wexford decides to pretend that this "abasement" never happened, but once again his high opinion of himself is shaken. At a blue-collar lounge, he is joined by a group of young veterans. "[They] came noisily through the entrance," the narrator explains, "wearing Army pants and pea coats and other remnants of service uniforms. They bellied up to the bar next to Wexford and ordered beers. All were wearing the 'Ruptured Duck' discharge insignia. Here were the national heroes and celebrities of 1946, veterans" (88). One of the men assumes that Wexford is another former serviceman and asks why he isn't wearing his discharge pin. Too embarrassed to admit that he is a schoolboy on vacation, Wexford claims that he forgot to put on his pin that morning. The veterans recognize that Wexford is lying, and they are not amused. "Look," one of them says, "I don't give a damn if you were 4-F or a sex pervert or what, but I do care when some punk goes around impersonating a veteran" (89). Then the veterans grab him by the collar and toss him out on the sidewalk. The reader might expect Wexford to be humbled after this incident, but instead he dreams about getting a gun or throwing a Molotov cocktail into the bar. His narcissism, in other words, is so extreme that he seems incapable of learning from his mistakes. "Someday, some year, sometime," he thinks, "I will be able to retaliate and win. There won't be any humiliation, no, nor any challenges either, no one someday will want to challenge me. Not me. I'd rather be dead than ground down by goons like that. I've got pride. I deserve to have it and I've got it: pride" (90-91). Wexford's misadventures in Boston seem disconnected from the rest of *Peace Breaks Out* at first, but in fact they play an important role in Knowles's plot. They prove beyond all doubt that the school community takes Wexford too seriously. He may seem to be an "incipient monster" (193) at Devon, but the reader knows that he is a deeply confused teenager who does not frighten anyone outside the boundaries of his school.

In J. D. Salinger's *The Catcher in the Rye* (1951), the headmaster of Pencey Prep tells Holden Caulfield that life is a "game" that must be played "according to the rules" (12). Holden listens patiently, but he feels certain that Dr. Thurmer is wrong. "Some game," he thinks. "If you get on the side where all the hot-shots are, then it's a game, all right—I'll admit that. But what if you get on the *other* side, where there aren't any hot-shots, then what's a game about it?" (12). *Tea and Sympathy* and *Peace Breaks Out* are, among other things, responses to Holden's question. In both works, students who find themselves on the "other side" at Northeastern prep schools are severely mistreated. Young men like Tom Lee and Eric Hochschwender are required to fit in with the popular boys, or else. If they cannot shed their reputations as "off-horses," they will have nowhere to hide from their enemies. (The key distinction between the two characters, of course, is that Hochschwender deliberately encourages the community at Devon to think of him as a Nazi sympathizer, while Tom Lee is bullied simply because he is misunderstood.) At private academies, Anderson and Knowles insist, isolation breeds conformity and conformity breeds suspicion of outsiders. The criminal defense lawyer Edward Bennett Williams often said that Washington's political culture burns a witch every three months, and that to succeed there it is important not to be the witch. Robert Anderson and John Knowles suggest that this warning also applies to boarding schools. The "witches" are identified early in *Tea and Sympathy* and *Peace Breaks Out*, and their persecution continues until one is on the verge of suicide and the other is dead.

Conclusion:
An Indestructible Myth

In *A Good Life* (1995), Ben Bradlee writes with gratitude about his education at St. Mark's School:

> I played varsity football and hockey, without getting my letter, but in baseball I was the starting first baseman for the team that beat Groton. My mother and grandmother had cried noisily a few weeks earlier when I hit a home run and thundered around the bases like a freight train. [A classmate] and I were the school doubles champions in tennis. My marks stayed up, and I ended up as a class monitor and editor-designate of the school yearbook.... I was the original round peg waiting for the round hole—programmed to do well at schools like St. Mark's [38, 39].[1]

Bradlee marveled at his old school's ability to turn "good students and good athletes into better students and better athletes" (35). He admired an English teacher who smuggled banned books through Customs for his students. And he enjoyed getting to know schoolmates like Blair Clark, who went on to become vice president of CBS News, and a student known as "Cal," who went on to become the poet Robert Lowell. In short, Bradlee's schooldays were pleasant and rewarding. He was lucky to spend several years as "an insider" (35) at St. Mark's and he knew it.[2]

Ben Bradlee, that is to say, tells a story about boarding school that American novelists and short story writers in the 1950s, '60s, and '70s refused to tell. If our knowledge of prep-school life were drawn entirely from the works I've discussed, we would find it hard to believe that "round pegs" existed at Northeastern prep schools in the middle decades of the twentieth century. The writers featured in this book use a wide range of plots and characters, but their representations of private academies have one thing in common. They all suggest that F. Scott Fitzgerald had it right in his short story "The Freshest Boy": life is "always difficult" (74), even if you spend your adolescence on a stately boarding-school campus. With the exception of *The Rector of Justin*, every novel examined here echoes "The Freshest Boy" by focusing on angst-ridden preppies and the "certain delicacies of torture" (65) they endured at school. These works pay scant attention to money, sports, education, and other subjects that come to mind when we hear the term "boarding school." Instead, they chronicle various forms of distress suffered by teenagers who leave home to attend private academies.

Why do these narratives harp on the troubles of young men who seem to be highly privileged? One possible explanation is that most of them are at least partly autobiographical. By all accounts, J. D. Salinger was a misfit at Valley Forge Military Academy. A former classmate recalls that Salinger's conversation was "frequently laced with sarcasm about others and the silly routines we had to obey and follow at school. Both of us hated the military regime and often wondered why we didn't leave the school" (Hamilton 23). Louis Auchincloss was unhappy throughout the six years he spent at Groton, and his posthumous memoir *A Voice from Old New York* (2010) reveals that his schooldays were even more traumatic than he let on during his lifetime. In particular, he recalls that he was a "social leper" at school and was "even subject to a sexual violation that would have created a major scandal today" (63). Auchincloss insists, however, that it would be unfair to hold officials at Groton responsible: "I must emphasize that every person in the administration of that school would have been horrified had they known what was going on. They were helpless then just as their counterparts are these days. Boys cannot be shielded from one another" (63–64). James Kirkwood attended Brewster Academy, where, readers of *Good Times/Bad Times* will not be surprised to learn, he mourned the death of a schoolmate and did not get along with the headmaster. The real-life model for Franklyn Hoyt was Brewster's headmaster, Walter G. Greenall, Jr. Brewster alumni have often described Greenall as stuffy and aloof, but Kirkwood seems to have truly despised him. As Sean Egan explains, the author recalled many years after he left Brewster that "[t]he headmaster was rather sadistic. He was also a latent homosexual. He took a shine to me and we had a very unhealthy time of it for a while. I was terrified of him and I disliked him intensely" (53). William Grove's campus ordeal in *A Good School*, moreover, is based on Richard Yates's experiences as one of the most unpopular boys at Avon Old Farms School in the early 1940s. Blake Bailey reports that "Yates's first year at prep school 'was almost unalloyed in its misery.' Apart from being poor, unathletic, untidy, and immature in every respect, Yates had to endure ... the sort of everyday hazing that, however silly and unfounded, the victim never quite forgets" (*A Tragic Honesty* 49). The pattern could hardly be clearer: all of these writers suffered at the private academies they attended, so their novels challenge the notion that boarding-school students are privileged and fortunate.

It's also possible that American school fiction grew darker and more turbulent in the decades following World War II for literary reasons. From Salinger to Yates, the writers I have discussed seem to have assumed that modern fiction required unfamiliar characters, themes, and emotional atmospheres. Readers remained curious about prep schools, but by the middle of the twentieth century they had lost interest in comic tales about athletic rivals and schemes to get even with campus bullies. The postwar generation of American novelists came of age admiring Faulkner, Hemingway, and other standard-bearers of modernism. Accordingly, they stayed clear of the formulaic approaches which had dominated British and American boarding-school fiction before "The Freshest Boy." I have not come across a single "retro" school novelist who has published a present-day counterpart of *The Lawrenceville Stories* and other lighthearted school narratives of the early twentieth century. Even John Knowles, who thoroughly enjoyed the years he spent at Phillips Exeter Academy, appears to have believed that a novel about a young man who enrolls at an exclusive prep school and proceeds to earn excellent grades and thrive as a varsity athlete would have struck his contemporaries as hopelessly old-fashioned and cloying. In his essay "The Art of Fiction," Henry James asserts that "[t]he only obligation to which in advance we may hold a novel, without incurring the accusation of being arbitrary, is that it be interesting" (170). The novelists discussed here patently did not believe that readers would be interested in nostalgic, uplifting tales about privileged adolescents. As Ben Bradlee's former schoolmate Robert Lowell observed in 1965, "I have a feeling that the arts are in a very funny position now—that we are free to say what we want to, and somehow what we want to say [has to do with] the confusion and sadness and incoherence of the human condition" (qtd. in Berthoff 15).

It seems to me that Salinger, Knowles, Auchincloss, Kirkwood, and Yates highlighted the troubles of ostensibly fortunate students mainly because they wanted to document the realities of prep-school life. Taken together, their novels suggest that most Americans have the wrong idea about private academies. The prep-school myth tells us that these institutions are extraordinarily posh, but few observers today seem to know that Andover, Groton, et al. were originally meant to be harsh environments. In the late nineteenth century, American boarding schools had a good deal in common with boot camps. They were marked by strict discipline, long winters, Spartan dormitories, and violent sports. As David V. Hicks explains, their raison d'etre was to toughen up young men accustomed to high levels of privilege and luxury:

> At Groton and other schools the students were provided with a considerable amount of corrective salutary deprivation. At St. Paul's and Groton the boys roomed in barren little cubicles, and if they were ever indulged in anything as sybaritic as a warm shower, the fact has gone unrecorded. Historically, one did not send one's son to a school like Groton to secure his place in society. That place was already secure. One sent a boy to Groton to save him from the selfishness and softness of his secure place [528].

Preparatory schools began the process of "preparing" students for higher education and future careers, Christopher Brookeman explains, by separating them from the comfort and security of their homes:

> The evolution of single-sex boarding schools like St. Mark's and Choate ... had a specific function.... In its purest form this kind of school was created in the nineteenth century to educate, socialize, and monitor the male offspring of the professional and business classes. As modern society developed its diverse industrial and administrative systems, such institutions as the church, the ancient universities, and the family began to cede power and responsibility for educating and controlling children to others. Throughout the nineteenth and twentieth centuries, the dominant role of the family has been steadily supplanted, though not entirely

replaced, by a whole range of institutions such as the school, the college, the firm, and the state bureaucracies. These institutions became places where the young future professionals of the middle and upper classes experienced an extended period of training and socialization [59].

Moreover, boarding schools were regarded as a means of giving a sense of responsibility to wealthy young men. "In the eighteen eighties and nineties, the education of the rich boy was considered to be a particularly grave problem. 'Inherited wealth,' said Charles W. Eliot, president of Harvard, 'is an unmitigated curse when divorced from culture.' Conscientious parents, of old and new wealth alike, were eager to believe that large doses of 'muscular Christianity,' sternly administered by Endicott Peabody at Groton, were the magic cure for juvenile indolence and indifference" (Kintrea 100).

More than any other American writer, Auchincloss understood the origins of the nation's boarding-school culture. As a child, he had expected to suffer at Groton, and the school met his expectations. In fact, in a letter to his mother written ten years after he graduated, Auchincloss confessed that his schoolboy angst once became so overwhelming that he poisoned himself to avoid returning to Groton at the beginning of a new semester: "I never turned much over to you because I felt that Groton was something that one *had* to get through, that it was part of the cruel fabric of life.... And when I one time broke down and drank mercurochrome ... to make myself sick so I wouldn't have to go back and you saw red on my tongue, I told you I had been sucking on my tie.... I could never admit the shame of what seemed the equivalent of suicide" (qtd. in Gelderman 47). Auchincloss persevered, however, because he considered boarding school an indispensable rite of passage: "I knew that such things had to be. If one had to endure homesickness and hazing and snowballs, if one had to take ice-cold showers and play rough sports, it was part of the indoctrination required of my sex. Left at home with Mother in a woman's world of cushions and caresses, one would turn into a sissy, and that was to be damned" (*A Writer's Capital* 36).

Several Presidents and other American political leaders attended New England boarding schools, but most of them were unhappy during their schooldays. Franklin D. Roosevelt was unusually lighthearted during his adolescence, but even he found it hard to convince his parents that he was "getting on very well" at Groton. Part of the problem was that he was so accustomed to being popular and carefree: "It had been the natural order of his childhood world that he be liked by everyone, and he worked almost desperately to replicate that world at Groton. His inevitable failure to do so confused and frustrated him. 'I always felt entirely out of things,' he admitted to one close friend many years later, and to his wife he would confess that something had gone 'sadly wrong' at Groton" (Ward 180). Like Auchincloss, Roosevelt was mocked and bullied by schoolmates. During his first year, for instance, "a group of older boys ... trapped him in a corner of the corridor and ordered him to dance, jabbing hard at his ankles with hockey sticks to make sure he stepped fast enough. [He] did better than that. Refusing ever to seem a victim, even to himself, he pirouetted and toe-danced in apparent high spirits as if he were part of the fun instead of its object" (182).[3]

John F. Kennedy disliked both of the private academies he attended. During the year he spent at Canterbury School, Kennedy (then 13 years old) earned mediocre grades and grumbled in letters to friends and relatives that there was little to enjoy in his new surroundings:

> Although attending a boarding school marked Jack as a privileged child, he did not appreciate being sent so far away from home.... He was "pretty homesick the first night" and at other times thereafter. The football team looked "pretty bad." Worse, "you have a whole lot of religion and the studies are pretty hard. The only time you can get out of here is to see the Harvard-Yale and the Army-Yale [football games]. This place is freezing at night and pretty cold in the daytime" [Dallek 30].

Kennedy transferred to Choate School the following year, but he struggled there, too.[4] In the fall of 1934, he became so sickly that his doctors feared he was dying of leukemia. Throughout the years Kennedy spent at Choate, he felt overshadowed by his brother Joseph P. Kennedy, Jr.: "When his brother won the school's coveted Harvard Trophy at his graduation in 1933, an award to the student who best combined scholarship and sportsmanship, it confirmed in Jack the feeling that he could never win the degree of approval his parents—and, it seemed, everyone else—lavished on his elder brother" (36). And when Kennedy and several classmates started a "Muckers Club" based on finding new ways to "buck the system more effectively" (Goodwin 486),[5] George St. John, the headmaster, publicly reprimanded them: "Although the [club] represented no more than a small rebellion on Jack's part, in the cloistered atmosphere of a rural private school, where such defiance took on a larger meaning, St. John responded angrily. He 'let loose' at the thirteen club members in chapel, naming names and denouncing their corruption of the school's morals and integrity" (Dallek 39).

In *True Compass* (2009), Edward M. Kennedy tells a number of stories about fear and anguish at boarding school. In 1941, Rose Kennedy decided to send Teddy to Portsmouth Priory, a Catholic school run by Benedictine monks, mainly because she wanted him to attend the same school as his brother Robert.[6] That decision was a "recipe for disaster," Kennedy recalls, because he was only nine years old and Portsmouth Priory "started with the seventh grade; it had no elementary school":

> "No problem," said Mother. Bobby, a fourteen-year-old eighth grader, would be there to look after me, and after all, she was planning to keep me at Priory just until the end of the school year. Unfortunately, "just until the end of the school year," even if it's just two or three months, can be a very long time [61].

Not long after Kennedy arrived, some of his schoolmates "proved as cruel as only children can be." When Kennedy's pet turtle died, he gave the creature "my own nine-year-old version of a funeral" (62). That night, several older students dug up the turtle's carcass, played catch with it in the hall outside of Kennedy's room, and placed it under his blanket while he was sleeping. A few days later, he was horrified to learn that his dorm master coerced students to play a "game" that required them to strip for "inspection" and was notorious for taking "a private interest" in certain boys:

> I could not believe this was happening. There were whispers that [the dorm master] ... took a private interest in some boys and would send [two upper-classmen] to round them up. I spent many terror-filled nights under my bunk, hiding lest I too become one of those victims. I kept telling myself that this would pass. That I would get through this nightmare. That my brothers had survived boarding school and I would too. *It's going to be okay*, I told myself. I had to believe that.... The dorm master was eventually caught and fired. But his activities were all hushed up; nothing was ever said to the parents [63–64].

Conclusion

Even George W. Bush, the scion of a family that has been associated with exclusive prep schools for generations, describes his secondary education as an unpleasant experience. In *A Charge to Keep* (1999), Bush recalls that in his early teens he was a happy, energetic public school student and Little League baseball player in Texas. Then, after he turned 15, his parents arranged for him to transfer to his father's old school, Phillips Academy Andover. At first, Bush writes, Andover seemed "cold and distant." He missed his family and friends and received some extremely low grades. (One exam was returned "with a 'zero' marked so emphatically that it left an impression visible all the way through to the back of the blue book" [20].) The school's inflexible rules were "a shock to [his] system" and the Massachusetts winters were "long, bitterly cold, and confining" (21). Bush does what he can to describe his boarding-school education as beneficial in retrospect ("One of the most valuable lessons of Andover was what I learned about myself. I could … make my way, no matter where I found myself" [22]), but the unmistakable message of his recollections is that he was forced to make the best of a difficult situation.

The political implications of the works discussed in this book are hard to discern. On the one hand, these prep-school narratives often seem left-leaning because they suggest that there is something specious about the Eastern old-money establishment. These elites pose as American Brahmins and yet they are plagued by insecurity and angst. On the other hand, it could be argued that mid–twentieth-century prep-school literature is conservative because it suggests that low- and middle-income Americans should not monopolize our sympathy. One of its central messages is that elites struggle and suffer, too. As John Cheever's stories illustrate repeatedly, the world of affluent suburbs, country clubs, and preparatory schools should not be mistaken for Shangri-la. It may *seem* idyllic, but only when viewed from a distance by outsiders. The human predicament is the human predicament, Cheever insists, and it cannot be swept aside by money and prestige. Both arguments have merit, but ultimately political messages are beside the point because these works portray boarding school as a sphere in which partisan views are rarely mentioned. It may seem odd to label works that highlight class and gender issues as politically neutral, but how else can we label novels and short stories set in the 1940s, '50s, and '60s that are virtually silent about the Cold War, civil rights, and women's rights?

A Good School marks the end of an era in American boarding-school fiction. After Yates published his bittersweet novel, writers of school literature started to avoid plots centering on adolescent angst as carefully as their forerunners from the 1950s through the mid-1970s had avoided plots centering on athletic rivalries. This shift began with John Irving's *The World According to Garp* (1978). *Garp* presents, among other things, a baby boomer's rejection of the histrionics which had pervaded the American school literature published when he was young. Chapters 2-4 of *Garp*, the section of the novel set at "the vast and famous Steering School" (33), amount to a novella wedged into a longer narrative about T. S. Garp, a novelist, and his mother Jenny Fields, a nurse who becomes a leader of the women's rights movement. Throughout the Steering chapters, Irving (a graduate of Exeter) refuses to treat prep-school life as though it were a big deal. Steering is the secondary school Garp happened to attend, nothing more. Instead of imagining some sort of campus ordeal, Irving loads the chapters with eccentric characters and comic vignettes. When she is not caring for sick and injured students, Nurse Fields reads avidly and baffles the school community by keeping her thoughts about the books she has studied to herself:

> [T]he book someone wanted was always discovered to be checked out to Nurse Fields. Phone calls were politely answered; Jenny frequently offered to deliver the book directly to the party who wanted it, as soon as she finished it. She finished such books promptly, but she had nothing to say about them. In a school community, someone who reads a book for some secretive purpose, other than discussing it, is strange.... Her books spilled out of the tiny wing apartment in the infirmary annex. She spent ten years at [Steering] before discovering that the bookstore offered a ten percent discount to the faculty and staff (which the bookstore had never offered her). This made her angry. She was generous with her books, too—eventually shelving them in every room of the bleak infirmary annex [37].

Instead of a tragically injured Finny, Irving presents Hathaway, a bland, athletic teenager laid up with two leg injuries, one of which he suffered while falling down Irving's version of the marble stairs in Exeter's Academy Building: "Hathaway was a lacrosse player who had done ligament damage to his knee; two days after they put him in a cast and turned him loose on crutches, Hathaway had gone out in the rain and his crutch tips had slipped at the top of the long marble stairway of Hyle Hall. In the fall, he had broken his other leg. Now Hathaway, with both his long legs in casts, sprawled in the bed on the fourth floor of the infirmary annex, a lacrosse stick held fondly in his large-knuckled hands" (41). This is surely not a coincidence. Like Finny in Knowles's *A Separate Peace,* Hathaway suffers two injuries, and like Finny he falls down those white marble stairs. In *Garp,* however, the young man's injuries are mishaps, not occasions to ponder the thin line between friendship and rivalry or the psychological impact a war fought overseas can have on young civilians. Meckler, a "sarcastically brilliant" 16-year-old (43), alternates between writing dazzling term papers and getting away with practical jokes involving, among other things, a condom filled with egg whites and a pot of tea flavored with polliwogs. And Dean Bodger offers these words of advice after five-year-old Garp hurts himself while trying to catch pigeons on a rooftop:

> "Do you like living here?" Bodger asked him....
> "Yes, sir," Garp said.
> "Well, if you *ever* go out on that fire escape, or anywhere near that roof again," Bodger said, "you won't be *allowed* to live here anymore. Do you understand?"
> "Yes, sir," Garp said.
> "Then be a good boy for your mother," Bodger told him, "or you'll have to move to some place strange and far away" [49, 50].

In a novel by Yates or Kirkwood, or a film like *Dead Poets Society*, this exchange undoubtedly would have underscored the pomposity and insensitivity of prep-school authorities. In *Garp,* it is one of several episodes in which Bodger proves an ineffectual dunce. He does not mean to scare little Garp; he is simply too slow-witted to think of a better way to prevent similar accidents in the future.

Garp's schooldays are so ordinary that they stand apart from those of almost every other major character in American school fiction. He earns above-average grades, largely because his mother has audited virtually every course offered at Steering and guides him toward the most engaging subjects and teachers. He joins the varsity wresting team and takes a few steps toward a future career as a novelist. He falls in love with one young woman and loses his virginity with another. A key message of the Steering School chapters, then, is that there is nothing inherently melodramatic about boarding school. As Irving's plot progresses, the reader finds that for Jenny Fields and her son, Steering was a preamble. The most important events in their lives (Fields's career as an activist and Garp's experiences as a husband, father, and writer) take place after they leave the school. *Garp*'s depictions of boarding-school culture are not as lighthearted as those in *The Lawrenceville Stories* and other early school narratives, but unlike Salinger, Knowles, et al. Irving focuses on sports, schoolboy pranks, bumbling teachers, and other topics that figured prominently in British and American school literature published before the 1920s.

Like *The World According to Garp*, most American boarding-school novels published since the late 1970s have paid little attention to the sorrows of privileged teenagers. Richard Hawley's *The Headmaster's Papers* (1983) recounts an unhappy year in the life of a school administrator. Tobias Wolff's *Old School* (2003) brings academics to the fore by examining the literary ambitions of students at a private academy in the early 1960s. Curtis Sittenfeld's *Prep* (2006) stresses the impact of class distinctions on contemporary boarding schools. And in Anita Shreve's *Testimony* (2008), a town in Vermont is shaken by a scandal involving a small group of students and the headmaster's misguided efforts to cover it up. In one respect, however, the authors of these novels echo the school novelists of the fifties, sixties, and seventies. Each of them views the prep-school myth in a deeply skeptical way. Like their forerunners from Salinger to Yates, they imply that exclusive private academies are not all they are cracked up to be.

In spite of these writers' attempts to demythologize Northeastern private academies, the prep-school myth is alive and well. Tales highlighting the glamour and prestige of exclusive private schools are a staple of contemporary young-adult fiction. In fact, the television series *Gossip Girl* is based on a series of novels by Cecily von Ziegesar, a graduate of the Nightengale-Bamford School. Pete Campbell, an advertising executive featured on *Mad Men*, frequently mentions that he attended Deerfield Academy. In *The Social Network* (2010), Jesse Eisenberg wears a Phillips Exeter Academy sweatshirt while performing as Mark Zuckerberg, the co-founder of Facebook. (Zuckerberg graduated from Exeter in 2002.) And in a recent article in *Rolling Stone*, Ezra Koenig, the lead singer in the indie rock band Vampire Weekend, recalls that when he was in college he wrote a short story set at a private academy in New England. "'At the time,' Koenig explains, 'I was really obsessed with boarding school as a concept. It seemed so ... fantastical.' When a classmate asked Koenig if he had attended that kind of school, he thought, 'Oh, right! People actually go to boarding school! It's not like Narnia!'" (Eels 50).[7] Why did Koenig consider private academies as "fantastical" as C. S. Lewis's magic kingdom? The answer, I suspect, is that his "obsession" sprang from some of the narratives discussed in this book. The creators of these narratives set out to associate prep schools with cruelty, bigotry, snobbery, and suffering, yet their critiques seem to have left the prep-school myth essentially intact.[8] Clearly, it is going to take more than a few unflattering fictional portraits of boarding-school culture to do away with the glamorous aura that captivated Fitzgerald's Basil Lee and continues to attract millions of readers and viewers today.

Chapter Notes

Introduction

1. "The Freshest Boy," one of the nine "Basil stories" Fitzgerald wrote between 1928 and 1932, is based on the author's first year at the Newman School in Hackensack, New Jersey. As Matthew J. Bruccoli explains, "Scott arrived at Newman ... and promptly established himself as the most unpopular boy at school. He was bossy and boastful; he irritated the teachers and students.... He was rebuffed when he tried to join groups of boys and criticized when he kept to himself" (*Some Sort of Epic Grandeur* 32). Fitzgerald's first fictionalized memories of his unhappy debut at school appear in *This Side of Paradise* (1920): "He went all wrong at the start, was generally considered both conceited and arrogant, and universally detested.... He was resentful against all those in authority over him, and this, combined with a lazy indifference toward his work, exasperated every master in school. He grew discouraged and imagined himself a pariah.... Miserable, confined to bounds, unpopular with both faculty and students—that was Amory's first term" (27, 28).

2. Ted Coy, the son of the Hotchkiss School's headmaster, is said to have popularized "the new tactic of running down opposing tacklers instead of dodging them" (Kolowrat 85). Several years earlier, Fitzgerald mentioned Coy in *This Side of Paradise*. When Amory Blaine plays well in a prep-school football game, the narrator reports that "[f]or those minutes courage flowed like wine out of the November dusk, and he was the eternal hero, one with the sea-rover on the prow of a Norse galley, one with Roland and Horatius, Sir Nigel and Ted Coy..." (31–32). In "The Bowl," a story published a few months before "The Freshest Boy," a drunken spectator at a football game shouts "'Stob Ted Coy!' under the impression that [he was] watching a game played a dozen years before. When he realized finally that he was funny he began performing for the gallery and aroused a chorus of whistles and boos until he was dragged unwillingly under the stand" (391).

3. Two notable exceptions are F. W. Farrar's *Eric, or Little by Little* (1858), a novel about an unruly student who tries, usually without much success, to reform his behavior, and Rudyard Kipling's *Stalky and Co.* (1899), a collection of stories in which traditional school-fiction plots give way to tales of brutality and revenge at an English public school. For historical surveys of English boarding-school fiction, see Isabel Quigly, *The Heirs of Tom Brown: The English School Story* (1984); P. W. Musgrave, *From Brown to Bunter: The Life and Death of the School Story* (1985); Jeffrey Richards, *Happiest Days: The Public Schools in English Fiction* (1988); Benjamin Watson, *English Schoolboy Stories: An Annotated Bibliography of Hardcover Fiction* (1992); and Beverly Lyon Clark, *Regendering the School Story: Sassy Sissies and Tattling Tomboys* (1996).

4. As the novelist John R. Tunis observes, *The Lawrenceville Stories* are extremely entertaining and, at the same time, extremely dated: "Good writing, like good clothes, stands the test of time. But like good clothes, some good writing may seem old-fashioned. Inevitably, some of these stories sound like General Montgomery declaiming Kipling's 'If'

to his assembled staff before the Battle of Alamein. Yet Johnson was essentially a supreme storyteller" (8).

5. See note 1.

6. As Louis Menand points out, critics and social historians did not begin to regard *The Catcher in the Rye* as an "important cultural statement" until several years after it was published: "[It] was a bestseller when it came out, in 1951, but its reception as some sort of important cultural statement didn't happen until the mid-fifties, when people started talking about 'alienation' and 'conformity' and 'the youth culture'—the time of *Howl* and *Rebel Without a Cause* and Elvis Presley's first records. It is as a hero of that culture that Holden Caulfield has survived" (85). Even after Salinger's novel became enormously popular and influential, it was widely assumed that few readers would be drawn to fiction about the sorrows of young men at private academies. John Knowles recalled that he was not surprised when a dozen American publishers passed on *A Separate Peace* before it was initially published in England in 1959. Even he had wondered "Who's going to want to read about a bunch of prep-school boys and what happened to them long ago in the past?" ("My Separate Peace" 106).

7. Indeed, as Alice Hall Petry observes, most of Basil's social blunders at St. Regis spring from the fact that he has gleaned "all his knowledge of prep schools from popular literature" (158).

8. In his biography of the Scribner's editor Maxwell Perkins, A. Scott Berg explains that this characterization of Fitzgerald is misleading. The often-repeated remark about "the very rich" should not be attributed directly to Fitzgerald—it is spoken by the narrator of his story "The Rich Boy": "Let me tell you about the very rich. They are different from you and me. They possess and enjoy early, and it does something to them, makes them soft where we are hard, and cynical where we are trustful, in a way that, unless you were born rich, it is very difficult to understand" (177). In 1938, Fitzgerald wrote that he was fascinated by the American upper class in part because he had felt excluded from it in many ways: "That was always my experience—a poor boy in a rich town; a poor boy in a rich boys' school; a poor boy in a rich man's club at Princeton.... I have never been able to forgive the rich for being rich, and it has colored my entire life and works" (qtd. in Turnbull 150).

Chapter 1

1. When Armstrong died in 1971, Collier continues, "the tens of millions of people all over the world who mourned him remembered him as an endearing child of nature who became famous singing improbable tunes like 'Hello, Dolly' and 'Blueberry Hill' in a voice choked with gravel.... What only a tiny fraction of those people knew ... was that Louis Armstrong was one of the most important figures in twentieth-century music. Indeed, a case can be made for the thesis that he was *the* most important of them all, for almost single-handedly he remodeled jazz and, as a consequence, had a critical effect on the kinds of music that came out of it..." (3).

2. The reader learns only two additional details about D.B.'s career in Hollywood: his girlfriend is going to appear in one of the films he has written and he is considering working on a screenplay set at the U.S. Naval Academy.

3. Virtually all of the male characters who annoy Holden are conspicuously successful. By his lights, taxi drivers, elevator operators, and other working-class men are ineligible to be classified as "hot-shots" and "phonies."

4. Even boarding-school chaplains are "hot-shots" in Holden's eyes. "If you want to know the truth," he explains, "I can't even stand ministers. The ones they've had at every school I've gone to, they all have these Holy Joe voices when they start giving their sermons. God, I hate that" (131).

5. As Kenneth B. Kidd points out, another common hypothesis in masculinity studies suggests that "since boys have trouble establishing a masculine self against [the] maternal bond, it follows that 'being a boy or being masculine is not so much based on the positive identification with father but on the negation of the male child's tie to mother.' In other words, '*Being a boy becomes defined in the negative: Not being a girl*'" (178; qtd. Pollack).

6. In his essay "The Salinger Cult," Irving Howe notes that Holden's reluctance to struggle against "his perceptions of the world's evil" was shared by many of Salinger's earliest readers. Salinger's fiction, Howe writes, "is a cult that flourishes mainly among the academic young: those well-scrubbed boys and girls who have inherited the material good of this world and find themselves stirred neither to conquest nor rebellion, but instead remain bright, 'cool,' and estranged" (93).

7. This kind of abstention from organized athletics is commonplace in American boarding-school literature. Only one major character in the works discussed in this book—Peter Kilburn, the narrator of James Kirkwood's novel *Good Times/Bad Times* [1968]—is shown in competition as a varsity athlete.

8. American prep schools have often defined themselves as institutions that train young people to compete and win. For example, a school song declares that St. George's is a "testing ground for victory makers."

9. As John Seelye points out, Reisman noticed the popularity of *The Catcher in the Rye* and made it required reading in some of his sociology courses: "Appearing one year after ... *The Lonely Crowd*, Salinger's novel would be assigned to his Harvard undergraduates as a casebook in point" (24).

10. This reading, it seems to me, is more persuasive than David Castronovo's assertion that *The Catcher in the Rye* is a "wisdom book" that dispenses "pronouncements about living well and discovering usable truths" (59). If Holden—traumatized, hospitalized, and overwhelmed by anxiety, exhaustion, and despair—is, as Castronovo concludes, the author of "a strict code for living" (63), it would surely be a mistake to take that code at face value. Gary Cross concludes that most adolescent readers do not interpret *The Catcher in the Rye* as a novel about post-traumatic stress disorder: "Caulfield's alienation could be explained as a psychological disorder, but that is not how many young people read it (I certainly didn't when I read it as a sixteen-year-old.) Youth saw Caulfield as true to their own lives, alienated from the 'phoniness' of school and the hypocrisy of adulthood" (95). For an incisive discussion of Holden's reactions to Allie's death, see Edwin Haviland Miller's "In Memoriam: Allie Caulfield."

11. Pencey Prep is modeled on Valley Forge Military Academy, a school in Pennsylvania that Salinger attended during his junior and senior years (1934–36). As Ian Hamilton writes, "[t]he academy ... was founded in 1928 and, according to its manifesto, [its] mission from the start was to turn out 'young men fully prepared to meet their responsibilities, alert in mind, sound in body, considerate of others, and with a high sense of duty, honor, loyalty, and courage.'... Pencey, it will be recalled, boasted of 'molding boys into splendid, clear-thinking young men'" (18–19). Kenneth Slawenski explains that although Salinger tended to be angry and unmotivated in his late teens, he "did well" at Valley Forge: "Whatever his inward rebellion against the authority of the place, it did indeed provide the discipline necessary for him to apply himself. His grades improved markedly ... [and he] became involved in campus activities, including intramural sports and, uncharacteristically, the glee club" (17).

12. Although only the first seven of *The Catcher in the Rye*'s twenty-six chapters are set at Pencey Prep, the novel is widely regarded as a key text in American boarding-school literature. Sanford Pinsker, for example, argues that *The Catcher in the Rye* is "the best account of prep-school despair we are likely to get" (16), and Christopher Brookeman observes that "Salinger locates Holden's story within a very specific social world in which the most significant influence is not some generalized concept of American culture or society, but the codes and practices of a particular instrument of social control—the American prep school" (58).

13. Salinger attended The McBurney School, a private school in Manhattan, for two years before he flunked out and then enrolled at Valley Forge Military Academy. The story of Salinger's exit from McBurney should sound very familiar to readers of *The Catcher in the Rye*: "By the end of the spring term of 1934, he had performed so badly in his classes that McBurney administrators asked him not to return in the fall.... Upon his departure, a school official wrote the following note on his transcript: 'Character: Rather hard-hit by [adolescence] his last year with us. Ability: plenty. Industry: did not know the word'" (Alexander 38).

14. This sensation of "disappearing" returns later in the novel, when Holden flees from the apartment of his former English teacher Mr. Antolini: "Every time I came to the end of a block and stepped off the goddam curb, I had this feeling that I'd never get to the other side of the street. I thought I'd just go down, down, down, and nobody'd ever see me again.... Every time I'd get to the end of a block I'd make believe I was talking to my brother Allie. I'd say to him, 'Allie, don't let me disappear. Allie, don't let me disappear. Allie don't let me disappear. Please, Allie'" (257).

15. Holden's rage in this episode, Peter Shaw contends, is fueled by his fear that Stradlater has seduced Jane Gallagher: "[W]hen Holden imagines not just a kiss but Stradlater and Jane having sex, he [ends] up 'practically bawling' (after maneuvering Stradlater into beating him up).... [H]aving had a relationship with Jane that only once reached the stage of (chaste) kissing, [Holden] is frozen at a painful stage of development. In contrast, Stradlater has, to Holden's dismay, broken through this stage. Accordingly, when Stradlater hints at having had sex with Jane, Holden takes a swing at him..." (105).

16. Pinsker suggests that Spencer's main objective during this meeting is to relieve his guilty conscience, not to chastise his former student: "Mr. Spencer is obviously disturbed by having to fail a Pencey student, especially if the grade contributed to the boy's being expelled; but he is also interested in exonerating himself, in getting the student in question to admit that he had no other choice, that what he did was right" (34).

17. In light of these passages, Charles Poole's description of Holden's attitude toward Pencey Prep seems overstated: "Like most of the rest of the world in Holden's ambiance, Pencey was bulging with decrepit and idiotic adults of thirty or forty or even older, and loathsome contemporaries who are pinned along the walls of Holden's wandering memories" (101). Holden's mistrust of adults, Henry Anatole Grunwald writes, calls to mind the attitudes of the title character in Mark Twain's *Adventures of Huckleberry Finn* (1885): "Like Huck Finn, with whom Holden Caulfield is constantly compared, the hero of *The Catcher in the Rye* is usually described as a rebel, either against the materialism and ugliness of 'our society' or against the realities of the adult world. But he does not make a very satisfactory rebel because he is not for anything" (xiv). Similarly, Charles McGrath suggests that *The Catcher in the Rye* appealed to young readers in part because of Holden's "distrust of the adult world" ("J. D. Salinger, Literary Recluse" A1), and Peter J. Seng points out that Holden tends to reject all of the values he associates with adulthood: "What disturbs Holden about the world in which he finds himself is adults and adult values. He sees that the world belongs to adults, and it seems to him that they have filled it with phoniness, pretense, [and] social compromise" (206).

18. Holden's most scathing remarks about Pencey are prompted by trivial things. When he recalls that only seniors were allowed to bring dates to football games, for instance, he insists that "[i]t was a terrible school, no matter how you looked at it" (5), and when he notices that his dorm room is too warm he grumbles that "I was yawning all over the place. For one thing, the room was too damn hot. It made you sleepy. At Pencey, you either froze to death or died of the heat" (30).

19. Purity, Oldsey argues, may be the most striking feature of Holden's vision of "the catcher": "He must be pure to be the catcher in the rye, saving little children who might be rushing to their doom, and living in his own peaceful cabin. There, one of his few visitors would be Phoebe. As for his brother D.B., a proviso is necessary: 'I'd let D.B. come out and

visit me for a while if he wanted a nice, quiet place for his writing, but he couldn't write any movies in my cabin, only stories and books'" (266). Adam Gopnik notes that the influence of childhood innocence on emotionally battered adults and adolescents is the dominant theme of Salinger's fiction: "The message of his writing was always the same: that, amid the malice and falseness of social life, redemption rises from clear speech and childlike enchantment, from all the forms of unself-conscious innocence that still surround us..." (21).

20. In a recent *New York Times* article, Jennifer Schuessler reports that teenagers who study *The Catcher in the Rye* in high school English classes today are often exasperated by Holden's short-tempered, judgmental tendencies: "Teachers say young readers just don't like Holden as much as they used to. What once seemed like courageous truth-telling now strikes many of them as 'weird,' 'whiny,' and 'immature'" (WK5).

Chapter 2

1. Macmillan published the first American edition of *A Separate Peace* in February 1960. The true first edition was published in Great Britain by Secker & Warburg in 1959.

2. According to a recent estimate, there are more than nine million copies of *A Separate Peace* in print.

3. Joseph McElroy argues that the real subject of "Do You Like It Here?" is not Roberts's guilt or innocence; it is the neurotic, self-important behavior of Mr. Van Ness: "The boy doesn't slip once, not even into cleverness; the man, petty and cruel but more pompous than sadistic, prepared for the kill as if he were ambushing a belligerent equal, but he looks steadily bad, a tyrant here, doubtless a sycophant elsewhere, and instead of setting an example of clarity and frankness, he is so overcome by the mysterious mess (as I read the story) inside him that he upholds alma mater's honor by the vainest attempt to demoralize an adolescent" (154).

4. In *The Finest Education Money Can Buy* (1972), Richard L. Gaines also writes about the uncanny stillness of a deserted boarding school: "All the kids had left, and the campus lay mute—exposed and somehow strangely vulnerable, as deserted schools always are.... The thing is that a school shouldn't be quiet or peaceful or empty. A school is supposed to have a lot of kids and noise and laughter and confusion and things going on. A school during vacation is useless, dead" (17, 18).

5. As Thomas Hassan, Exeter's current principal, explains on the school's Internet site, "Over 75 years ago, [Exeter] was transformed by a generous gift from Edward S. Harkness, a gift that changed our classrooms and the experiences within them. The open give-and-take of Harkness pedagogy has enabled not only students but also faculty and staff to consider together what '*great end* and *real business* of living' really means. In this process, students have learned from teachers and teachers have learned from students, both inside and outside the classroom." (When John Phillips founded Exeter in 1781, he declared that the school's principal objective would be to help young men learn about "the great end and real business of living.") In *Palimpsest* (1995), Gore Vidal wryly observes that the Harkness Plan helped him to cheat on his exams. "Each class sat at a round table with pull-out leaves," he writes. "During a written test, the master would wander about the room or look out the window while we answered the test questions.... [H]onesty now requires me to say that I cheated in almost every mathematics examination; otherwise, I could not have graduated.... My breach of Exeter's honor system never gave me the slightest pause. After all, it was their honor system, not mine, a means of getting us to sneak on one another" (92, 93).

6. As Nelson W. Aldrich, Jr., explains, American boarding-school officials in the mid-twentieth century prohibited radios to limit students' access to the "outside world": "Schools

like Groton and St. Paul's were once as isolated from potentially bad influences as Cuba, say, is from the United States. More so: Cubans can listen to American radio. At St. Paul's when I was there in the early 1950s, radios were contraband. There were many other things we couldn't have: no cars or motorcycles or bicycles, no playing cards or backgammon boards, no cigarettes or liquor or drugs, no sexual relations. Visits to and from the 'outside' world were limited to a few weekends a year" (42).

    7. Nothing reveals Gene's insecurity and eagerness to conform as fully as his remarks about Finny's pink shirt. In "Phineas," a 1956 short story in which Knowles began to develop the characters and themes highlighted in *A Separate Peace*, Gene recalls that "[i]t was a finely woven broadcloth, carefully cut, and very pink. No one else at the school could have worn it without some risk of having it torn from his back. But Finny put it on with the air of a monarch assuming the regalia" (103).

    8. Similarly, Knowles writes that the Devon School "did not stand isolated behind walls and gates but emerged naturally from the town which had produced it" (11).

    9. Bryant, for instance, notes that when Gene returns to the "areas of order" on Devon's campus, he senses that "it is logical ... to hope that the individual can find a similar balance" (37). In a review of *A Separate Peace*, Paul Pickrel argues that Knowles's rendering of his emotionally fragile narrator introduces a new kind of school-fiction protagonist: "*A Separate Peace* makes a break with the usual novel of preparatory school life in several ways, but most notably in its reassessment of the 'sensitive' boy. In most recent novels about schoolboys (in the nineteenth century it was different), the sensitive boy has been the hero.... Yet Knowles is right in recognizing the possibility of cruelty in sensitivity, the impulse of the acutely self-conscious to make the world pay them back for what they suffer" ("The Curse of Goodness" 108).

    10. Kathy Piehl points out that students' "physical isolation from society" in boarding-school fiction "enhances a crucial feature of the genre: the minimal presence of adults. The lack of constant and direct adult supervision places more power in the hands of adolescents" (67, 68). Knowles explained that the generation gap between students and teachers in *A Separate Peace* is mainly attributable to the war: "All of the faculty on the campus were so much older than we were that we had no connection with them. They just were too old, too tired, and too busy. One of the reasons that Gene and Finny develop this intensely close friendship is that they had no one to relate to; no older person to pattern themselves on, to look and talk things over with, they only had each other" ("John Knowles on *A Separate Peace*" 2).

    11. Gene, in particular, knows very well that the leaps are dangerous. The first time he yields to Finny's peer pressure, he jumps from the limb "[w]ith the sensation that I was throwing my life away" (17). And in the next chapter Gene recalls that he once came close to losing his balance and falling from the limb: "There was a moment of total, impersonal panic, and then Finny's hand shot out and grabbed my arm, and with my balance restored, the panic immediately disappeared.... It was only after dinner, when I was on my way alone to the library, that the full danger I had brushed on the limb shook me again. If Finny hadn't come up right behind me ... if he hadn't been there ... I could have fallen on the bank and broken my back!" (31-32).

    12. Desertion was classified as a capital offense, and forty-nine American soldiers were court-martialed and sentenced to death during World War II. Only one, however, Pvt. Eddie Slovik, was executed.

    13. For illuminating discussions of desertion and post-traumatic stress disorder in the World War II era, see Robert Fantina, *Desertion and the American Soldier, 1776-2006* (2006) and Gerald F. Linderman, *The World Within War: America's Combat Experience in World War II* (1997).

    14. The summer session in *A Separate Peace* takes place in 1942. Phillips Exeter offered its first summer classes the following year.

    15. Similarly, in "Phineas," Gene explains that at Devon, "kidding people, or 'cutting

them down,' as it was called, gave place only to athletics as a field of concentration. No one could be allowed to grow above the prevailing level; anyone who threatened to must be instantly and collectively cut down" (102). The *Washington Post* reviewer Jonathan Yardley has written incisively about *The Rector of Justin* and other works of prep-school literature, but his reading of *A Separate Peace* overlooks the Devon boys' strong reluctance to express their emotions. Yardley calls the book "a novel about lachrymose preppies" ("Holden Caulfield, Aging Gracelessly" 3), when in fact it is a novel about young men who habitually conceal their sorrow and fear.

16. Knowles started to read *The Catcher in the Rye* for the first time while writing *A Separate Peace*. "When I was about a third of the way into my own book," he recalled, "I ran across a copy of *The Catcher in the Rye*. Always having meant to read it, I started in. Oh my God, I said to myself on about page 10, a teenage boy! In a prep school! This thing could influence me, if I let it. I closed the book and only returned to it when mine was in galleys. Then I read and admired it very much. They are very different books. His is a 360-degree circumambulating of one fascinating character. Mine is linear, a narrative involving two and then four interrelating characters" ("My Separate Peace" 108). For a comparison of the narrative approaches in *The Catcher in the Rye* and *A Separate Peace*, see Ronald Weber's "Narrative Method in *A Separate Peace*" (1964).

Chapter 3

1. In addition to publishing 47 novels and short-story collections and 19 works of nonfiction and criticism, Auchincloss practiced law at two firms in Manhattan: Sullivan & Cromwell (1941–51) and Hawkins, Delafield & Wood (1953–86). In a 2008 profile in *The New Yorker*, Larissa McFarquhar summarizes Auchincloss's experiences at Groton this way: "There was no privacy ... and no rest from endless, pointless activity.... Auchincloss was a disaster from the start. He had no friends. He was a failure both as an athlete and as a scholar, but, more than that, he was, as he later put it, 'naturally unpopular,' possessing that indefinable but unmistakable quality that signals to his peers that a boy is to be ostracized and tormented" (61).

2. Auchincloss eventually won a measure of acceptance by performing in school plays, but long after he graduated he described his education at Groton, particularly his first two years there, as a "black and bitter" experience (Swaim, *Wired for Books* interview).

3. Although *The Rector of Justin* was Auchincloss's first boarding-school novel, it did not mark the first time his fiction had concentrated on prep-school life. The protagonist of "A World of Profit" (1938), an unpublished novel Auchincloss wrote three years after he left Groton, is a prototype for Frank Prescott. Dr. Mintern, headmaster at the Chelton School, began his career eager to "raise his boys 'with the ideals of public service and a sense of noblesse oblige, [but] the lure of Wall Street enticed the graduates whom he had trained to be leaders of church and state and made them into prosperous men of affairs'" (Piket 145). Later in his career, Auchincloss returned to "[i]mages of boarding schools and headmasters" (145) in several novels, including *The Indifferent Children* (1947), *Sybil* (1952), *Venus in Sparta* (1958), and *Pursuit of the Prodigal* (1959), and in the short-story collections *The Injustice Collectors* (1950) and *The Romantic Egoists* (1954).

4. In a 1994 interview, George Plimpton asked Auchincloss how *The Rector of Justin* was received at Groton. The novelist replied that "The school didn't like it. I was absolutely persona non grata for a while. But at last they came around; on the centennial of the school they asked me to make the chief address. So we all became friends again.... [Peabody's family] minded quite a lot at the start, but they were eventually conciliated by ... a granddaughter of Peabody, who told me, 'I can't see anything of my grandfather in that book at all.' It makes

me realize that people didn't really know him. They think of a headmaster as just a loud noise" (4).

5. Peabody's biographer Frank Ashburn was not persuaded by Auchincloss's remarks about the famous judge: "[Ashburn] maintained that no book about Groton had caused such a stir.... He conceded the preponderance of dissimilarities between the fictional and actual headmaster, but 'to old Groton hands,' he insisted, 'much of the setting, many of the details, some of the minor characters, and at least one major episode were familiar. The result was confusion and unhappiness. Many felt it a pity that such an important work should be popularly considered as an authoritative portrait of a man, his school, and his family.' Even Peabody's children acted as if they believed Prescott was Peabody" (Gelderman 154–55).

6. In an earlier entry, Aspinwall mentions that "the famous Dr. Peabody of Groton" had recently visited Justin Martyr and points out that Peabody did not share Prescott's interest in secular art. "Peabody," he writes, "would not see the beauty in Swinburne or be tempted by the Lorileis of art. His is a simpler path" (43). Thus, as Virgilia Peterson observes, "Any resemblance ... between Dr. Prescott and that other leading headmaster, Dr. Endicott Peabody, is purely fanciful, as demonstrated by the fact that Dr. Peabody himself appears in the story briefly as a visiting preacher" (1). Similarly, Jonathan Yardley notes that "[r]eaders who are tempted to see Groton's Peabody in [Prescott] must be dissuaded. Physically, they are completely different: Peabody was tall, while Prescott is 'short for one that dominating, about five feet six, which is accentuated by the great round shoulders, the bull neck, the noble square head, the thick shock of stiff, wavy grey hair'" (2).

7. As Parsell points out, Frank Prescott seems to be the only major character in *The Rector of Justin* who is not interested in writing about his career and his private life: "Notably absent from the assembled documentation is any word from Prescott himself; in keeping with his character as revealed, the old gentleman has committed little or nothing to paper in the course of his long, distinguished career, choosing instead to be remembered by his actions" (49). James Tuttleton argues that Auchincloss's use of multiple narrators highlights the elusiveness of any biographical subject: "In this novel Frank Prescott ... is recreated through the differing recollections and impressions of several characters—the priggish young admirer, the irreverent daughter, the wife, the friends, the students and alumni. What the novel suggests is that we can never know what Prescott was really like because none of the narrators knew the real Prescott—he presented a different side to each of them. It might well be asked whether there was any 'real' Prescott behind his various masks. The answer is yes, but we can never know him except as a composite of the limited points of view of his various biographers" (618–19).

8. Aspinwall becomes even more panic-stricken when the students in his dormitory make him the butt of a practical joke: "Dear God, if I become a pitiable creature, spare me at least from the sin of self-pity. I have a terrible leaning to it.... I found a dead frog in my bed last night, and the touch of it against my bare foot scared me so that I was sick to my stomach. I wonder if such a trick has ever before been played on a master at Justin. But obviously I'll never know, as I shall never dare admit that it happened. Dear God, will it ever be over?" (9–10).

9. Christopher Dahl attributes the close relationship between Prescott and Aspinwall to the fact that both men are devout Christians: "In spite of the great differences in their ages the two men are drawn to each other by their common faith. Unlike most of the other people at the school, they are motivated by ideals of selfless Christian service" (16).

10. Virgilia Peterson argues that Cordelia Turnbull's most vexing problem is that her actions and temperament are so unlike those of Lear's youngest daughter: "Her recriminations against her father, a deliberate attempt to disillusion Brian, prove her quite unlike her namesake..." (20).

11. As Frank Kintrea points out, no student at Groton was exempt from the threat of pumping: "Little Teddy Roosevelt, Jr., a few weeks before his father was inaugurated as Vice President, was pumped for being 'fresh and swell-headed.' Half-drowned but still spouting

Notes. Chapter 3

defiance after two immersions, he escaped being put under for a third time; the boys admired his pluck. Malcolm Peabody, the rector's own son, was pumped because the older boys didn't like his 'tone'" (102).

12. A July 1964 *Newsweek* review of *The Rector of Justin* makes the curious argument that the many cultural references made by Jules Griscam and other characters reveal that Auchincloss himself was a "name dropper": "Every five pages he drops a name, and whether he does it to 'place' a pasteboard character, milk a stock emotion, or inject the dry veins of sentimentality with a dose of second-hand atmosphere, the end result is to make the reader think that he himself knows or cares about Caresse Crosby and Frank Crowninshield, Rossetti and Rousseau, Redon and Julia Ward Howe's Newport" (83).

13. During a conversation with Brian Aspinwall, Prescott offers this account of Jules Griscam's accident and his own role in causing it: "I have always dreaded to think to think [he crashed deliberately], for if it was suicide, it was also murder. Jules' car, a Bugatti sports model, left the highway between Nice and Cannes and crashed into a rock pile. It was traveling at eighty miles an hour, and Jules, as usual, had been drinking. But Jules was not the only person killed. There was a girl in the car. Why should he have made that poor little Riviera tart pay the price of his own mad follies?" (240).

14. Horace Havistock explains that "[i]t is important briefly to describe St. Andrew's, as it existed in the seventies, because it later become the model of all that [Prescott] thought a school should not be. Life there, outside of classes, was totally disorganized. The boys played informally at football and baseball, making up their own rules, but they were quite at liberty, if they pleased instead, to roam the New Hampshire countryside and fish or trap in their afternoons. They were equally at liberty to haze the weak and to group themselves into fierce little competing clubs.... I will admit that they seemed to enjoy themselves, but to me the school was another Dotheboys Hall" (61–62). (Dotheboys Hall is a boys' school in Charles Dickens's novel *Nicholas Nickleby*, managed by a sadistic headmaster named Wackford Squeers.) This feature of Frank Prescott's story does seem to have been drawn from the life of Endicott Peabody. As James McLachlan explains, "Peabody later said that about all he learned from Cheltenham [the English boarding school he attended] 'were things to be avoided and not to do'" (246, qtd. Ashburn 16).

15. Paul Pickrel argues that Prescott's idealism early in his career derived in part from the loss of his parents and his respect for their generation: "[T]he son's impulse to found a school springs from his attachment to the idealism of the Civil War generation and his desire to keep it alive in the money-grubbing decades that followed the war" ("Manners of Mammon" 100).

16. J. Carter Brown, a 1951 graduate of Groton, recalls in the documentary *Smithsonian World: American Dream at Groton* that the school did all that it could to guide students in the direction of public service: "The school had a great sense of tradition, and this tradition was very much rooted in that straight-laced, New England, late nineteenth-century sense of discipline and of doing things for other people. Unto those to whom much has been given, much is expected." This emphasis on the importance of service is reflected in Groton's motto, *Cui Servire Est Regnare* ("to serve is to rule").

17. In *The Finest Education Money Can Buy* (1972), Richard Gaines, a former teacher at the Lawrenceville School, also worries about the tendency of Northeastern prep schools to turn out graduates who fit a narrow, familiar profile. While describing a class reunion at Lawrenceville, Gaines points out that "everything is so predictable, everybody so much alike. The same clean-shaven, neatly trimmed, carefully groomed, well-scrubbed appearance; the same half-forced hearty smiles; the same dark suits or quietly expensive sports jackets; the same eager small talk about family and sports and 'the economy,' and vacations at Aspen and Nantucket; the same confident awareness of success subtly contradicted by that tightness around the corners of the mouth which hints at something somewhere gone wrong—the little doubt gnawing away, deep down and unconfessed. The students are nicer people to be with, more alive" (27).

Chapter 4

1. Vidal and John Knowles were contemporaries at Exeter. Knowles modeled Brinker Hadley, the student who organizes the mock trial of Gene Forrester in *A Separate Peace*, on Vidal.

2. As Sean Egan has pointed out, the eloquence of Peter's document is probably the most unconvincing feature of *Good Times/Bad Times*: "Notwithstanding the fact that Peter is an articulate, intelligent, thoughtful, middle-class eighteen-year-old—and despite the fact that Kirkwood seems to try to cover himself by having [Mr. Hoyt] state that he has a high IQ—the prose he writes is too eloquent. No matter how intelligent an eighteen-year-old might be, he would not use the little stylistic devices and flourishes of a seasoned author the way Kilburn does" (227).

3. See Chapter 6 for a discussion of *Tea and Sympathy*.

4. Alex Shoumatoff explains that St. Paul's School was originally designed to put Pestalozzi's theory of education into practice: "The school was founded in 1856 by a Boston doctor named George Shattuck, who hoped to implement the beliefs of an early-19th-century Swiss pioneer in progressive education named Johann Heinrich Pestalozzi. Pestalozzi espoused the Rousseauian idea that society was irredeemably compromised but that children were a fount of natural goodness. The only hope for reforming society, therefore, was to begin with children and give them a 'natural' education.... This meant removing the sons of the Gilded Age's ruling class from their corrupting environs and building a school for them in some pristine place where they could experience the sublime directly through their senses. Green fields and trees, streams and ponds, beautiful scenery, flowers and minerals, are 'educators,' Shattuck wrote" (145).

5. As William G. Saltonstall points out, the "great headmasters" also seem to have gone out of their way to support one another. When Deerfield Academy was plagued by financial problems in the 1920s, for instance, Exeter's Lewis Perry wrote that "I know of no school in the country which I believe in more thoroughly than [Deerfield]" (55) and, with the help of Andover's Alfred Stearns and Horace Taft (founder of the Taft School), he raised $300,000 to help Deerfield avoid filing for bankruptcy.

6. In 1974, Auchincloss explained that "[w]hen I wrote *The Rector of Justin* I was trying to paint the portrait of a headmaster of a New England boarding school who would be characteristic of the great era of headmasters which began, roughly speaking, at the end of the last century and ended some time before World War II. It was the era which produced Endicott Peabody of Groton, Samuel Drury of St. Paul's, William Thayer of St. Mark's, Mather Abbott of Lawrenceville, and many others. I read all the privately printed biographies (a dreary lot) and made notes of what I deduced to be the salient characteristics of their subjects" (35).

7. When Auchincloss created his fictional Rector of Justin, he gave Frank Prescott Peabody's habit of supervising every aspect of day-to-day life at his school: "[I]n the course of a week he visits every part of the school grounds, some of them many times over: the playing fields, the infirmary, the gymnasium, the locker rooms, the dormitories, even the cellars and lavatories" (41).

8. Samuel Drury, a former missionary who served as rector of St. Paul's School from 1911 to 1936, was particularly conscious that he and the majority of his students came from different socioeconomic backgrounds: "Shabby genteel in origins, a Harvard-educated retainer of the class rather than a full-fledged member of it, Drury never got over the envy ... of the steward for the objects of his stewardship.... In his diary he railed against the people he'd been 'called' to educate: '[The school] must not become a place of fashion, an exclusive retreat where like-minded sons of like-minded parents disport themselves.... Our function is not to conform to the rich and prosperous world which surrounds us, but rather, through its children, to convert it'" (qtd. in Aldrich 148). Evan Thomas and Daniel Klaidman note that many exclusive boarding schools shared this determination to "convert" the rich:

Notes. Chapter 5

"The so-called St. Grottlesex schools (Groton, St. Paul's, St. Mark's, St. George's and Middlesex) were regarded as playgrounds of the spoiled rich. But, in part to rebut the stereotype, they attempted to be moral incubators, preaching 'muscular Christianity' and the duty to serve 'in the larger light of the world'" (1).

9. This notion that there is something effeminate about young men who choose to play tennis also surfaces in *The Rector of Justin*. When David Griscam expresses his surprise that Frank Prescott allows some of the boys at Justin Martyr to play varsity tennis, Prescott acknowledges that he once regarded tennis as "a game for mollycoddles" (118), but Brian Aspinwall convinced him that it takes courage for students at private academies for boys to "stand out against organized sports" (119).

10. As Thomas A. Atwood and Wade M. Lee have noted, *Good Times/Bad Times*, like several other American school narratives, contains elements of Gothic fiction: "Works of school-based fiction, especially those set at preparatory schools, are well-studied ... as Bildungsroman, or coming of age novels, but they have rarely been examined in terms of their Gothic sensibilities" (202).

Chapter 5

1. As Martin Naparsteck observes, it could be argued that Dorset Academy is the most compelling "character" in *A Good School*: "[The school] is the dominating, ever-present character that undergoes, as all well-developed characters do, a significant change as the story progresses. In a sense, the stories of the boys and the faculty and a few others are almost digressions, except that their personalities contribute to the personality of the school" (107).

2. Blake Bailey describes Cheever's education at Thayer this way: "Thayer Academy was an old-fashioned New England day school.... The atmosphere was, in almost every sense, austere.... Cheever did not shine in such a climate, though at the time he was not shining generally. Sloppy and depressed, he refused to improve his abysmal math skills ... nor did he make more than a token effort in classes that might otherwise have interested him. His freshman English teacher, Louise Saul, remembered him as a young man who did perfunctory work and 'didn't take well to discipline'; in her class and in history he managed a low C, while receiving D's or E's (failing) in pretty much everything else" (37–38).

3. Thayer's files are unequivocal about the cause of Cheever's departure: "John Cheever, ex '31, was not expelled, but in the interest of drama considered himself to be" (Donaldson 39).

4. Meanor points out that Charles's glance through the window at the school's lawns and trees would be reenacted in various ways in Cheever's subsequent work: "Time after time throughout Cheever's fiction, and especially when a character is undergoing severe stress, he looks out a window, takes a walk down a street or through the woods, and is momentarily granted entrance into a natural realm of grace that mysteriously refreshes him and spiritually removes him from the painful constraints of time and duty.... Cheever is a genuine American romantic in his attitude toward nature and its ameliorative role in human affairs" (30–31).

5. One of Britain's most notable anti-public-school polemics is "Such, Such Were the Joys," an essay in which George Orwell describes Crossgates, the school he attended, as a site of endless intimidation and shame: "'*Report yourself* to the headmaster after breakfast!' I do not know how many times I heard that phrase during my early years at Crossgates. It was only very rarely that it did not mean a beating. The words always had a portentous sound in my ears, like muffled drums or the words of a death sentence" (11). Roald Dahl's *Boy: Tales of Childhood* (1984) also stresses the cruelty of officials at an English public school.

6. Mailer's essay "The White Negro: Superficial Reflections on the Hipster" asserts

that after World War II a small cohort of young white Americans expressed their dissatisfaction with the mainstream by associating themselves with African-American culture, which they viewed as a model of authenticity and street smarts. These "White Negroes," Mailer writes, became "a new breed of adventurers, urban adventurers who drifted out at night looking for action with a black man's code to fit their facts. The hipster had absorbed the existential synapses of the Negro, and for practical purposes could be considered a white Negro" (341). Roger Ebert notes that one of the most curious features of Tom Shulman's screenplay is its failure to mention the Beat Movement: "[*Dead Poets Society*] is set in 1959, but none of these would-be bohemians have heard of Kerouac, Ginsberg or indeed of the beatnik movement" (1).

7. Orr goes on to endorse a third approach articulated by the English actor and writer Stephen Fry in his book *The Ode Less Traveled: Unlocking the Poet Within*: "Rather than pull a Keating, and attempt to turn poetry into a Doors concert circa 1969, Fry's goal is to demystify the art without deadening it; to make it seem as open to the interested amateur as 'carpentry and bridge and wine and knitting and brass-rubbing and line-dancing and the hundreds of other activities that enrich and enliven the daily toil of getting and spending'" (14).

8. These insults are nothing out of the ordinary for David. Before he leaves home, he gets into a fistfight with a Scranton kid who calls him a Christ-killer and a "Sheeny bastard."

9. Once the school community learns the truth about David's religious affiliation, David Ansen observes, "out of the mouths of the well-bred bigots at St. Matthew's come pouring vile anti–Semitic epithets" (78).

10. *The Emperor's Club* (2002; directed by Michael Hoffman, screenplay by Neil Tolkin) also highlights the treachery of a privileged schoolboy. Its main character, a history teacher named William Hundert, begins the film as a man of exemplary character and teaching ability, but his integrity is compromised by one of his students, the charismatic, amoral son of a United States Senator.

11. In *School Ties*, *Dead Poets Society*, and other previous prep-school films, attractive young women had been presented as insufferable snobs or as trophies. *Outside Providence* does not contain even a trace of that stereotype. As Stephanie Zacharek observes, the actress Amy Smart "ends up giving a "completely charming and natural performance [as Jane] ... knowing exactly how to show that a blond, beautiful, privileged co-ed can also be just really neat" (1).

12. Castronovo and Goldleaf also note that the struggles of Dorset Academy have a good deal in common with those of John Wilder, the main character in Yates's novel *Disturbing the Peace* (1975): "Just as *Disturbing the Peace* charts the downfall of a little man, *A Good School* studies the breakup of 'a funny little school.' Dorset Academy ... is the institutional equivalent of John Wilder: it lacks stature, dignity, basic survival skills. It fails during World War II, just at the time when America was gearing up for victory" (81).

Chapter 6

1. The narrator of *Peace Breaks Out* explains that prep-school students in the 1940s impressed their schoolmates only if they could show "the easy touch, the everyday manner, the effortless gift for camaraderie which made for popularity" (20).

2. Similarly, David V. Hicks explains that after Dr. George Cheney Shattuck founded St. Paul's School in 1855, he stated that the school's main objective was "to educate the sons of wealthy inhabitants of large cities" (530).

3. The same principle applies to teachers in American boarding-school literature. Some are more popular or well-respected than others, but student characters seldom pay compliments to faculty members. After Pete Hallam makes a positive first impression on

the boys in his history class in *Peace Breaks Out*, this is what passes for a rave review of the new Master: "Since Pete Hallam was Nick's History teacher and Tug's faculty adviser, they had both met this interesting new Master. 'I think he's okay,' conceded Tug. This, coming from one of The Boys in Pembroke House, constituted high praise" (21). This aspect of American prep-school literature makes the film *Dead Poets Society* (1989) seem sui generis. I cannot think of another work in which young preppies respond to a teacher with the kind of hero-worship shown by several of John Keating's students at Welton Academy.

4. Robert Anderson (1917–2009) attended Phillips Exeter Academy where, like Tom Lee, he struggled with loneliness and fell in love with an older woman. *Tea and Sympathy* was first performed in New York at the Ethel Barrymore Theater, where it proved an enormous success. The role of Laura Reynolds attracted a number of famous actresses, including Deborah Kerr, Joan Fontaine, and Ingrid Bergman. A film adaptation of the play (directed by Vincente Minnelli) was released in 1956. In this watered-down retelling, Tom is ostracized because his peers consider him effeminate: a "Sister-boy" who keeps his room tidy and knows how to sew. No one in the film suggests that Tom is gay.

5. Some of Harris's remarks after he is fired raise the suspicion that he is a closeted gay man. Before he leaves the school, for example, he stops by Tom's dorm room, asks Tom what he told the dean about their afternoon at "the dunes," and says "It probably wasn't your fault. It was my fault. I should have been more ... discreet" (33). This comes close to answering the question about Harris's sexual orientation, but Anderson leaves open the possibility that Harris is blaming himself for creating a misleading impression, not for trying to seduce Tom. Later in the play, Tom is astounded when his father says that Harris was fired because he is a "fairy" who had been caught "doing a lot of suspicious things" (70).

6. In this respect, the play is reminiscent of John O'Hara's "Do You Like It Here?" (1930), a short story in which a 12-year-old student struggles to convince his housemaster that he did *not* steal a wristwatch from one of his schoolmates.

7. Reynolds acknowledges that he was once very much like Tom: "When I was a kid in school here, I had my problems too. There's a place up by the golf course where I used to go off alone Sunday afternoons and cry my eyes out. I used to lie on my bed just the way Tom does, listening to phonograph records hour after hour. But I got over it, Laura. I learned how to take it" (51).

8. *Peace Breaks Out* is set at the Devon School (a fictional campus modeled on Phillips Exeter Academy) and mentions by name two characters (Mr. Patch-Withers and Dr. Stanpole) who also appear in *A Separate Peace* (1959), but it is not a sequel to *A Separate Peace*. The plot of *Peace Breaks Out* is unrelated to that of Knowles's earlier Devon novel, and the second book contains only one very brief reference to the friendship/rivalry of Gene Forrester and his roommate Finny.

9. Roscoe Latch, the teacher Hallam admired most during his schooldays, thinks about Hallam's new life at Devon in more or less the same way: "'Here you are back from the wars!' Roscoe exclaimed cheerily in his swallowed, marbles-in-the-mouth British voice. 'And I'm sure you'll find little old Devon a risible backwater after the great world and the great war'" (7).

10. As an adult, Hallam is amused (and slightly embarrassed) when he recalls his eagerness to be popular when he was a teenager: "He certainly had wanted the other guys ... and the Masters, too, to like him, and he had certainly succeeded at that.... He had been popular, very popular. And so what? Captain of this team, president of that club: what possible good had it done him or could it do him? He wasn't going to go into politics. It was demeaning to scrape affection from virtually everyone you encountered" (11–12).

11. When Wexford reads this letter for the first time, he can hardly believe that his enemy has done something so foolish: "Hochschwender, mused Wexford, has all the charm of a Panzer attack. The crew-cut blond hair, the bony face, ice-blue eyes, too-rigid posture: he was like a parody of a Prussian. His reason for living seemed to be solely to irritate others" (62).

Conclusion

1. St. Mark's, an Episcopal school founded in 1865, is located in Southborough, Massachusetts. Bradlee's fond memories of the years he spent there are particularly striking because he contracted—and was temporarily paralyzed by—polio at St. Mark's when he was in the third form.

2. In fact, Bradlee's boarding-school memories convey a deeper sense of exhilaration than his account of covering the 1960 presidential race from his unique vantage point as a neighbor and close friend of two other famous graduates of New England boarding schools: Senator and Mrs. John F. Kennedy.

3. Years later, Eleanor Roosevelt suggested that her husband's loneliness at Groton "helped foster [his] sympathy for outcasts" (Ward 184).

4. In 1973, Choate School became coeducational and was renamed Choate Rosemary Hall.

5. "Mucker" was Choate School slang for a rebellious, irresponsible student. The headmaster George St. John frequently used the term to describe "the boys who weren't trying hard enough to obey the time-honored rules of [the school], the goof-offs who were not diligent enough about their studies" (Goodwin 486).

6. Robert F. Kennedy, it seems, did not enjoy himself at Portsmouth Priory, either. As Evan Thomas explains, "[t]he monks who ran the school regarded him as a moody and indifferent student. 'He didn't look happy, he didn't smile much,' said Father Damian Kearney, who was two classes behind RFK and later became a teacher at Portsmouth Priory.... Kennedy was clearly not stupid, but paralyzed by the prospect of failure, he could not pull his grades out of the 60s or 70s. He seemed to be flailing, not studying" (31, 36).

7. As the critic John Lucas recently observed, fiction set in the world of elite private academies has also retained much of its popularity in Britain: "[T]he last few years, which have seen Stephen Fry's recordings of Anthony Buckeridge's Jennings stories for Radio 4 and Pamela Cox's updating of Enid Blyton's *Malory Towers* series, suggest these stories still resonate with readers" (1).

8. Like prep-school literature, preppy fashion seems in no imminent danger of going out of style. Carol McD. Wallace points out that "in the 1980s the preppy uniform became just clothes. Here's how you can tell: [Ralph Lauren] had a bad habit of putting his monogram on everything and nobody complained except my mother. The sourcing patterns for the lifestyle got blown open. A department store chain bought Brooks Brothers. L. L. Bean went from being the store in Maine where you got those lace-up boots to a national brand" (1). Christina Binkley argues that those who prefer preppy clothing today tend to be less "understated" than their forerunners in past generations: "The preppy look is ... what the people who run the nation have always worn at their country homes. Now, as in the 1980s, people who want to suggest they live that lifestyle are wearing it, too. Never mind that preppies were traditionally old-money understated; now the look is about flamboyant colors and embroidered whales" (D1).

Works Cited

Adams, Henry. *The Education of Henry Adams*. 1907. New York: The Library of America, 2009.
Aldrich, Nelson W., Jr. *Old Money: The Mythology of America's Upper Class*. New York: Vintage, 1988.
Alexander, Paul. *Salinger: A Biography*. Los Angeles: Renaissance, 1999.
Ambrose, Stephen E. *Citizen Soldiers: The U.S. Army from the Normandy Beaches to the Bulge to the Surrender of Germany, June 7, 1944–May 7, 1945*. New York: Simon & Schuster, 1997.
Anderson, Robert. *Tea and Sympathy: A Drama in Three Acts*. 1953. New York: Samuel French, 1983.
Ansen, David. Review of *School Ties*. *Newsweek* 21 September 1992: 78.
Ashburn, Frank D. *Peabody of Groton: A Portrait*. New York: Coward McCann, 1944.
Atwood, Thomas A., and Wade M. Lee. "The Price of Deviance: Schoolhouse Gothic in Prep School Literature." 35 *Children's Literature* (2007): 102–26.
Auchincloss, Louis. "Afterword: Origins of a Hero." *The Rector of Justin*. 1964. New York: Modern Library, 2001.
———. *The Education of Oscar Fairfax*. New York: Houghton Mifflin, 1995.
———. *Honorable Men*. New York: McGraw Hill, 1986.
———. *The Rector of Justin*. Boston: Houghton Mifflin, 1964.
———. *A Voice from Old New York: A Memoir of My Youth*. New York: Houghton Mifflin Harcourt, 2010.
———. *A Writer's Capital*. Minneapolis: University of Minnesota Press, 1974.
Avon Old Farms School: A Brief History. www.avonoldfarms.com/page.cfm?p=1287.
Bailey, Blake. *Cheever: A Life*. New York: Knopf, 2009.
———. *A Tragic Honesty: The Life and Work of Richard Yates*. New York: Picador, 2003.
Balliett, Whitney. "A Model Novel." *The New Yorker* 1 August 1964: 76–78.
Barbour, Ralph Henry. *For the Honor of the School*. New York: D. Appleton, 1904.
———. *The Half-Back*. New York: D. Appleton, 1899.
"The Bart Wants What It Wants." *The Simpsons*. Dir. Michael Polcino. Fox. 17 February 2002.
Baum, Robert. "John Cheever Faces the Demands of Fame." *Conversations with John Cheever*. Ed. Scott Donaldson. Oxford: University of Mississippi Press, 1987.
Baumbach, Jonathan. "The Saint as a Young Man: A Reappraisal of *The Catcher in the Rye*." *Critical Essays on Salinger's* The Catcher in the Rye. Ed. Joel Salzberg. Boston: G. K. Hall, 1990.
Berg, A. Scott. *Max Perkins: Editor of Genius*. New York: Dutton, 1978.
Bergman, David. *Gaiety Transfigured*. Madison: University of Wisconsin Press, 1991.
Biddle, Francis. *A Casual Past*. Garden City: Doubleday, 1961.
Bienen, Leigh Buchanan. "Review: New American Fiction." 20 *Transition* (1965): 46–51.

Works Cited

Binkley, Christina. "Plaid Taste: The Return of the Preppy." *Wall Street Journal* 19 July 2007: D1.
Bowden, Edwin T. *The Dungeon of the Heart*. New York: Macmillan, 1961.
Bradlee, Ben. *A Good Life: Newspapering and Other Adventures*. New York: Simon & Schuster, 1995.
Brookeman, Christopher. "Pencey Preppy: Cultural Codes in *The Catcher in the Rye*." *New Essays on* The Catcher in the Rye. Ed. Jack Salzman. New York: Cambridge University Press, 1991.
Bruccoli, Matthew J. Preface to *The Short Stories of F. Scott Fitzgerald: A New Collection*. New York: Scribner, 1989.
_____. *Some Sort of Epic Grandeur: The Life of F. Scott Fitzgerald*. New York: Harvest/HJB, 1981.
Bryant, Hallman Bell. A Separate Peace: *The War Within*. Boston: Twayne, 1990.
Bryer, Jackson R., and John Kuehl. Introduction to *The Basil and Josephine Stories*. New York: Collier, 1987.
"Bunch of Phonies Mourn J. D. Salinger." *The Onion* 28 January 2010. www.theonion.com/articles/bunch-of-phonies-mourn-jd-salinger,2901.
Bush, George W., and Mickey Herskowitz. *A Charge to Keep*. New York: William Morrow, 1999.
Canby, Vincent. "Shaking Up a Boys School with Poetry." *New York Times* 2 June 1989: C8.
Canin, Ethan. "The Palace Thief." *The Palace Thief*. New York: Random House, 1994.
Castronovo, David. *Beyond the Gray Flannel Suit: Books from the 1950s That Made American Culture*. New York: Continuum, 2004.
_____, and Steven Goldleaf. *Richard Yates*. New York: Twayne, 1996.
Cheever, John. "Expelled." *John Cheever: Collected Stories and Other Writings*. New York: The Library of America, 2009.
_____. "Expelled." *The New Republic* 1 October 1930: 171–74.
_____. *The Stories of John Cheever*. New York: Ballantine, 1978.
Clark, Beverly Lyon. *Regendering the School Story: Sassy Sissies and Tattling Tomboys*. New York: Garland, 1996.
Collier, James Lincoln. *Louis Armstrong: An American Genius*. New York: Oxford University Press, 1983.
Cowley, Malcolm. "Editor's Note." *The Stories of F. Scott Fitzgerald*. New York: Collier, 1987.
Crosier, Louis M. *Casualties of Privilege: Essays on Prep Schools' Hidden Culture*. Gilsum, NH: Avocus, 1991.
Cross, Gary. *Men to Boys: The Making of Modern Immaturity*. New York: Columbia University Press, 2008.
Dahl, Christopher C. *Louis Auchincloss*. New York: Ungar, 1986.
Dahl, Roald. *Boy: Tales of Childhood*. New York: Farrar, Strauss & Giroux, 1984.
Dallek, Robert. *An Unfinished Life: John F. Kennedy, 1917–1963*. New York: Little, Brown, 2003.
Dead Poets Society. Dir. Peter Weir. Walt Disney Studios, 1998.
Delderfield, R. F. *To Serve Them All My Days*. New York: Simon & Schuster, 1972.
DeMarr, Mary Jean, and Jane S. Bakerman. *The Adolescent in the American Novel Since 1960*. New York: Ungar, 1986.
Donaldson, Scott. *Conversations with John Cheever*. Oxford: University of Mississippi Press, 1988.
_____. *John Cheever: A Biography*. New York: Random House, 1988.
Ebert, Roger. Review of *Dead Poets Society*. www.rogerebert.suntimes.com/apps/pbcs.dll/article?AID=/19890609/REVIEWS/906090301/1023.
Eels, Josh. "The Semi-Charmed Life of Vampire Weekend." *Rolling Stone* 4 February 2010: 50–51.
Egan, Sean. *Ponies & Rainbows: The Life of James Kirkwood*. Duncan, OK: BearManor, 2012.

Works Cited

Ely, Sister M. Amanda, O.P. "The Adult Image in Three Novels of Adolescent Life." *English Journal* 56 (1967): 1127–31.
The Emperor's Club. Dir. Michael Hoffman. Universal, 2003.
Erens, Pamela. *The Virgins: A Novel.* Portland, OR: Tin House, 2013.
Exeter Remembered. Ed. Henry Darcy Curwen. Exeter, NH: Philips Exeter Academy Press, 1965.
Fantina, Robert. *Desertion and the American Soldier, 1776–2006.* New York: Algora, 2006.
Farrar, F. W. *Eric, or Little by Little.* Edinburgh: A. & C. Black, 1858.
Fitzgerald, F. Scott. "The Bowl." *The Short Stories of F. Scott Fitzgerald: A New Collection.* Ed. Matthew J. Bruccoli. New York: Scribner's, 1989.
_____. "The Freshest Boy." 1928. *The Basil and Josephine Stories.* Ed. Jackson R. Bryer and John Kuehl. New York: Collier, 1987.
_____. "The Rich Boy." 1926. *The Short Stories of F. Scott Fitzgerald: A New Collection.* Ed. Matthew J. Bruccoli. New York: Scribner's, 1989.
_____. *This Side of Paradise.* 1920. New York: Collier, 1986.
French, Warren. *J. D. Salinger, Revisited.* Boston: G. K. Hall, 1988.
Fry, Stephen. *The Ode Less Traveled: Unlocking the Poet Within.* New York: Gotham, 2006.
Gaines, Richard L. *The Finest Education Money Can Buy.* New York: Simon & Schuster, 1972.
Gaztambide-Fernández, Rubén A. *The Best of the Best: Becoming Elite at an American Boarding School.* Cambridge, MA: Harvard University Press, 2009.
Gelderman, Carol. *Louis Auchincloss: A Writer's Life.* New York: Crown, 1993.
Goldleaf, Steven. *John O'Hara: A Study of the Short Fiction.* New York: Twayne, 1999.
Gopnik, Adam. "Postscript: J. D. Salinger." *The New Yorker* 8 February 2010: 21–22.
Gossip Girl. The CW. 2007–2012. Television.
Grunwald, Henry Anatole. Introduction to *Salinger: A Critical and Personal Portrait.* New York: Harper & Row, 1962.
Hall, Alice Petry. *Fitzgerald's Craft of Short Fiction: The Collected Stories, 1920–1935.* Ann Arbor: UMI, 1989.
Hamilton, Ian. *In Search of J. D. Salinger.* London: Minerva, 1988.
Harrington, Walt. "George Bush: Born to Run, Born to Rule." *American Profiles.* Columbia: University of Missouri Press, 1992.
Hassan, Ihab. *Radical Innocence: The Contemporary American Novel.* Princeton: Princeton University Press, 1961.
Hassan, Thomas E. "Learning from Each Other." www.exeter.edu/exeter_bulletin/12984_6089.aspx.
Hawley, Richard. *The Headmaster's Papers.* 1984. Forest Dale, VT: Paul S. Eriksson, 2002.
Heckscher, August. *St. Paul's: The Life of a New England School.* New York: Scribner's, 1980.
Heiserman, Arthur, and James E. Miller, Jr. "Some Crazy Cliff." *Salinger: A Critical and Personal Portrait.* Ed. Henry Anatole Grunwald. New York: Harper & Row, 1962.
Hersey, John. "John Cheever, Boy and Man." *New York Times Book Review* 26 March 1978: 3.
Hicks, David V. "The Strange Fate of the American Boarding School." *The American Scholar* (Autumn 1996): 523–35.
Hicks, Granville. "The Search for Wisdom." *Salinger: A Critical and Personal Portrait.* Ed. Henry Anatole Grunwald. New York: Harper & Row, 1962.
Hilton, James. *Goodbye, Mr. Chips.* 1934. New York: Little, Brown, 1962.
"History of Harkness Teaching." www.exeter.edu/admissions/147_5238.aspx.
Holmes, Oliver Wendell. *The Poetical Works of Oliver Wendell Holmes.* Boston: Houghton Mifflin, 1975.
Howe, Desson. Review of *Dead Poets Society. Washington Post* 9 June 1989.
Howe, Irving. "The Salinger Cult." *Celebrations and Attacks: Thirty Years of Literary and Cultural Commentary.* New York: Harcourt Brace Jovanovich, 1979.

Works Cited

Hughes, Thomas. *Tom Brown's Schooldays.* 1857. New York: Signet, 1986.
Irving, John. *The World According to Garp.* New York: Dutton, 1978.
James, Henry. "The Art of Fiction." *The Art of Criticism: Henry James on the Theory and Practice of Fiction.* Ed. William Veeder and Susan M. Griffin. Chicago: University of Chicago Press, 1986.
"J. D. Salinger: Author of *The Catcher in the Rye*." *The Times* 29 January 2010. www.times online.co.uk/tol/comment/obituaries/article7007023.ece.
Johnson, Owen. *The Lawrenceville Stories.* 1908–1911. New York: Simon & Schuster, 1987.
Kael, Pauline. "Stonework." *The New Yorker* 2 June 1988: 70–71.
Kanfer, Stephan. "Holden Today: Still in the Rye. *Time* 7 February 1972: 50–51.
Karabel, Jerome. *The Chosen: The Hidden History of Admission and Exclusion at Harvard, Yale, and Princeton.* New York: Houghton Mifflin Harcourt, 2005.
Kennedy, Edward M. *True Compass: A Memoir.* New York: Twelve, 2009.
Kidd, Kenneth B. *Making American Boys: Boyology and the Feral Tale.* Minneapolis: University of Minnesota Press, 2004.
Kimmel, Michael. *Manhood in America: A Cultural History.* New York: The Free Press, 1996.
Kintrea, Frank. "'Old Peabo' and the School." *American Heritage* (October/November 1980): 98–106.
Kipling, Rudyard. *The Complete Stalky & Co.* 1899. New York: Oxford University Press, 1999.
Kirkwood, James. *Good Times/Bad Times.* New York: Simon & Schuster, 1968.
Knowles, John. "John Knowles on *A Separate Peace.*" www.exeter.edu/libraries/4513_5177.aspx.
_____. "My Separate Peace. *Esquire* (March 1985): 106–109.
_____. "On *A Separate Peace.*" *The Exonian* 1 November 1972: 2.
_____. *Peace Breaks Out.* New York: Holt, Rinehart & Winston, 1981.
_____. "Phineas." *Phineas: Six Stories.* New York: Random House, 1968.
_____. *A Separate Peace.* 1960. New York: Scribner Classics, 1996.
_____. "A Special Time, A Special School." www.exeter.edu/libraries/4513_4621.aspx.
Kolowrat, Ernest. *Hotchkiss: A Chronicle of an American School.* New York: New Amsterdam Books, 1998.
Kourkounis, Jessica. "J. D. Salinger Slept Here (Just Don't Tell Anyone)." *New York Times* 20 March 2011: A1.
Leverenz, David. "Manhood, Humiliation and Public Life: Some Stories." 71 *Southwest Review* (Fall 1986): 442–62.
Levin, James. *The Gay Novel in America.* New York: Garland, 1991.
Lewis, Michael. "Greed Never Left." *Vanity Fair* April 2010: 126–29.
Linderman, Gerald F. *The World Within War: America's Combat Experience in World War II.* New York: Free Press, 1997.
Lucas, John. "Has Public School Fiction Passed the Test of Time?" *The Guardian* 4 January 2011. www.guardian.co.uk/books/booksblog/2011/jan/04/public-school-fiction.
Lunn, Arnold. *The Harrovians.* London: Methuen, 1913.
Mad Men. AMC. 2007–2014. Television.
Madison, William V. "Decoding Kirkwood's Good Times/Bad Times." *Billevesées.* www.billmadison.blogspot.com/2011/10/decoding-kirkwoods-good-times-bad-times.html.
Mailer, Norman. *Harlot's Ghost.* New York: Random House, 1991.
_____. "The White Negro: Superficial Reflections on the Hipster." *Advertisements for Myself.* New York: Putnam's, 1959.
Maslin, Janet. "What's Up at Prep School? Culture Shock." *New York Times* 1 September 1999: E5.
McElroy, Joseph. Excerpt from "Reflections on at Least One Story of John O'Hara's." *John O'Hara Journal* 3, no. 1–2 (Fall/Winter 1980). Reprinted in *John O'Hara: A Study of the Short Fiction.* New York: Twayne, 1999.

Works Cited

McFarquhar, Larissa. "East Side Story." *The New Yorker* 25 February 2008: 54–63.
McGavran, James Holt. "Fear's Echo and Unhinged Joy": Crossing Homosocial Boundaries in *A Separate Peace.*" *Modern Critical Interpretations: John Knowles's* A Separate Peace. Ed. Harold Bloom. New York: Chelsea House, 1999.
McGrath, Charles. "The First Suburbanite." *New York Times* 1 March 2009: MM36.
———. "J. D. Salinger, Literary Recluse, Dies at 91." *New York Times* 28 January 2010: A1.
———. "Still Paging Mr. Salinger." *New York Times* 30 December 2008: C1.
McLachlan, James. *American Boarding Schools: A Historical Study.* New York: Scribner's, 1970.
McPhee, John. *The Headmaster: Frank L. Boyden of Deerfield.* New York: Farrar, Strauss & Giroux, 1966.
Meanor, Patrick. *John Cheever Revisited.* New York: Twayne, 1995.
Menand, Louis. "Holden at Fifty: *The Catcher in the Rye* and What It Spawned." *The New Yorker* 1 October 2001: 82–87.
Miller, Edwin Haviland. "In Memoriam: Allie Caulfield." *Holden Caulfield.* Ed. Harold Bloom. New York: Chelsea House, 1990.
Miller, James E., Jr. *J. D. Salinger.* Minneapolis: University of Minnesota Press, 1965.
Mills, C. Wright. *White Collar: The American Middle Classes.* New York: Oxford University Press, 1951.
Musgrave, P. W. *From Brown to Bunter: The Life and Death of the School Story.* London: Routledge & Kegan Paul, 1985.
"Name Dropper." *Newsweek* 20 July 1964: 83.
Naparsteck, Martin. *Richard Yates Up Close: The Writer and His Works.* Jefferson, NC: McFarland, 2012.
O'Hara, James E. *John Cheever: A Study of the Short Fiction.* Boston: Twayne, 1989.
O'Hara, John. "Do You Like It Here?" *Selected Stories of John O'Hara.* Ed. Frank MacShane. New York: Modern Library, 2003.
Oldsey, Bernard S. "The Movies in the Rye." 23 *College English* (December 1961): 209–15.
O'Nan, Stewart. "The Lost World of Richard Yates." *Boston Review.* October/November 1999. www.bostonreview.net/BR24.5/onan.html.
Orr, David. "School of Verse." *New York Times Book Review* 1 October 2006: 14.
Orwell, George. "Such, Such Were the Joys." *The Collected Essays, Journalism, and Letters of George Orwell.* Ed. Sonia Orwell and Ian Angus. New York: Harcourt, Brace & World, 1968.
Outside Providence. Dir. Michael Corrente. Miramax, 1999.
Parsell, David B. *Louis Auchincloss.* Boston: Twayne, 1988.
Peterson, Virgilia. "A Crucible Covered with Ivy." *New York Times Book Review* 12 July 1964: 1.
Petry, Alice Hall. *Fitzgerald's Craft of Short Fiction: The Collected Stories, 1920–1935.* London: UMI Research Press, 1989.
Pickrel, Paul. "The Curse of Goodness." *Harper's* March 1960: 106–108.
———. "Manners of Mammon." *Harper's* July 1964: 99–100.
Piehl, Kathy. "Gene Forrester and Tom Brown: *A Separate Peace* as a School Story." *Children's Literature in Education* 14:2 (Summer 1983): 67–74.
Piket, Vincent. *Louis Auchincloss: The Growth of a Novelist.* New York: St. Martin's, 1991.
Pinsker, Sanford. The Catcher in the Rye: *Innocence Under Pressure.* New York: Twayne, 1993.
Plimpton, George. "Interview: Louis Auchincloss." *The Paris Review* (Fall 1994). www.theparisreview.org/interviews/1759/the-art-of-fiction-no-138-louis-auchincloss.
Pollack, William. *Real Boys: Rescuing Our Sons from the Myths of Boyhood.* New York: Random House, 1998.
Poole, Charles. "This Madman Stuff." *Harper's* August 1951: 101.
Powell, Arthur G. *Lessons from Privilege: The American Prep School Tradition.* Cambridge, MA: Harvard University Press, 1996.

Works Cited

Prescott, Peter S. *A World of Our Own: Notes on Life and Learning in a Boys' Preparatory School*. New York: Coward-McGann, 1970.
Price, Richard. Introduction to *Richard Yates: Revolutionary Road, The Easter Parade, Eleven Kinds of Loneliness*. New York: Knopf, 2009.
Quigley, Isabel. *The Heirs of Tom Brown: The English School Story*. Oxford: Oxford University Press, 1984.
Reed, Talbot Baines. *The Fifth Form at St. Dominic's*. 1887. London: Dakers, 1955.
Reisman, David, with Nathan Glaser and Reuel Denney. *The Lonely Crowd: A Study of the Changing American Character*. New Haven: Yale University Press, 1950.
Richards, Jeffrey. *Happiest Days: The Public Schools in English Fiction*. Manchester: University of Manchester Press, 1988.
Rosen, Gerald. "A Retrospective Look at *The Catcher in the Rye*." *Critical Essays on Salinger's* The Catcher in the Rye. Ed. Joel Salzberg. Boston: G. K. Hall, 1990.
Ross, Lillian. "Bearable." *The New Yorker* 8 February 2010: 22–23.
Rossoff, Meg. *What I Was*. New York: Viking, 2008.
Rowe, Joyce. "Holden Caulfield and American Protest." *New Essays on* The Catcher in the Rye. Ed. Jack Salzman. New York: Cambridge University Press, 1991.
Rowling, J. K. *Harry Potter: The Complete Collection*. New York: Scholastic, 2007.
Salinger, J. D. *The Catcher in the Rye*. Boston: Little, Brown, 1951.
Saltonstall, William G. *Lewis Perry of Exeter: A Gentle Memoir*. New York: Atheneum, 1980.
Salzman, Jack. *New Essays on* The Catcher in the Rye. New York: Cambridge University Press, 1991.
Samuels, Ernest. Introduction to *The Education of Henry Adams*. New York: Wadsworth, 1972.
Sargent, J. Katherine. *The Handbook of Private Schools: A Descriptive Summary of Independent Education*. Boston: Porter Sargent, 1988.
Sarotte, Georges-Michel. *Like a Brother, Like a Lover: Male Homosexuality in the American Novel and Theater from Herman Melville to James Baldwin*. Garden City: Anchor Press/Doubleday, 1978.
Scent of a Woman. Dir. Martin Brest. Universal Studios, 1992.
Scheussler, Jennifer. "Get a Life, Holden Caulfield." *New York Times* 20 June 2009: WK5.
Schlesinger, Arthur M. "Exeter 1931–1933: In the Eye of the Hurricane." *Exeter Remembered*. Ed. Henry Darcy Curwen. Exeter, NH: Phillips Exeter Academy Press, 1965.
School Ties. Dir. Robert Mandel. Paramount, 1992.
Seelye, John. "Holden in the Museum." *New Essays on* The Catcher in the Rye. Ed. Jack Salzman. New York: Cambridge University Press, 1991.
Shapiro, Anna. *Living on Air*. New York: Soho, 2007.
Shaw, Peter. "Love and Death in *The Catcher in the Rye*." *New Essays on* The Catcher in the Rye. Ed. Jack Salzman. New York: Cambridge University Press, 1991.
Shoumatoff, Alex. "A Private-School Affair." *Vanity Fair* January 2006: 136–48.
Shreve, Anita. *Testimony*. New York: Little, Brown, 2008.
Sims, Yvonne D. *Women of Blaxploitation: How the Black Action Film Heroine Changed American Popular Culture*. Jefferson, NC: McFarland, 2006.
Sittenfeld, Curtis. *Prep*. New York: Random House, 2005.
Skow, John. "More Loneliness." *Time* 21 August 1978: 83–84.
Slawenski, Kenneth. *J. D. Salinger: A Life*. New York: Random House, 2010.
Smithsonian World: American Dream at Groton. Dir. David Grubin. PBS Video, 1991.
The Social Network. Dir. David Fincher. Columbia, 2010.
Stephen, Katherine. "John Updike Still Finds Things to Say About Life, Sex, and Religion." *Los Angeles Times* 4 January 1987: Section VI, 1, 4.
Swaim, Don. "Interview: Louis Auchincloss." *Wired for Books*. 23 September 1986. www.wiredforbooks.org/louisauchincloss/index.htm.
Thomas, Evan. *Robert Kennedy: His Life*. New York: Simon & Schuster, 2000.

Works Cited

Tribunella, Eric. "Refusing the Queer Potential: John Knowles's *A Separate Peace*." *Children's Literature* 30 (2002): 81–95.
Tunis, John R. "A Man of Distinction." *New York Times* 24 September 1967: 8.
Turnbull, Andrew. *Scott Fitzgerald*. London: The Bodley Head, 1962.
Tuttleton, James W. "Louis Auchincloss: The Image of Lost Elegance and Virtue." 43:4 *American Literature* (January 1972): 616–32.
Updike, John. *Odd Jobs*. New York: Knopf, 1991.
Varner, Greg. "James Kirkwood (1924–1989)." www.glbtq.com/literature/kirkwood_j.html.
Vidal, Gore. *Palimpsest: A Memoir*. New York: Penguin, 1995.
———. "The Zenner Trophy." *Clouds and Eclipses: The Collected Short Stories*. Cambridge, MA: Da Capo, 2006.
Wakefield, Dan. "The Search for Love." *Salinger: A Critical and Personal Portrait*. Ed. Henry Anatole Grunwald. New York: Harper & Row, 1962.
Waldeland, Lynne. *John Cheever*. Boston: Twayne, 1979.
Walker, David, Andrew J. Rausch, and Chris Watson, eds. *Reflections on Blaxploitation: Actors and Directors Speak*. Lanham, MD: Scarecrow Press, 2009.
Wall Street. Dir. Oliver Stone. 20th Century–Fox, 1987.
Wall Street: Money Never Sleeps. Dir. Oliver Stone. 20th Century–Fox, 2010.
Wallace, Carol McD. "We're All Preppies Now." *New York Times* 24 October 2005. www.nytimes.com/2005/10/24/opinion/24hamlin.html.
Ward, Geoffrey C. *Before the Trumpet: Young Franklin Roosevelt, 1882–1905*. New York: Harper & Row, 1985.
Watson, Benjamin. *English Schoolboy Stories: An Annotated Bibliography of Hardcover Fiction*. Lanham, MD: Scarecrow Press, 1992.
Weber, Ronald. "Narrative Method in *A Separate Peace*." *Modern Critical Interpretations: John Knowles's* A Separate Peace. Ed. Harold Bloom. New York: Chelsea House, 1999.
Wodehouse, P. G. *The Gold Bat*. 1904. New York: Penguin, 1986.
———. *The Pothunters*. 1902. New York: Penguin, 1986.
———. *Tales of St. Austin's*. 1903. New York: Hard Press, 2006.
Woititz, Janet Geringer. *Adult Children of Alcoholics*. Deerfield Beach, FL: HCI Books, 1990.
Wolcott, James. "It's Still Cheever Country." *Vanity Fair* April 2009: 74–78.
Woolf, Tobias. *Old School*. New York: Vintage, 2004.
Yardley, Jonathan. "Holden Caulfield, Aging Gracelessly." *The Washington Post* 19 October 2004: C1.
———. "Valuable Lessons from 'The Rector of Justin.'" *The Washington Post* 9 July 2008: C1.
Yates, Richard. *The Easter Parade*. New York: Delacorte, 1976.
———. *A Good School*. New York: Delta/Seymour Lawrence, 1978.
———. *Revolutionary Road*. New York: Little Brown, 1961.
———. *A Special Providence*. New York: Knopf, 1969.
Zacherek, Stephanie. Review of *Outside Providence*. Salon 1 September 1999 www.saloncom/entertainment/movies/review/1999/09/01/outside/index.html.

Index

Adams, Henry 72
Ambrose, Stephen E. 48
Anderson, Robert 87, 134–35, 138–45, 148, 159; *Tea and Sympathy* 87, 102, 134–35, 138–45, 148, 155, 159
Armstrong, Louis 11
Auchincloss, Louis 5, 41, 46, 54–76, 78–79, 90–95, 97, 107, 139, 156, 161, 164, 165; *The Education of Oscar Fairfax* 41, 92–95; *Honorable Men* 41, 90–92; *The Rector of Justin* 5, 6, 46, 54–76, 78–79, 97, 130, 139, 156, 161; *A Voice from Old New York* 161; *A Writer's Capital* 55, 92, 97, 164; "A Writer's Use of Fact in Fiction" 55–56
Avon Old Farms School 123, 125, 162

Bailey, Blake 109, 110, 111, 123, 125, 129, 130, 162
Bakerman, Jane 131
Balliett, Whitney 53
Barbour, Ralph Henry 2
Baum, Robert 114
Baumbach, Jonathan 25
Bergman, David 84
Bernstein, Carl 120
Biddle, Francis 66
Bienen, Leigh 74
"Blaxploitation" films 89
Bowden, Edwin T. 18
Boyden, Frank 97
Bradlee, Ben 160, 163; *A Good Life* 160
Brest, Martin 117
Brewster Academy 82, 161
Brookeman, Christopher 163
Bruccoli, Matthew 5
Bryant, Hallman Bell 36, 39, 44, 46
Bryer, Jackson 5
Bush, George H.W. 6–7, 118
Bush, George W. 167

Canby, Vincent 115
Canterbury School 165
Cape Cod 62, 157
Castronovo, David 12, 123, 129, 132
The Catcher in the Rye 5, 6, 11–32, 49, 52, 53, 78, 119, 127, 128, 137, 158
Cheever, John 108–14, 136–37, 167; "Expelled" 108, 110–14
Choate School 98, 102, 163, 165
Clark, Blair 160
Collier, James Lincoln 11
Corrente, Michael 118, 119
Cowley, Malcolm 4, 110, 111
Coy, Ted 2
Crosier, Louis M. 7

Dallek, Robert 165, 166
Dead Poets Society 7, 108, 114–15, 121, 169
Deerfield Academy 97, 125, 170
Delany, Samuel R. 84
Delderfield, R.F. 6
DeMarr, Mary Jean 131
Do the Right Thing 148, 156
"Do You Like It Here?" 33–35

The Education of Oscar Fairfax 41, 92–95
Egan, Sean 88, 161
Eliot, Charles W. 164
Ely, Sister M. Amanda, O.P. 47
English public schools 6
Erens, Pamela 4
Esquire 5
"Expelled" 108, 110–14

Farrelly, Bobby 118, 119
Farrelly, Peter 118, 119
Faulkner, William 162

Index

Fitzgerald, F. Scott 5, 8, 15, 129, 161, 171; "The Freshest Boy" 1–5, 8–10, 15, 161, 162; *The Great Gatsby* 5, 129
French, Warren 31
"The Freshest Boy" 1–5, 8–10, 15, 161, 162

Gardner, William Amory 92–93
Gaztambide-Fernández, Rubén 6, 8
Gelderman, Carol 54, 75, 98, 164
Goldleaf, Steven 35, 82, 123, 129, 132
Goldman, Bo 117
A Good Life 160
A Good School 6, 49, 108–9, 122–33, 135, 137, 146, 162, 168
Good Times/Bad Times 6, 41, 49, 53, 77–107, 139, 161, 169
Goodwin, Doris Kearns 165
Gossip Girl 170
Gothic literature 77, 106
The Great Gatsby 5, 129
The "great headmasters" 74, 96–100, 136, 148, 156
Greenall, Walter G., Jr. 161
Groton School 29, 54, 55, 56, 60, 66, 70–71, 74, 75, 93, 97–98, 135, 160, 161, 163, 164, 165

Hackett, David 51
Halberstam, David 74
Hamilton, Ian 161
Hand, Learned 55, 56
The Harkness Plan 37
Harlot's Ghost 41, 95–96, 96
Harrington, Walt 7
Hassan, Ihab 12
Hawley, Richard 170; *The Headmaster's Papers* 170
Heiserman, Arthur 12
Hemingway, Ernest 162
Hersey, John 109
Hicks, David V. 7–8, 20, 93, 135, 136, 148, 163
Hicks, Granville 19
Hightower, Jim 7
Hilton, James 6
Holmes, Oliver Wendell 74
Honorable Men 41, 90–92
Howe, Desson 115
Hughes, Thomas 2, 42

Irving, John 168–70; *The World According to Garp* 168–70

James, Henry 59, 162
Johnson, Owen 3; *The Lawrenceville Stories* 3, 162, 169
Joyce, James 112

Kael, Pauline 115
Kanfer, Stefan 16
Karabel, Jerome 60
Kennedy, Edward M. 166
Kennedy, John F. 165–66
Kennedy, Joseph P., Jr. 165
Kennedy, Robert F. 51, 166
Kennedy, Rose 166
Kimmel, Michael 18
Kintrea, Frank 135, 164
Kirkwood, James 6, 41, 49, 77–107, 139, 161; *Good Times/Bad Times* 6, 41, 49, 53, 77–107, 139, 161, 169
Knowles, John 5, 33–53, 78, 107, 132, 134–35, 137, 145–59, 162, 169; "My Separate Peace" 44; *Peace Breaks Out* 5, 36–38, 134–35, 145–59; *A Separate Peace* 5, 6, 33–53, 78, 119, 130, 135, 137, 169; "A Special Time, A Special School" 50–51, 52, 132
Koenig, Ezra 171
Kourkounis, Jessica 12
Kuell, John 5

The Lawrenceville School 135
The Lawrenceville Stories 3, 162, 169
Lee, Spike 148
Leverenz, David 18
Levin, James 83, 86–87, 88
Lewis, C.S. 171
Lewis, Michael 11
Lowell, Robert 160, 163
Lunn, Arnold 3

Mad Men 170
Madison, William 88–89
Mailer, Norman 41, 95–96, 115; *Harlot's Ghost* 41, 95–96, 96; "The White Negro: Superficial Reflections on the Hipster" 115
Mandel, Robert 115
Maslin, Janet 120
McGavran, James Holt 40, 49
McGrath, Charles 12–13, 111
McLachlan, James 41, 99, 136
McPhee, John 97
Meanor, Patrick 111, 114
Menand, Louis 22

Index

Miller, Edwin Haviland 128
Miller, James E., Jr. 12, 31
Mills, C. Wright 22, 130
Musgrave, P.W. 42

Naparsteck, Martin 132
The New Republic 110, 111
The New York Times 12
The New York Times Book Review 109
The New Yorker 115

O'Hara, James E. 111
O'Hara, John 33–35, 38; "Do You Like It Here?" 33–35
Oldsey, Bernard 14
O'Nan, Stewart 128, 129
The Onion 11–12
Orr, David 115
Outside Providence 108, 118–21

Parsell, David 55, 56, 65, 72
Peabody, Endicott 29, 55, 56, 58, 92, 97, 98, 135, 164
Peerce, Larry 50
Perry, Lewis 29, 99
Phillips Academy Andover 8, 51, 118, 125, 163, 167
Phillips Exeter Academy 29, 37, 39, 41, 50–51, 52, 80, 99, 125, 132, 139, 162, 168, 170–71
Piehl, Kathy 45
Piket, Vincent 68, 68–69, 72
Pinsker, Sanford 12
Ponicsan, Darryl 115
Portsmouth Priory 166
Powell, Arthur 9
Preece, W. E. 130
Prescott, Peter 98, 102
Price, Richard 129

The Rector of Justin 5, 6, 46, 54–76, 78–79, 97, 130, 139, 156, 161
Reed, Talbot Baines 2
Reisman, David 22, 130
Richards, Ann 6–7
Richardson, Maurice 44
Richardson, Samuel 58, 60
Riddle, Theodate Pope 124, 125
Robinson, Jackie 116
Roosevelt, Franklin D. 93, 98, 124, 164–65
Roosevelt, Theodore 98
Rosen, Gerald 23

Rosoff, Meg 6
Ross, Lillian 21
Rowe, Joyce 27
Rowling, J.K. 6

Sacco and Vanzetti 112
St. John, George 98, 165–66
St. Mark's School 160, 163
St. Paul's School 7, 125, 136, 163
Salinger, J. D 5, 11–32, 49, 78, 96, 107, 110, 128, 130, 137, 158, 161; *The Catcher in the Rye* 5, 6, 11–32, 49, 52, 53, 78, 119, 127, 128, 137, 158
Saltonstall, William G. 99
Samuels, Ernest 72
Sarotte, Georges-Michel 40
The Saturday Evening Post 5
Scent of a Woman 7, 29–30, 108, 117–18, 121
Schlesinger, Arthur M., Jr. 37
School Ties 108, 115–17, 119, 121, 121–22
Seelye, John 24
A Separate Peace 5, 6, 33–53, 78, 119, 130, 135, 137, 169
Shapiro, Anna 4
Shreve, Anita 4, 170
Shulman, Tom 114
The Simpsons 7
Sims, Yvonne 89
Sittenfeld, Curtis 4, 170
Skow, John 132
The Social Network 170
"A Special Time, a Special School" 50–51, 52, 132
Spector, R.D. 130
Stone, Oliver 11

Tea and Sympathy 87, 102, 134–35, 138–45, 148, 155, 159
Thayer Academy 109, 109–10, 112, 114
The Times 11
Tribunella, Eric 40

Updike, John 111
Ursinus College 12

Valley Forge Military Academy 161
Vanity Fair 110
Varner, Greg 88
Vidal, Gore 79–82, 91, 139; *Palimpsest* 139; "The Zenner Trophy" 79–82, 91, 139
A Voice from Old New York 161
von Ziegesar, Cecily 170

Wakefield, Dan 12
Waldeland, Lynne 110
Walker, David 89
Wall Street 11
Wall Street: Money Never Sleeps 11
Ward, Geoffrey C. 58, 66, 93, 98, 165
Watson, Benjamin 3, 6
Weir, Peter 114
Williams, Edward Bennett 159
Wilson, Sloan 130
Wilson, Woodrow 135
Wodehouse, P.G. 2
Woititz, Janet G. 103
Wolcott, James 110
Wolf, Dick 115
Wolff, Tobias 170
Woodward, Bob 120

The World According to Garp 168–70
World War I 6
World War II 36, 39, 124, 130, 145, 146, 147, 153, 155, 158
A Writer's Capital 55, 92, 97, 164

Yardley, Jonathan 69
Yates, Richard 6, 49, 108–09, 122–33, 137, 146, 162, 168, 169; *The Easter Parade* 129; *A Good School* 6, 49, 108–09, 122–33, 135, 137, 146, 162, 168; *Revolutionary Road* 129, 130; *A Special Providence* 130

Zacharek, Stephanie 120
"The Zenner Trophy" 79–82, 91, 139
Zuckerberg, Mark 170–71

www.ingramcontent.com/pod-product-compliance
Lightning Source LLC
Chambersburg PA
CBHW032059300426
44116CB00007B/815